COUNTY AND TOWNSHIP GOVERNMENT
IN THE UNITED STATES

THE MACMILLAN COMPANY
NEW YORK · BOSTON · CHICAGO · DALLAS
ATLANTA · SAN FRANCISCO

MACMILLAN & CO., LIMITED
LONDON · BOMBAY · CALCUTTA
MELBOURNE

THE MACMILLAN CO. OF CANADA, LTD.
TORONTO

COUNTY AND TOWNSHIP
GOVERNMENT IN
THE UNITED STATES

BY
KIRK H. PORTER, Ph.D.
ASSISTANT PROFESSOR OF POLITICAL SCIENCE
STATE UNIVERSITY OF IOWA

New York
THE MACMILLAN COMPANY
1922
All rights reserved

COPYRIGHT, 1922
BY THE MACMILLAN COMPANY

Set up and electrotyped. Published September, 1922.

Printed in the United States of America

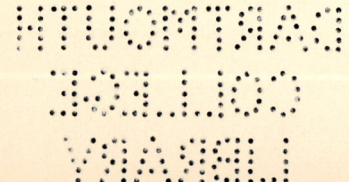

PREFACE

THIS book is intended to describe county and township government in the United States. In addition to this description there is developed throughout the volume a consistent plan for the reorganization of county government which is summarized in chapter fifteen. It is hoped the book will be considered suitable for use in colleges and universities as the basis for a course of study in county and township government. For one reason or another this field has been neglected in the class room. And yet the average citizen comes in contact with offices and institutions of local government much more frequently than he does with the organs of state and national government. It is hoped therefore that this volume will stimulate teachers of political science to offer courses on local government in those institutions where it has been neglected, and serve as an aid to those who are already teaching courses in this subject.

Variations in type were found to be so numerous as almost to discourage any effort to continue with the work. It seems as if for every definite statement concerning an office or institution of local government forty-seven qualifying comments must be added. Yet out of all these variations it has been possible to pick certain very essential facts about local government in general; and the purpose has been to present them without undue confusion. The nature of local government, the historical origins, the characteristic types to be found in the United States today, the legal status of local areas of government, the functions exercised through them, the methods pursued, and the characteristic officers and institutions have been discussed, though not in terms that are as explicit as could have been used were it not for all the manifold variations. An actual enumeration of the facts concerning local government in each of the forty-eight states is left to a work of different character.

In discussing the functions of different officers a somewhat unconventional method has been followed. The effort has been to conjure up a picture of local officers actually at work. Thus many of the homely details of their every-day activities are set forth at some length. Many of their duties when described in this way seem rather petty and unimportant; but they do affect the daily life of every citizen most intimately. So for this reason it was thought well to discuss them even though the treatment might seem rather elementary.

Chapter seventeen is devoted to small municipalities such as villages, boroughs, and towns, although it is believed these areas ought more properly to be considered in connection with a study of city government. This matter is discussed at some length in the first pages of chapter seventeen.

In most of the chapters will be found numerous critical comments concerning existing types of local government organization, and many constructive proposals with regard to the possibility of reform. So much adverse criticism is being directed upon institutions of local government that it was believed these comments and proposals would lend this volume a greater value than as if it merely afforded a descriptive account of existing conditions.

Appreciation is expressed for the aid rendered by Professor Benjamin F. Shambaugh, Professor Frank E. Horack, and Professor John E. Briggs, all of the State University of Iowa.

The manuscript was read by them and their criticisms and suggestions helped greatly to make this volume a better work than it otherwise could have been.

K. H. P.

Iowa City, June, 1922.

CONTENTS

	PAGE
PREFACE	v
NOTE ON BIBLIOGRAPHY	xi

CHAPTER

I.	MINOR AREAS OF GOVERNMENT	1
II.	ORIGIN OF LOCAL SELF-GOVERNMENT IN AMERICA	21
III.	VARIATIONS FROM THE NEW ENGLAND TYPE	42
IV.	PRESENT DAY TYPES OF LOCAL GOVERNMENT ORGANIZATION	58
V.	THE LEGAL STATUS OF THE COUNTY AND THE TOWNSHIP	76
VI.	FUNCTIONS OF THE COUNTY AND THE TOWNSHIP	92
VII.	THE COUNTY BOARD AT WORK	114
VIII.	THE CLERICAL OFFICES	136
IX.	COUNTY POLICE FUNCTIONS	162
X.	THE LAW OFFICERS	189
XI.	THE FINANCE OFFICERS	212
XII.	LOCAL CHARITIES AND PUBLIC HEALTH	239
XIII.	SCHOOLS AND COUNTY SCHOOL OFFICIALS	262
XIV.	ROADS AND HIGHWAYS	275
XV.	REFORM OF COUNTY GOVERNMENT	287
XVI.	TOWNSHIPS AND COUNTY DISTRICTS	307
XVII.	SMALL MUNICIPALITIES	323
	INDEX	341

NOTE ON BIBLIOGRAPHY

THERE is given below a very brief list of the best secondary sources that deal with county and township government in the United States. No student of the subject can afford to neglect any of them, and the writer of this volume is much indebted to them all.

The thorough student will find an abundance of material in constitutions, statutes, cases, monographic literature, official records and reports. The general and special histories add their bits of information and there is more or less periodical literature dealing with the subject. But even the most casual investigator will find interest in the following:

Geo. E. Howard—*Local Constitutional History of the United States.*

Johns Hopkins University Studies in Historical and Political Science.

Clarence Aurner—*History of Township Government in Iowa.*

J. A. Fairlie—*Local Government in Counties, Towns, and Villages.*

H. G. James—*Local Government in the United States.*

Annals of the American Academy of Political and Social Science, Vol. 47.

H. S. Gilbertson—*The County.*

C. C. Maxey—*County Administration.*

Documents on County Government—published by The National Short Ballot Organization.

National Municipal Review.

There is no work that can compare with Howard's *Local Constitutional History* as a source of information concerning the origin and early history of institutions of local government in America. In addition to this work there are to be found a number of monographs running through the volumes of the *Johns Hopkins Studies*, that deal with historic origins.

Concerning the history of the development of institutions of local government during the nineteenth century very little has been written. The best work of this sort is Aurner's *History of Township Government in Iowa*, published by the State Historical Society of Iowa. Although this work deals with but a single state it treats of a situation that was essentially characteristic of the entire Middle West.

A descriptive account of county and township government in the United States today is to be found in Fairlie's work on *Local Government in Counties, Towns and Villages*. This was the first work of its kind in the field, and it deals with conditions that have not changed in many essential aspects. This volume also contains an excellent bibliography on local government.

Local Government in the United States, by H. G. James, is the latest work dealing with counties and townships in the same descriptive manner. Four chapters deal with the subject, the rest of the volume being devoted to local government in England and France, and to city government in the United States.

Volume 47 of the *Annals of the American Academy of Political and Social Science* contains a descriptive and critical account of various county offices and institutions.

H. S. Gilbertson's *The County*, and C. C. Maxey's *County Administration*, are two of the most recent volumes that have appeared, the latter dealing only with the situation in Delaware. Both are highly critical and point to the need of reform.

But the most stimulating source of information on present

day conditions is the loose leaf volume of *Documents on County Government,* published by the National Short Ballot Organization. The folders and pamphlets in this volume come from many sources, some not so reliable as others, but all devoted to a striking exposition of conditions as they are. A tendency to hostile criticism is to be observed in most of them.

The attention of the student is further invited to the splendid articles appearing regularly in the *National Municipal Review.*

K. H. P.

COUNTY AND TOWNSHIP GOVERNMENT
IN THE UNITED STATES

COUNTY AND TOWNSHIP GOVERN-MENT IN THE UNITED STATES

CHAPTER I

MINOR AREAS OF GOVERNMENT

Areas of Local Government.—The county and the township are usually spoken of as areas of local government. In this connection the phrase local government is acceptable not because it serves to indicate any distinctive characteristics of the county and the township, but rather simply because no other term can be found that is at once brief and adequate. Cities and villages are certainly areas of local government. Indeed a small city is more truly an area of local government than is the average county; and a school district, too, falls into the same category. It is therefore desirable to differentiate clearly between these various areas of government with a view to arriving at some distinctive characteristics of the areas with which this volume is particularly concerned.

Greater Areas of Government.—It is very easy to fall into a careless way of speaking about political units. Thus one sometimes speaks of other "countries," and other "nations," and other "states," using the three terms interchangeably. Curiously enough, the latter term, while most nearly accurate in a majority of cases, is used the least often. The so-called "country" or "nation" is of course the political unit that is most significant in all political relations to-day, and as a political unit it is more properly spoken of as a "state" than as a "country" or a "nation." The word "country" may imply a geographical area that is not quite coterminous with the political area in question, and the word "nation" may imply a race of people who do not all reside within the same political jurisdiction. But it is not necessary here to go further into the meaning of these words, except to say that the term state should be used to indicate the most nearly sovereign political unit with which the science of politics is familiar to-day. Thus Great Britain, France, Spain, the United States, Holland, Switzerland, and some forty others are political units known in the language of political science as states.

Sovereign States.—Usually these states are called sovereign states, and the word sovereign is supposed to imply complete independence, a capacity to do anything that may be desired, the absence of any obligation to recognize the authority of any external power, and freedom to control internal polity in every respect. But as the sanctions of international law come to be looked upon as possessing greater authority and come to be more surely enforcible by orderly legal process, the word sovereign will cease to have some of its old significance. Indeed in recent decades it has been little more than an empty compliment when applied to such states as Belgium, or even China.

A World State.—All this is important for the present purpose only in so far as it is suggestive of the possibility that the future may witness the emergence of a political unit larger than the present day so-called sovereign state. It is easily conceivable that a league of nations might develop into a world state or a political unit that would be superior to all of the present-day sovereign states. But until such an organization shall appear, the state, spoken of carelessly as the nation or country, will be recognized as the largest significant political unit. The terms monarchy, republic, empire, kingdom, democracy—all have to do with the character of internal organization and the type of government. The word state indicates the political unit.

Self-Governing Dependencies.—It follows, therefore, that all other political units must be more or less subordinate to the authority of the state and embrace a smaller area. How small this area must be before it can properly be called an area of "local" government is impossible to say. The largest areas or units within the jurisdiction of a single state are the self-governing portions of an imperial state. Such are Canada and Australia. They stand as political units that are but portions of the greater union known as the British Empire. Except for some of their international relationships these political units are so far independent as to be properly classed, rather loosely, with the sovereign states themselves.

Portions of a Federal State.—Proceeding further into the classification of political areas one comes upon the component units in a state such as the United States, where a federal type of government obtains. Here a little confusion may arise, for when the American has used the word "state" to indicate the United States he finds himself somewhat at a loss for a word to apply to California, or Massachusetts, or any of the other forty-six so-called states. The original thirteen colonies did actually possess many of the attributes of real statehood if indeed they were not really sovereign. As soon as the colonies ceased to be colonial possessions the term state was appropriated and the present forty-eight commonwealths constituting the United States no doubt always will be called states even though the use of the word is not altogether appropriate. Yet as a matter of fact these commonwealths do possess many of the important attributes of sovereignty. Each has a complete structure of political machinery entirely adequate to cope with all the governmental problems that could face a people. Like sovereign states they have legislatures, executive departments, judiciaries, administrative machinery, and all the governmental organs and institutions that are essential to the maintenance of political existence. While they do not at present exercise any control over certain matters such as foreign affairs, the mails, and coinage, their governmental organization is such that the functions in these connections could be assumed with a very little readjustment of existing machinery. The twenty-six states composing the late German Empire were in much the same position, and possibly the cantons of Switzerland could be placed in this category.

All these political units, called states,—some of them sovereign, some of them parts of a greater union or empire,—may properly be designated major areas of government for the sake of simplifying discussion.

Minor Areas of Government.—But more important in the present connection is the differentiation and classification of political units that may be called minor areas of government. These areas of government are invariably created by, or exist on sufferance of, the major area. Any such minor area or geographical subdivision of a state may be considered a political unit when it exists for the purpose of carrying on some governmental function. Thus a city is created for the purpose of carrying on all the so-called municipal functions: its governmental machinery is adapted to this purpose. The city is a political unit and is a minor area of government.

On the other hand, a state may be divided arbitrarily into a number of geographical districts within each of which some governmental functionaries will carry on their duties, as do collectors of internal revenue within their districts. These districts, too, may be called political units and classed as minor areas of government. Again, the state may be divided into districts within each of which a judge will hold sessions of his court; or districts may be created that will serve as areas from which representatives may be chosen to sit in some legislative assembly; or districts may be created that will stand alone for some special function, having each its own peculiar organization for the purpose, as for instance, park districts. All such districts may properly be designated minor areas of government.

It is obvious that as the business of government grows more complex and these various political units or areas are multiplied they are sure to overlap, and together with the counties and the townships compose a complicated and more or less confusing system of many unrelated jurisdictions. It is possible, however, to classify all of these minor areas with some fair measure of success, according to the purposes for which they exist.

1. Cities.—First in such a classification are the cities—minor areas of government that are perfectly familiar the world over. In the United States they are created by state authority and their governmental machinery is prescribed in considerable detail. They may be given charters by which their boundaries are clearly indicated and their powers and duties set forth; or, as more frequently is the case to-day, these matters may be determined in a general law. The city is largely independent of all other areas of government except that of the state itself, though other areas may overlap the city without seriously impairing its independence. Though obviously the city exists to satisfy local needs it is not usually referred to as an area of local government, that phrase being reserved by common usage for the county and the township.

2. Villages, Boroughs, Towns.—Villages, boroughs and towns are in the same class with cities. Their functions are similar and their governmental organization is about the same. The principal differences have to do with size and extent of power. Like the cities, each one has a chief executive, a legislative council, and all the other organs of government and institutions necessary to the exercise of municipal functions. It is customary for these small urban communities to seek the status of cities as soon as the population has become great enough. And since it is primarily the purpose of this volume to discuss the distinctly rural areas rather than the urban, such communities might well be dismissed from any further consideration. But this matter is discussed in a later chapter,* and suffice it for the present to give these small municipalities a place in the classification of governmental areas.

3. Judicial Districts.—The judicial district is also well known. It is an area marked out in order to facilitate the administration of justice. In the past, when counties have served as judicial districts, as has often been the case, the judicial district as a distinct political unit or area of government has not existed. As a rule each county maintained its court and the jurisdiction of the court would extend no further than the county lines. But it often proved to be the case that one county would not supply enough judicial business to occupy the full time of a court, and for this and other reasons, too, it has been desirable to embrace two or more counties within the jurisdiction of a single court. When this occurs a new political entity—quite distinct from the counties themselves—comes into existence, and it may be called simply a judicial district. There may be only ten or twelve such districts in a state containing a hundred or more counties,

* Chapter XVII.

and thus these districts comprise a system of political units quite distinct and apart from all other areas of government.

It is by no means necessary that the boundaries of a judicial district should not cut athwart the boundaries of a county, thus embracing only parts of several counties instead of an even number of entire counties. But it has been customary, for diverse reasons, not to cut athwart of county lines in marking out judicial districts.

On the other hand, it might well be desirable to have two or more judicial districts within the limits of one very populous county. The chief point to bear in mind is that a system of judicial districts may exist quite independently of other governmental areas.

4. Representative Districts.—Familiar, likewise, as a political unit is the representative district—a local area designated for the purpose of choosing representatives to sit in a legislative assembly, when the members thereof are not selected at large. It is natural to assume that such districts would be marked out according to population, and that no other factor need be taken into consideration. But as a matter of practice, other factors do almost invariably have weight in determining the lines of such districts. Thus every state enjoys representation in the United States Senate regardless of population, and not infrequently every county in a given state enjoys representation in the state assembly, regardless of population. But a system of representative districts may, and sometimes does, exist quite independently of other areas of government, having been marked out solely according to population. They may then be called political units, for they are areas for governmental purposes. The purpose is very limited to be sure, and the degree of political organization within the district is very slight, but even so, the representative district has a character all its own and deserves a place in the classification of minor areas of government.

Pure representative districts of course possess essentially the same characteristics the world over. At stated times the people within the district proceed to elect one or more representatives to sit for that district in a legislative assembly for a given period. Representative districts in the United States are: the states themselves, from which the United States senators are elected; state senatorial districts and state representative districts (oftentimes identical in area with the counties); county board districts (oftentimes identical in area with the townships); and city wards. All are representative districts.

5. *The Pure Administrative District.*—Another sort of minor area or district that exists for governmental purposes is what may be called the pure administrative district. It has not been very fully developed in the United States, and is more or less unfamiliar to the average American. But on the continent of Europe the administrative district and the ideas of government which it serves to fulfill are much more common. Primarily, the administrative district exists for the purpose of carrying out a governmental programme conceived by authority superior to and outside of the district itself. The idea involved does not admit any considerable amount of local self-government. There lies the principal reason why the system of administrative districts has not been popular in the United States, for that system does provide a highly centralized and efficient organization for carrying on government activities.

By way of illustration, let it be supposed for a moment that one of our state governments should centralize and concentrate within itself all political authority, and exercise that authority directly, without permitting the exercise of what is called local self-government. Picture this state arbitrarily divided into a considerable number of districts upon the authority of the state central government. Within each of these districts there might be officers with varying functions—all appointed upon the authority of the state central government. The state central authorities would make all the law for the entire state, and the district officers would administer it strictly in accordance with instructions from state authorities. These district officers might then proceed to exercise direct control over police functions, roads and bridges, the assessment and collection of taxes, school affairs, the administration of justice, and the care of the poor, the insane, and those who were sick and indigent. They would look after public health and sanitation, and might even exercise the function of fire protection, and supervise the management of parks and the construction of drainage systems. They might exercise direct control over public utility corporations, gas and electric light companies, water supply, and street railway corporations. They might supervise the financial operations of all public officers within the district, and even control the letting of contracts for public works and supplies. And at all times these district officers would act in strict subordination to the state central authorities, and often with small regard to local sentiment.

Here then would be a splendid system of pure administrative districts, wherein administrative responsibility would be highly centralized and a very high standard of efficiency attained with a minimum of cost. But what of local self-government? The thought of being governed from above in all such matters of local concern without having an opportunity to determine policies or control administration is so repugnant to the American mind that such a governmental system as has been outlined above would probably be quite unacceptable even in these days when efficiency in government is sought after with such eagerness.

At the same time it is to be observed that the administrative district is by no means entirely foreign to the American system of government, else there would be slight justification for discussing it in this connection. Indeed the idea has always been appropriated in connection with the exercise of certain governmental functions, and it is becoming more and more common in the United States every decade. In a word, the pure administrative district and the centralization of authority which it involves are entirely acceptable to the American mind when used in the exercise of functions which are thought proper for state authorities to control directly. For the most part these functions have been so few and unimportant, and the officers so few and inconspicuous, as largely to escape public attention; and the districts within which they function are so unimportant as areas of government that they scarcely deserve mention. But as the states undertake more activities and functions that require elaborate administrative machinery, and furthermore, functions which in the past have been exercised by local authorities, the administrative district is bound to come into greater prominence and the theory of government involved is sure to be challenged by those who are jealous of the older democratic institutions of local self-government.

A state, for instance, may be divided into districts for the purpose of administering a pure food law, and state inspectors exercise their functions within these districts without exciting much attention. But suppose it were proposed to divide the state into districts and to appoint district officials to exercise all police functions, with the consequent abolition of all the county sheriffs, township constables and other local peace officers! Although such a proposition would merely involve an extension of the administrative district idea it would certainly excite a great deal of comment and vigorous opposition.

In those states where an income tax is operating the state is divided into administrative districts for the purpose of collecting it. But suppose the assessment and collection of all taxes were intrusted to state authorities, and they functioned through similar districts! There again would be a decided extension of the administrative district idea.

These districts have existed for such inconspicuous purposes in the past that the public does not realize how easily the ideas could be worked out in connection with a radical programme of state government reorganization, a programme which might involve a taking over of many functions never exercised before under direct supervision of the state authorities. But the movement is afoot and gaining headway. Already state authorities are gaining control over school affairs, and districts are arbitrarily created in order to facilitate school administration. State authorities are gaining control over road improvement projects and districts are created for the purpose. In Pennsylvania, New York, and Texas, and in some other states to a lesser extent, the central authorities are exercising police functions. So it may be expected that a steady extension of the administrative district idea will continue.

There are two principal factors that account for the slowness with which this system of government has developed in the United States. The first has already been hinted at: it is the desire for local self-government that is latent in the Anglo-Saxon temperament. Ever since this continent was first settled the people have been exceedingly jealous of their right to control their own local affairs directly, instead of through the instrumentality of central, and more or less remote, authorities. This desire is a manifestation of an early concept of democracy. Contemporary students of politics know that democratic political machinery cannot be static. No one system of government is intrinsically democratic to the exclusion of all others. Democracy cannot be expressed in any particular rigid formulæ. But the statesmen of a century ago were very sure that real democracy involved the right of the people to manage all of their local concerns directly themselves. This meant the right to determine policies as well as the right to control administration. It meant for instance the right to determine what roads should be improved, and how, what schools should be maintained, what methods of caring for the poor and insane should be followed, what type of police protection should be afforded, the amount and method of collecting taxes, and many other things as well.

There is much of this same spirit manifest to-day, and it is a spirit of which the present generation may well be proud, although it is not always possible to approve of its present-day application to the practical problems of government. This spirit is particularly vigorous in the cities and finds expression in demands for home rule, and local control over public utilities and other institutions. Unfortunately it is often perverted and kept aflame by unscrupulous politicians and demagogues who, actuated by ulterior motives, find plenty of ignorance and stupid prejudice to play upon. But at any rate the presence of this particular spirit of democracy and the desire for this particular kind of self-government have been important factors in blocking the centralization of authority and the development of the administrative district. And, as a corollary it might be added, it has served to keep alive the county and the township.

Writers on the subject of state administration are inclined to deplore this situation. They point out that it makes for gross inefficiency, lack of uniformity, failure to attain proper standards (as in school matters, road improvement, and the care of dependents), and worst of all gross wastefulness. But these constitute the price that the American people seem to have been willing to pay for the enjoyment of their particular type of democracy. Experts insist that the public pays the price, as measured in terms of inefficiency and wastefulness, and fails to gain real democracy. They are partly right of course, and yet the present generation might view with some indulgence this heritage of conservatism that has come down from those who established democratic institutions upon this continent.

The second chief point to be held in mind as an explanation of the slow development of centralization and the administrative district idea, is the ready acceptance in the United States of the doctrine of administrative decentralization. This doctrine is based upon the assumption that locally elected officers are entirely competent to administer the law enacted by central authorities. Thus it implies that a state government may enact laws in great variety that involve many problems of interpretation, and that county, city and town authorities will enforce them; that criminal statutes may be written upon the statute books and all the county prosecutors, locally elected, will proceed to enforce them; that health regulations and building codes may be enacted, and that local officers can be relied upon to enforce them to the letter. In a word, it implies the absence of state authorities whose business it would be to enforce state laws.

Fortunately this idea has not been carried out in connection with the operations of the federal government. When Congress passes an income tax law federal agents are appointed to collect the tax; when Congress enacts legislation to enforce the eighteenth amendment federal agents proceed to enforce it; and in general it is the business of federal prosecuting attorneys to enforce all federal legislation.

There is an historical explanation of the fact that the doctrine of administrative decentralization became fastened upon the state governments and not upon the federal government; but the significant thing is that it clings with such tenacity. Local authorities, elected in small areas, responsible to no one except to the people, are supposed to enforce state and local law with entire impartiality. The state legislature might pass an act concerning gambling, and instead of its being enforced by state officers responsible to central authorities it would be enforced by a hundred or more different prosecuting attorneys in as many counties, no one of them responsible to any superior officer, and each one interpreting the law as he might see fit. Illustrations could be multiplied indefinitely, but they may better be presented when the functions of the officers involved are under consideration.

This doctrine of administrative decentralization, like the desire for literal self-government and home rule, grows out of old-fashioned democratic philosophy. It puts in practice that somewhat vague and belligerent principle which demands a government of laws and not of men, the implication being that any honest officer will enforce the law as he finds it written, and need not be accountable to any superior.

The most significant consequence of the practice of administrative decentralization in the states is the existence of relatively independent rural areas of local self-government that are more or less peculiar to the United States. These areas are the counties and the townships.

6. *Special Districts.*—There is still another distinct type of governmental area that deserves mention. It is not a pure administrative district for it does not exist for the purpose of executing a legislative programme enacted by central authorities and is not officered by centrally appointed officials. The particular type of area now in question is usually created because of the ineptitudes of existing city, county and township governments, and in order to avoid doing violence to the desire for self-government. Park and drainage districts are the most familiar in this particular class. It may be desirable for instance to set aside a considerable tract of land for park or drainage purposes. The area may overlap several city, county and township jurisdictions. It would be impossible to carry out the project of drainage construction or park building unless certain officers were selected and given power to control and direct the operations in hand quite independently of the governing authorities. To turn the whole business over to state authorities would be to do considerable violence to democratic sentiment; on the other hand, existing local government machinery could not function easily when the operations overlap several distinct jurisdictions. Therefore a compromise scheme has been worked out. The area is set aside usually as a result of popular referendum. Officers are elected within the newly created area and they are given very limited, specific, and minutely defined powers to proceed with the project for which the area has been marked off.

7. *Counties and Townships.*—Having come finally to the county and the township, a word may be said in order to give them a distinctive character as contrasted with all other minor areas of government. It is evident that a

map of a typical state would present a very complicated maze of crossing lines if all of the minor areas of government were marked upon it. And yet each area established for governmental purposes has its own distinctive characteristics. Any area becomes a political unit when it possesses some degree of organization for the purpose of carrying out a governmental programme, no matter how simple it may be. Even if there be only one officer, exercising just one trifling function, the area of his operations becomes a political unit.

Areas for Local Self-Government.—The outstanding characteristic of the county and the township is that they are, and always have been, areas for local *self*-government. In none of the areas described above, except the municipality, is there an opportunity for any real self-government, —self-government that provides an opportunity for the inhabitants to determine for themselves through their own locally elected officials, a governmental programme which they can finance and carry through without regard to any external authority. Self-government involves the determination of policies. What shall be done during the current year? What institutions shall be established? How much money shall be spent? How shall the money be raised? When a community is in a position to answer these questions to its own satisfaction, without regard to external authorities, it enjoys a very considerable measure of self-government.

One would not call a judicial district an area of local self-government; nor yet could a representative district be so described; and certainly an administrative district is not an area of local self-government; for in none of these areas is there to be found governmental machinery through which the inhabitants can determine a programme of action and carry it out to suit themselves. This is just exactly the sort of opportunity which the organization of the county and township do afford. It is therefore proper to call the county and the township areas of local self-government in a sense that is not possible when referring to the other types of district.

Significance of Self-Government.—The importance of this point cannot be too firmly emphasized. Contemporary political thinkers are by no means convinced that local self-government is essential to democracy, but the fact remains that local self-government has been looked upon as an essential feature of democracy in America, and it has been through the county and the township that self-government has been exercised. If it were not for the political machinery of county and township all the people living outside the boundaries of urban districts would have no opportunity to enjoy this peculiarly American form of democracy. And after all, so far as area is concerned, the municipalities are but dots upon the map.

To be sure this particular feature of American democracy is rapidly losing its hold. The measure of real discretion resting with the county or township comes to be less and less each year, and the functions which local authorities have to perform simply as agents of their own community are less and less important. This is a result of the extension of state activity and control as well as a declining interest in local governmental institutions. But American democracy has its roots down deep in the county and the township, and the county particularly is the very basis of the political structure in most of the states. This doubtless will continue to be the case notwithstanding the fact that the county is losing its place as an area of local self-goverment strictly speaking.

Combining Functions.—While the function of self-government is the distinguishing feature about the county and the township, it will be found that frequently they function also in the same capacity as do the other minor areas of government; and it is the exercise of these other functions that will guarantee the county at least, a very important position in the governmental structure no matter what happens to the function of self-government. County government therefore presents numerous complexities in the way of functions and as regards the status of officers. For instance, the county may be itself a judicial district, the judge will be known as the county judge and the court will be spoken of as the county court. Indeed there may be no other state judicial districts. But as a judicial district the county is not strictly speaking an area of local self-government: it merely happens occasionally, for one reason or another, that the county serves this purpose as well as other purposes.

Again it is quite likely that the county will be discovered as a representative district. In each county a representative may be chosen to sit in the state legislature. It will be found that this has been done in a great many of the states, whereas it might have happened that the state would have been divided arbitrarily into representative districts without regard to county lines, just as the states are divided into congressional districts. Thus when the county serves as the unit of representation in the state legislature it is nothing more nor less than a representative district, it merely happens that the representative district lines correspond with the county lines. But the fact does not have any bearing upon the status of the county as an area of local self-government.

Counties as Administrative Districts.—The scarcity of pure administrative districts has been mentioned. One reason for this scarcity is that the county and the township have been accepted in a great many cases as administrative districts for a variety of purposes. The process of tax collection illustrates the point. Instead of permitting state authorities to collect taxes through administrative districts it has been the custom to leave this function entirely to the county and township officers. And to this extent the county and the township are mere administrative districts for the purpose of collecting taxes for the state. As the functions of the state increase the county and township prove to be very convenient areas through which central authorities may function. Thus the county particularly tends to assume the character of a pure administrative district for the purpose of carrying out a state programme.

Compromising with Self-Government.—It is easily possible to compromise with the demand for self-government to the extent, at least, of permitting the administrative officers to be locally elected. Indeed this has always been the case so far as the county sheriff and the prosecutor are concerned. They function for the state and enforce state law, while their area of operation is almost invariably the county, wherein they are popularly elected. The situation does not make for efficient and uniform administration. Furthermore, the status of many county and township officers is rather difficult to define because they perform some functions purely as administrative agents of the state and other functions purely as instruments in the machinery of local self-government.

Minor political areas have now been defined and classified, and attention has been called to the fact that each type of area has some distinguishing characteristic. And although the various districts are often coterminous, the area embraced being identical, it might well be that these districts could exist independently of each other. The distinguishing feature of the county and the township is that they are truly areas of local self-government and with this in mind it is now appropriate to turn to the consideration of the historical origins of county and township government.

CHAPTER II

THE ORIGIN OF LOCAL SELF-GOVERNMENT IN AMERICA

Conditions Favorable for Self-Government.—The county and the township have been characterized as areas for local self-government. But self-government cannot obtain unless certain very important factors have contributed to make the situation right for it. Other areas of government, the administrative district for instance, may be entirely artificial, they may be created arbitrarily to suit the plans of state central authorities. It makes but little difference whether or not the inhabitants of one of these artificial areas are conscious of any real bond of unity. They are entirely passive subjects in the governmental process carried on within the area. But if real self-government is to be attempted the inhabitants must necessarily coöperate and work together on their governmental problems. This cannot be done successfully unless there is a consciousness of unity amongst the people.

It can hardly be imagined that a group of people would desire local self-government unless they were keenly aware of very definite political interests in common. If a group of people do have definite political interests in common and are aware of governmental problems all their own, and do desire to work out these problems themselves through political machinery which they themselves can control directly, then an area of local self-government may be created and will function in a satisfactory manner. But if the group is not conscious of any common political interests,—if the people are not keenly aware of any political problems all their own, then they are not likely to have any real desire for local self-government, or at least it is a mere simulated desire, and the area of local self-government begins to degenerate. The machinery that was designed for self-government does not function, it proves to be ill-adapted to other methods of government, and local self-government proves to be a failure.

This is just what has been happening to the county and township for the past many years. They are organized and designed as areas for local self-government, and the desire for self-government, presumably growing out of a consciousness of political unity, is supposed to exist. But in truth this desire is rapidly disappearing, and in many of the western states never existed.

Factors that Develop a Sense of Unity.—But when the county and township struck roots on American soil and first appeared as areas of local self-government there was a very real and flaming consciousness of unity, political and social. This sense of unity gave birth to a keen desire for self-government which was jealously defended as a precious right. There are a great many factors that may combine to stimulate a sense of unity even before political institutions are thought of. They may be geographic, economic, religious, racial, cultural, or social. In fact there can be no hope of political unity and healthy self-government until some of these factors do appear. For instance, geographical configuration may be such as to throw a group of people together in a certain locality. It may be across a mountain, isolated from other habitation. It may be on the shore of some body of water at a vantage point for navigation purposes.

Other factors may be economic. A group may well find it desirable to coöperate and pool their interests in their economic relationships. They may all be producing the same commodity and seeking the most advantageous foreign market for their produce—a market which can be exploited to the best advantage only when they work together. Or there may be a diversity of occupation among the members of the group and they find themselves interdependent. Such a situation cannot but serve to develop a sense of unity. Many variations of this economic factor will suggest themselves.

The religious factor is just as readily appreciated. Common religious beliefs inevitably serve as a very strong bond amongst men, and when these beliefs must be defended against unsympathetic or actively hostile outsiders the bond is doubly strong. The racial bond is obvious enough and the cultural and social bond needs no discussion. But add to these the thousand and one minor influences that serve to bring men together—the fear of enemies, the fear of cold and starvation, the desire for liberty, the multitude of hopes and ambitions that can find fulfillment through coöperation—and there is a combination of factors that makes for real unity.

It is well known that these factors existed in colonial America, and when coupled with the Anglo-Saxon temperament and traditions gave rise to a very strong demand for local self-government. Small groups of men with their families found themselves isolated and far removed from external authority, and the situation was favorable in every respect for the establishment of political units for local self-government. Men were bound together by complex forces, and they sought to satisfy their own political needs and desires through governmental agencies of their own creation. They wished to do things for themselves through political machinery.

Such a situation cannot be brought about by artificial

means. If the bonds that make for unity do not exist, the desire for local self-government will not appear, and any attempt to set up machinery for self-government will meet with relative failure. Other areas of government, that are purely artificial in their nature, may be marked out arbitrarily; but an area for the realization of local self-government cannot be created with any expectation of success if the conditions that make for unity do not exist. Sometimes the sense of unity is latent and must be stimulated by artificial means, as when townships are marked out as formal squares upon a map and certain functions are left for the residents within each township to perform. But in modern times with each succeeding decade it becomes more difficult to stimulate the sense of unity and the desire for local self-government, simply because the factors described above no longer operate with the same force to bind men in small groups.

Origin of Counties and Townships.—In the early part of the seventeenth century, soon after the first settlements were established on the American continent, townships and counties were organized as areas of local self-government. In some places the township was the first to appear, in other places it was the county, and yet again both may have been established at about the same time.

In New England, however, it was the town that appeared first, and the circumstances surrounding its appearance were so significant as to deserve considerable attention. The institutions and methods of government established there have persisted throughout the years, even down to the present day.

Areas for local government were set up and functioned wholly on sufferance of the colonial authorities. Thus the colony of Massachusetts Bay bore much the same relation to minor areas of government established within its jurisdiction that state governments bear to-day toward modern townships and counties. The seat of the colonial government was usually to be found on the seaboard and was likely to be the most populous urban community within the colonial jurisdiction. Groups of dissatisfied or venturesome spirits might sally forth from the seat of government, or might indeed land from the sea many miles from any habitation but well within the colonial jurisdiction. Such a group would find it necessary to establish institutions of government immediately after they had decided to settle upon a certain spot and thus a "town" would literally be born.

Distinction Between Town and Township.—It should be said that the words "town" and "township" have been used interchangeably, and still are so used, oftentimes in error. The word "town" usually suggests a semi-urban district, a compact area rather thickly populated, though it may be very small. It is like a small city, from which it differs chiefly in size, variety of function, and extent of power. But these early "towns" embraced both urban and rural communities within their jurisdiction, the thickly populated center and the rural area surrounding it. When a group of settlers created a "town" a considerable area would be marked out as coming within their jurisdiction. Most of them might actually build their homes within a very small radius, which area, of course, would be relatively densely populated. Yet the rural area surrounding it would be within the same political jurisdiction. The same officers and the same institutions of government would function for both. There would be just one government embracing the thickly populated center and the surrounding rural area as well. It was as if the government of one of our modern cities were to have control over the township within which it might be located, and the same identical government were to function for the entire area, there being no township government distinct from the city government.

The New England Town.—This is the type of district which was known as, and still is known as, the "town" in New England. Outside of New England it has been the practice to separate the densely populated district from the rural area, provide it with governmental machinery of its own, and call it a "town," "village" or "borough," it being like a small-sized city. The purely rural area that remains, if it be organized at all into areas of local self-government smaller than the county, is organized into what are known as "townships," with meager governmental machinery quite distinct from that of the "town."

Thus the New England town is quite different from the town outside of New England; and it is also very different from the township. The town outside New England is like a small city. The township is a purely rural area that does not ordinarily include in its governmental jurisdiction the towns within its boundaries; while the New England town is much like a combination of the two.

The groups of settlers who established these New England towns marked out areas for themselves subject only to the colonial authority. A specific area might be assigned to them, or they might be quite at liberty to stake out their own claim as it were, or again they might simply appropriate a certain area of land and at some later date get the sanction of the colonial authorities. At any rate the colonial government owned the land and the towns secured title to their bits from the colonial government.

Political Power.—As to the political powers which the towns enjoyed, theory is somewhat in conflict with fact. In theory, whatever sort of town government might be set up, it would enjoy only delegated and enumerated powers. It could legally exercise only such powers as might be specifically bestowed upon it by the colonial government. The towns did not have inherent and residual powers, any more than minor areas of government of the present day enjoy inherent and residual powers. The city or the county of to-day enjoys exactly that measure of power bestowed upon it by the state. Just so, in theory, these early towns enjoyed powers delegated to them by the colonial governments.

But legal forms and theories played a very small part in the practical affairs of men in those early days, and to justify our theory we must fall back upon the proposition that "what the king permits he commands." Whenever the exercise of certain powers by the town was tolerated by the colonial government it must be assumed that by implication the colonial government had delegated those powers to the town. That the towns often exceeded the powers which colonial authorities thought they ought to exercise cannot be doubted. Not infrequently are to be found illuminating statements in the colonial records showing that the central authorities were inclined to curb the towns in their exercise of power, thus indicating clearly that the colonial authorities knew that they had the right to curb the powers of the towns.

As a matter of fact the towns did exercise practically all the powers they chose to exercise. Remote isolation from the central colonial government had much to do with this. Town authorities simply did whatever seemed necessary or desirable in their eyes without much regard to legal theories. Thus we find the town government exercising the most minute and paternalistic disciplinary powers over the inhabitants of their jurisdiction without much question being raised as to their power to do so.

Important civil and criminal cases of course found their way to the higher colonial courts, but in the everyday affairs of life the town government exercised an amazingly comprehensive power. And the colonial governments were for the most part indifferent to this assumption of power. So long as the towns sent in their quotas of the tax levy and furnished armed men and supplies when these were needed they seldom were molested by central authorities.

The Town Meeting.—The town meeting was the primary institution of government through which these powers were exercised. It was nothing more nor less than a mass meeting of all the adult men in the town. It would be very hard to find an institution of government more truly democratic than this. The town meeting was competent to exercise any and every power and function which may have been bestowed upon or permitted to the town, and every man's voice could be heard in the town meeting. The meeting was not in any sense a representative assembly, as are ordinary legislatures, conventions, modern township boards of trustees, and county boards of supervisors. The nearest counterpart to the town meeting that can be found in the modern political structure is perhaps the precinct party caucus—which also is in no sense representative but rather is composed of all the party voters in the district. The town meeting was thus a primary assembly in that it embraced all men, without distinction.

It has been stated that the town meeting enjoyed all powers of which the town might be possessed, and it follows that all town officers had need to look to the town meeting for authority and guidance. The meeting was all powerful and its activities are particularly significant. Meetings were held at least once a year, the date having been fixed by the previous meeting. But in the smaller towns meetings were often held more frequently than this. Sometimes they were held four times a year, regularly at stated intervals, and there was always a way left open for the calling of a special meeting if some emergency might require it. This could usually be done through the selectmen. But town meetings seem to have become rather burdensome as the towns grew larger; and so meetings once a year were considered quite enough for the most part, and pure democracy was thus sacrificed in favor of more efficient and mobile boards of selectmen.

The town meeting, having been properly announced by the constable and his assistants who went literally to every home to give the "lawful warning," would assemble on the appointed day at a place most convenient for the purpose. If the weather permitted it was always desirable to hold the meetings in the open. No one then could feel himself excluded, but town halls were usually at hand if it became necessary to go indoors.

The day of the meeting had something of the aspect of a general holiday. Ordinary business activities were suspended, farmers left their fields, and all men with their families turned out as to a festive occasion—barbecues, dancing, and games being second only to the serious business of the meeting.

But even though these town meetings were frequently characterized by an atmosphere of gayety and picturesque features the real business in hand was serious enough. Morning, afternoon, and evening sessions might be necessary. The first session would be called to order by the town clerk and immediately a presiding officer would be chosen. This dignitary was called a "moderator" and he had no other function than that of being the presiding officer at the meeting. He was in no sense a chief executive officer for the town, nor even a chairman of a permanent board. Selected merely for the occasion his office terminated with the final adjournment of the meeting.

On the other hand, the town clerk functioned as secretary for the meeting, and the constables with their deputies served as sergeants-at-arms. With this simple and meager organization the meeting was prepared to transact its business.

There can be no doubt that active and influential townsmen prepared, in an informal way, much of the business that was to come before the meeting. The selectmen of course had their programme to present. They presented lists of expenditures to be authorized, they sought authority to do certain things which they did not feel at liberty to do without special sanction of the meeting, and there would be scores of little matters on which they would want an expression of opinion from the meeting. But any townsman was free to bring a matter before the meeting, and those who were thoroughly prepared and experienced were likely to control its actions. Debate was in order throughout the session, and the rules of procedure were simplicity itself.

Functions of the Town Meeting.—Probably the most important function of the meeting was the business of determining who might be permitted to live in the town and what property rights were to be enjoyed by the inhabitants. These towns were exceedingly jealous, and suspicious of strangers. Whether or not they had the legal right to do so they did not hesitate to exclude from their jurisdiction people whom they did not want, and they sometimes expelled inhabitants for one reason or another—often because of unorthodox religious beliefs.

1. Concerning Inhabitants.—This power to determine who might live within the borders of the town was of great importance and does not seem to have been challenged in the earliest days. One might expect that the exercise of such arbitrary power as this might, in later days at least, have precipitated some legal controversy. But in the early day when these towns were isolated the practice was not seriously challenged, and as time went on economic and social forces came into play which induced the towns of their own accord to let down the barriers which at first they had erected; so the problem took care of itself. But for many years in old New England a man with unorthodox religious views, or a man without a trade, or one who had a bad reputation, or even a foreign accent or a strange look about him, might find the towns as effectively closed as were the walled citadels of mediæval Europe. With a blunt assumption of superiority that somehow does not seem to fit in with their boasted democratic spirit these townsmen would refuse to admit strangers; or they might let them stay for a time on probation, assign them a social and legal status in the community considerably below that of themselves and possibly indicate a time limit after which the stranger would be expected to depart.

The selectmen examined into the details of each case and had the final determination in the matter unless the town meeting chose to overrule them. A few extracts from their proceedings will illustrate the custom.*

"This day Clement Maxfield appeared, and desired that his brother John, being arrived lately from England, might continue in the town with him; and that he would secure the town against any damage during his residence—which was granted—that the said Clement Maxfield might entertain his brother, until such time as he shall settle himself, here or elsewhere."

* George E. Howard, *Local Constitutional History of the United States*, p. 87.

"Richard Way is admitted into the town, provided that Aaron Way do become bound in the sum of twenty pounds sterling, to free the town from any charge that may accrew to the town by the said Richard or his family."

And to make sure that no strangers found refuge without knowledge of the town officers, "It is ordered that no inhabitant shall entertain man or woman from any other towne or countrye as a sojourner or inmate with an intent to reside here, butt shall give notice thereof to the Selectmen of the Towne for their approbation within 8 days after their cominge to the town upon penalty of twenty shillings."

It can well be imagined that if the towns were as strict as this concerning the relatives of well-established townsmen, it must have been difficult indeed for an utter stranger to gain admission.

2. Property Rights.—Not only did the town meeting assume competence to determine who might live within its jurisdiction, but it also was the final arbiter in determining property rights. In earliest times the land belonged to the town—not to individuals. This was a perfectly natural situation. The central colonial government would grant a certain portion of land to a town, or it may have happened that the town would be established even before the central colonial government—in which case recognition of title on the part of the town would come sooner or later—either tacitly or formally. But be that as it may, the individual townsmen looked to the town for title to private property.

In some cases the towns chose to retain considerable portions of their land in common, not parcelling it out to private individuals. There might be a common pasture land, a common woodland, a common meadow or waste land, and other portions set apart for cultivation. These common lands were to be used by all the inhabitants strictly in accordance with regulations laid down in town meeting, each man's rights being carefully defined. But the desire to possess private property was strong in these men of Anglo-Saxon temperament and heritage and not many years passed before most of the land was portioned out to private owners. Not every man, however, was permitted to own land, and for many years no one was permitted to sell indiscriminately. When in later years the superior power of the central government came to be established everywhere the towns were not permitted to exercise such prerogatives in reference to private property; but in the early days their jurisdiction was undisputed. And it was the town meeting which had ultimate authority in such matters.

3. Taxes.—The town meeting had full control over the machinery of taxation. In addition to providing funds for local purposes each town was expected to contribute money to the central colonial government. Demands upon the towns coming from that source were in the form of a request for a lump sum. In later days this method gave way of course to the practice of fixing a certain rate, which was to apply upon all the property owned in the town. But in earliest times the demand came in the form of a request for a certain sum and it was the town meeting which provided a means of raising this amount in an equitable manner.

A much more complicated problem was that of providing for local needs. The meeting did not follow the simple expedient of adopting a budget and then fixing a tax rate that would be just high enough to produce the necessary revenue, but instead fixed many rates for diverse purposes. Thus a special rate would be fixed to provide the minister's salary, another rate to provide money for a new town hall, and still another to provide for building a new bridge. The application of these rates must have resulted in considerable confusion; but the idea seems to have been to deal with each individual undertaking separately, to pass upon its merits and then to provide the funds. The same idea is followed to-day in the matter of special assessments and the allowing of special rates for parks, new school buildings and like undertakings.

Rates also had to be applied in order to provide for ordinary running expenses. These expenses were all authorized by the town meeting. Often the smallest details were the subject of deliberation. Sums of only a few shillings were allowed to different individuals who may have performed certain services for the town, such as the repairing of a fence or work upon the meetinghouse. In the meeting the salaries of all town officials were determined and allowed. This was no simple matter, for there was a very large number of petty officials even if their salaries were inconsiderable.

In a word, the town meeting had complete and absolute jurisdiction over the financial affairs of the town, which involved particularly the raising of the sum demanded by the central authorities, the passing of rates for special purposes, and the preparation and authorization of what would to-day be called the town budget. This is significant especially in view of the fact that townships still retain a vestige of the same function. The modern township is as much a unit for the collection of state taxes as was the town of early days. The township budget must still be prepared and authorized, small as it may be. But the gradual decline of the township has proceeded to such a point that to-day it is not often that the township has much to say in the matter of authorizing special undertakings of any great importance.

ORIGIN OF LOCAL SELF-GOVERNMENT

4. Representatives.—Another function of the town meeting was to select a representative, one or more, to sit in the colonial assembly. For many years, as has been said before, the towns were the units of representation. In the early days, when towns were widely separated, it would have been quite unwise to have attempted to divide up the entire area of the colony into districts of approximately equal population, as is done to-day in marking out congressional districts. The generally accepted theory of representation to-day is that people should be equally represented, not that towns, or states, or cities, as such, should be represented. Thus has grown up the practice of dividing areas into districts of nearly equal population for purposes of representation. But this was not feasible in early times, and the towns as such demanded representation.

As some towns grew to be much larger than others the practice of allowing each town the same number of representatives regardless of size, was seen to be manifestly unfair, and so the larger towns were allowed extra representation. But the town, as a town, continued to be the unit of representation. The idea was no different from that which prevailed in England where boroughs enjoyed representation in Parliament regardless of their population. These boroughs each established a right to a representative in very early times, and it proved to be a difficult problem to deprive them of such representation in later years even though the population may have fallen to a very low figure. Some of the worst cases were known as "rotten boroughs," boroughs which continued to enjoy representation in Parliament but had only a few hundred inhabitants.

This older theory, that political units should enjoy representation rather than people, has many survivals in the United States to-day. The New England town is the earliest case and still persists to the present day in certain of the New England states where representatives are sent from the towns to the state assembly. The United States Senate provides another illustration, since two senators are sent from each state regardless of population. But one of the most interesting survivals, because it is least apparent, is the practice of accepting counties as units of representation for the state assemblies instead of arbitrarily dividing the state into areas of approximately equal population. Where glaring inequalities of population appear, the county having an exceptionally large population is given two or more representatives in the assembly.

An explanation of this survival is simple enough. Most states have been divided into a number of counties averaging between ninety and one hundred fifty. One representative from each of these makes an assembly of convenient size. The county lines being well established, it was an easy thing to accept counties as units of representation.

To be sure representatives from political units as such are much more likely to be provincial in their attitude toward public problems than representatives from arbitrarily defined districts. This was certainly true of the representatives sent from the towns to colonial assemblies, for not infrequently the representative would assume the rôle of champion for the town from which he had come and concern himself with but little else than getting taxes reduced and privileges extended.

They were chosen in open town meeting, and this practice continued as long as the meetings were held. Thereafter representatives were chosen by popular election like other town officers.

5. *Local Machinery and Institutions.*—It was further necessary for the town meeting to provide all the machinery

and institutions necessary to carry on local undertakings. The problem of poor relief early had to be met. Schools and churches were among the very first institutions to be established. Often the meeting would concern itself with the details of managing these institutions, but very soon this came to be left to boards of selectmen or special trustees. Jails had to be provided, bridges had to be built, and roads had to be cut through woods and rough places. All these matters were the concern of the town meeting. To be sure problems of management soon became too complex to be met in full meeting, but even so the full meeting did consider and adopt long resolutions intended to guide in the smallest particular those who had the matter in direct charge.

6. *Petty Ordinances.*—Acts of the colonial assembly could not possibly contain rules and regulations concerning social relations and for the guidance of personal conduct sufficiently minute to satisfy the townsmen. Local ordinances were required, not simply to provide for public health and safety but to put inhabitants into a moral strait-jacket, as it were. Such rules and regulations, or ordinances, were considered and passed in town meeting. They had to do with the obligation of inhabitants to attend church, and penalties were stipulated for absence. Rules were enacted requiring people to send their children to school. Regulations concerning apprenticeship, concerning fences and the care of stock, and concerning the right to engage in a business or profession were enacted. Curfew laws, for adults as well as children, were passed. Ordinances fixing the time in the evening after which all lights must be out in private homes were passed. No detail of personal conduct could be sure of escaping the careful scrutiny of the town meeting. Even after boards of selectmen assumed the function of writing these rules and

regulations, it was the town meeting that gave to them their sanction.

7. *Officers.*—After all other business had been finished, and just before adjournment, it remained for the town meeting to name all the town officers for the ensuing year. Thus every officer owed his position to the town meeting and could be controlled by it in the discharge of his duties. Offices could be created and abolished at will by the meeting, and incumbents seldom enjoyed a tenure of more than one year. The principal officers in each town had practically the same titles and the same functions as officers in neighboring towns, and indeed their counterparts can be found in the modern township.

Town Officers.—First in importance were members of the board of selectmen. These boards varied in size from three to a dozen, and their functions were prescribed by the meetings which created them. The selectmen were the principal officers of the town and enjoyed great prestige. There was no chief executive or any other officer that could possibly be looked upon as closely resembling a chief executive. The board of selectmen as a group was the highest authority in the town next to the meeting itself.

Next in importance to the selectmen were two other officers, appointed by the town meeting, and found in every town, then and now. They were the town clerk and the constable. Both were subordinate to the selectmen and performed their duties under the direction of the selectmen. The primary functions of these two officers have not changed in the course of three hundred years. Selectmen might disappear, of other officers there might be none, but a town to be a town must have its clerk and constable.

Officers next in importance would be those who had to do with the collection and disbursement of public funds.

In very small towns the constable did this work, but usually it was desirable at least to have a treasurer. He was named by the town meeting. For one reason or another, the meeting might decide to appoint a collector as well, thus relieving the constable or treasurer of part of these duties, and in time of course the town assessor appeared upon the scene.

This almost completes the list of officers who may be called principal, although the surveyor enjoyed considerable prestige as soon as the keeping of land transfer records came to be looked upon as important. As to still other officers, they were frequently numerous but of distinctly minor importance, and they disappeared as years went on. There were fence viewers, cow keepers, town drummers, hog reeves and a score of others appointed as the town might see fit.

Modern Significance of New England Town Organization.—This survey of the functions of that remarkable institution of government, the town meeting, has been carried to some length because in those meetings are to be found the very roots of the modern institutions of local government. The New England town meeting did not appear generally outside of New England, but the things which were done by these town meetings are the very things which are done by the people of a modern township, either through the ballot box or through the instrumentality of trustees and supervisors. It was in meeting that the towns of New England did these things. Towns and townships still do these same homely things, even though the meeting does not exist. Levying taxes, providing schools, taking care of roads, looking after the poor, electing officials, are the functions which towns and townships have always performed. It was in New England that the practice first began on American soil. The town meeting was literally the town itself. To-day the township often functions without a meeting, but the same duties must still be performed.

Development of Board of Selectmen.—But the town meetings came to be too big to function in all of the matters which they undertook to handle at first. And while they still continued to be the organ of government through which the people of the towns exercised their ultimate control, they contented themselves simply with reviewing the work of the town officers, giving instructions of a general nature, passing upon financial matters and the selection of new officers for the ensuing year. As this tendency continued, the rise of the board of selectmen was perfectly natural. As the meeting gave over the handling of matters of detail it was quite logical to vest control in a small group which could meet frequently and deliberate at their leisure.

Ability to do just this was the prime virtue of the board of selectmen. As years went on they undertook to do all that the meeting itself ever did and more besides. They assumed full charge of the budget, proposing revenue measures and making appropriations. They passed upon newcomers, regulated the use of common lands, gave licenses for conducting shops, bound out apprentices, and assumed jurisdiction over all public institutions such as the schools and churches, and charitable institutions such as there were. They passed an amazing number of regulations and rules concerning the public welfare, fixed the price of beer, provided for the inspection of chimneys and fences, and censored private morals.

Petty officers who were not chosen in town meeting were appointed by the selectmen. Perambulators, ringers of swine, town-bellmen, corders of wood and rebukers of boys were among the number. Instructions had to be given to all the functionaries and their work superintended in every respect.

Functions of Other Town Officers.—The more important officers were not appointed by the selectmen but were more or less responsible to them. Thus the constable served as peace officer of the town on his own responsibility, but he was also a functionary for the selectmen, announcing their proclamations, enforcing their orders and in every way assisting them in the administration of town business. In later years he came to be primarily a functionary of the justice court, carrying out the orders of the justice of the peace. And whenever the selectmen exercised petty judicial functions, as they did at times, it was the constable who executed their decisions.

The town clerk kept a record of the proceedings of the town meeting, and also kept records of the meetings of the selectmen. He was supposed to keep a record of all births, deaths, and marriages. An equally important duty was that of keeping records of all land titles. Failure on the part of town clerks to do this carefully led to a great deal of trouble and litigation in future years. The other principal officers, the finance officers and the surveyor, exercised functions which are obvious enough.

Modern Township an Outgrowth of New England Town.—The origin of the town having been traced, its structure described, and its character and functions as a unit of local self-government examined, it remains to observe in conclusion that the modern township has evolved directly out of it and that in the modern township are to be discovered the same characteristics, the same functions, and the same institutions of government.

CHAPTER III

VARIATIONS FROM THE NEW ENGLAND TYPE

Town Organization Outside New England.—One might be inclined to suspect that little towns, similar to those that have been described, sprang up all along the American coast wherever English settlers established themselves. The town type of organization seems so simple, so logical, so democratic, and so altogether admirable that one may well wonder why it was not established everywhere. If it had happened thus, then indeed the roots of our local government would have been everywhere the same and there would not be, in all probability, that bewildering variety of county and township combinations which are to be found to-day.

But if one is to attach any significance at all to the social and economic factors which contributed to make the New England town just what it was, it will clearly be appreciated that as those social and economic factors change, and certain of them disappear, the character of the town will change, and maybe even disappear. There can be no one single type of government that is altogether good to the exclusion of all others, and it were folly to attempt to foist a given type upon a community if social and economic factors combine to make it ill-suited.

Forms of government simply grow out of a vast "composition of forces,"—if we may borrow a phrase from the physical sciences, and use it as a figure of speech. Some of these forces have already been considered in more or less detail, and it is only necessary to offer a reminder that they may be economic, geographic, racial, cultural, social, religious, and what not? All too frequently the determining factor in the vast composition of forces appears in the shape of arbitrary external authority. The other factors still play their part, their influence cannot possibly be stamped out utterly by the most ruthless external authority; but their weight in the composition of forces is for the time heavily offset. But in New England it has been seen the element of external authority was fortunately almost negligible, and the town form of local government quickly emerged out of a composition of normal forces.

The Situation South of New England.—Now these normal forces had a very different complexion as one turns his gaze from New England to portions of the continent further south. And even though the factor of external authority was hardly more prominent than it had been in New England, the composition of normal forces produced a somewhat different situation, and being unobstructed by artificial pressure, gave rise to slightly different types of local government. These differing types which appeared in the various colonies are just as truly the roots of local government in the United States as are the New England towns, and indeed have been more generally copied. For the pure town organism appeared only in New England.

Further south the stimuli which induced the townsmen of New England to live together in small compact communities did not operate to the same degree. Rigors of the weather were not so forbidding, danger from the Indians was not so great. A more bountiful nature made it less necessary to rely upon each other for sustenance. More extensive agricultural operations were possible, tempting men away from industrial enterprises which would have brought them close together in compact communities. The religious and cultural heritage of the people farther south had been enough different so that the impulse to organize for religious purposes did not operate in just the same way, and furthermore the population farther south was not so homogeneous as it was in severe New England. Where the climate was less rigorous and the conditions of life did not demand as much physical exertion and more or less battling with the elements in pursuit of a livelihood, there was always to be found a goodly smattering of the well-born aristocrats. Their presence was a factor to be reckoned with, and as a factor it entered into the complex composition of forces which molded local government in the various communities. In Virginia, known as the Old Dominion, probably this factor was of greater importance than it was in any other place.

The Township.—What then, were the important changes wrought by these differing factors in the equation? In New York and Pennsylvania towns existed, but they were not so vigorous and did not have so much governmental power as the towns of New England had. Townsmen in these states were not so jealous of their rights nor inclined to insist so vigorously upon the privileges of self-government. In New York particularly there were numerous units of local government called villages, manors and towns; and originally they maintained direct relations with the central colonial government. For many years there were no areas of local government other than these little semi-urban communities. These little units maintained an organization and exercised functions very similar to those of the New England town. They were the compact, rather thickly populated districts which in New England would have been merely the centers of the towns. But in New York and Pennsylvania they tended to separate themselves from the surrounding rural area, and the distinctly rural area that remained became the township.

Obviously these townships did not have much vitality although they have always remained as clearly defined areas of government with a structure and functions distinctly their own. But the significant thing is that when finally another unit of local government, the county, did appear in New York, as indeed it did in New England too, the townships of New York were not able to maintain their independence in the same degree as the towns had been maintaining theirs and sacrificed many important functions to the county. The townships ceased to have control over tax levies, they ceased to be units of representation in the colonial assembly, and they no longer enjoyed the right to pass laws dealing with their own local concerns. But still the township in New York remained a very live institution with important functions to perform. The significant thing is that the factors which make for strong, aggressive town organization were not strong enough to resist the encroachments of the county which was a more acceptable area of local government to the wealthy, landed class.

In Pennsylvania the situation was even worse so far as the townships were concerned. Even the towns did not flourish there, and when counties were established they were able completely to overshadow the townships—reduce them to the status of virtual administrative districts and appropriate to the county all the principal functions of local government.

In Virginia the township did not appear at all, for again the factors that would have made for the emergence of the New England type of local government did not operate in Virginia. Even compact towns were few and far between. Men did not come together in small compact communities to live. It was impossible to make them do so even though legislation was passed with a view to stimulating the growth of towns. Legislation for instance that forbade the building of residences farther than a certain distance from the center of the community, frequently was passed. The mild weather, together with the opportunities for acquiring plantations induced men to go out from compact communities and develop the plantation life. Slavery helped to make this possible, of course, and plantation life appealed very strongly to the wealthy men who were able not only to buy land but to maintain large plantations as little feudal manors. These proprietors exercised very considerable authority over their tenants and their servants, legally and extra-legally, and circumstances altogether were not such as to lead to the development of towns.

The Parish.—An institution closely analogous to the town, however, did develop. This was the parish, an ecclesiastical jurisdiction. The functions of the parish as an institution of government were all closely connected with the church and the religious life of the community. But the duties of parish authorities frequently involved the exercise of power that is only associated with institutions of government. For instance, the parish authorities had power to levy and collect taxes for the maintenance of the church, and in some cases to impose punishment for offenses against church regulations.

The Vestry.—The governing authority in the parish was the vestry. The vestry is suggestive of town selectmen. Ordinarily there were twelve men in the vestry, sometimes popularly elected but more often co-öpted by the old vestry. That is, when a vacancy occurred the remaining members would choose a new man to take his place. This arrangement suited the wealthy class and effectively stifled democracy. The duties of the vestrymen were to apportion and collect the parish rate, or tax. They also selected churchwardens and employed a minister. But under their supervsion still other functions were exercised which ordinarily are performed through a strictly civil organization. They assumed responsibility for the care of the poor, a function that has always belonged to institutions of local government. They were responsible for keeping vital statistics—that is, records of births, deaths and marriages—the actual work being done through the minister or his clerk; and they exercised some power in connection with the maintenance of peace, thus assuming functions elsewhere exercised by constables or sheriffs. These were meager functions to be sure, but they are at least suggestive of the town.

The County.—Another unit of local government had appeared to take the place of the township in the South, and to challenge its right to its somewhat precarious position in New York and Pennsylvania. This unit of government was the county. It appeared everywhere, but usually some years after towns had been established. In some communities it did not flourish and held a relatively insignificant place in the structure of the government. In other communities it proved to be so much better adapted to the needs of the people that township government promptly decayed and the county took over its functions, leaving the township a mere skeleton in the structure of government with almost no functions to perform.

Counties in New England.—Turning again to New England it will be possible to discover the circumstances that gave rise to the county. For some years there was no occasion for establishing a unit of government substantially larger than the town and yet subordinate to the colonial government itself. The colonial government had jurisdiction over the entire area belonging to the colony, the towns exercised jurisdiction within their limited boundaries, and there were not enough people living in the wild tracts between towns,—that is outside the jurisdiction of any town—to make it necessary to establish institutions of local government for their benefit alone. But as population grew, and the "between-lands" were inhabited, it became apparent that existing institutions of government were not quite suited to the exercise of at least some important governmental functions.

The most important of these functions was the administration of justice. As regarded cases arising within town boundaries, the selectmen in each town exercised judicial functions involving minor breaches of the peace, or relatively small sums of money. The more important cases were necessarily transferred to the judicial authorities of the central colonial government. And so long as the towns were not numerous and the population in between them was very sparse the central colonial courts were able very easily to deal with all the cases that arose. But as the towns became more numerous and the population grew, the central courts were not able conveniently to handle all the judicial business that came to them; and furthermore it became desirable to establish courts nearer to the people, for the seat of government was far removed from a large share of the population.

Administration of Justice.—Courts of competent jurisdiction might, it is true, have been established in each town and persons could always have brought their cases to the nearest town; but no one town had enough judicial business to occupy the whole time, or anywhere near the whole time, of a single court. Hence the obvious expedient suggested itself of marking out a district embracing a number of towns, within which district a single court might function.

Such districts were called counties, and it is to be observed that the conditions giving rise to the establishment of counties for judicial purposes are quite different from conditions that give rise to true areas of local self-government. The problem in this case was merely one of administrative detail. The county did not grow out of the circumstances of social, economic, cultural, and political unity that gave rise to town government, but rather it grew out of a practical administrative problem.

Military Districts.—Another practical problem was that of maintaining armed forces. Every man within the colonial jurisdiction was subject to call for military service and was expected to receive some training. The towns were too small to serve as units in the military organization and again the obvious expedient occurred of marking out large areas, counties indeed, in each of which a commanding officer would have full charge of all the men from all the towns within his county. Here again it will be seen that it was a problem of administrative detail that helped give rise to county organization.

Collection of Taxes.—Still another problem of similar nature appeared. The levying and collection of taxes could be done much more effectively if carried on under the direction of officers functioning for a district embracing several towns. And indeed, as soon as the county was created for any purpose at all it was necessary to provide funds to keep the county government itself going, and officers were needed to collect and have custody of the funds. This meant the creation of finance offices and machinery to supervise the assessment and collection of taxes and the care of public funds.

All these and other, less significant circumstances combining at about the same time caused the colonial authorities in New England to lay out systems of counties. The first move in this direction was taken in 1665, some forty years after the first settlements. Originally the districts were called shires, after the practice in England, but the term county soon took root and was accepted universally.

County Officers.—A court composed of several justices was set up in each county—the justices were appointed by colonial assemblies or the governors and held their sessions periodically in the principal towns of the county.

The military officer of the county was a sergeant major and it was his business to organize the "train bands" of all the towns within his county into a regiment.

Finance officers of the county were a county treasurer, usually regularly elected, and later a board of assessors. Their functions are obvious enough, but it should be noted that there was a decided tendency to expand the powers of the county finance officers, particularly in the matter of assessments. Town officers did the actual work of assessing and collecting taxes, but gross inequalities in assessed values appeared as between towns, and it soon became necessary to have some higher authority competent to equalize these unfair assessments. This was done by county officials and has remained an important function of the county to this day.

The County Court.—But it will be observed that the functions of the county in New England were extremely meager, compared with the functions which it enjoyed in other portions of the country. However, there was a decided tendency in certain of the colonies even in this northern group, to permit county officers to appropriate certain powers at the expense of the towns. At first these functions were rather closely related to the judicial function. Thus the county court, composed of all the justices, provided for prisons and houses of correction. The county court imposed fines on towns and town officials for neglect of duty. Presently the courts assumed the function of granting licenses to engage in business or a profession. Licenses to sell liquor and to keep inns were the most important of these. And when it became necessary the county court undertook to mark out highways, provide for their establishment and maintenance and to build bridges.

These functions, of course, were not related to the strictly judicial function of a court; but it is to be observed that they were assumed simply as a natural consequence of the developing situation. Highways had to be built that would connect the various towns. The colonial assembly was too remote to be concerned with such a problem, —the county court was just the body to assume the function. This is simply an example of the tendency of governmental institutions to adapt themselves to changing needs of a community if no artificial factor is introduced into the normal composition of forces.

Still other functions which the county courts undertook to assume gave rise to some effective resistance. They sometimes undertook to impose petty ordinances upon the towns and to review the town by-laws, disallowing those which were not acceptable to them. This was of course a direct invasion of the town's cherished prerogative, and in New England the towns were vigorous enough to resist any serious extension of the practice.

Counties in New York.—A little farther south, however, in New York, a different set of conditions not only led to the establishment of counties but made it possible for the county to extend its functions still farther at the expense of the townships. In 1683 New York was divided into twelve counties with the customary judicial, military and financial functions to perform. And since the townships were not so vigorous; since the townsmen were not so jealous of local prerogatives; since the sentiment of unity was not so strong; it was easy for the county authorities to assume numerous administrative functions that involved more and more an invasion of township prerogatives. They assumed more authority over financial administration, they took jurisdiction of the problems of poor relief, the building of highways and schools; and they passed petty ordinances that completely supplanted the old town by-laws.

The Board of Supervisors.—And in the early part of the eighteenth century appeared a new institution of county government that grew directly out of this practice of exercising administrative functions. It was the board of supervisors. One or more supervisors were sent from each township and altogether they composed the county board. This board exercised, or had control over the exercise of, all administrative activities.

Other Officers.—Other county officers that appeared with the expanding activity of the county were the county clerk, the sheriff and the coroner. The two latter officers were responsible for the maintenance of peace, and the town constable promptly lost his prestige.

County Functions in New York.—The counties also became units for elections, and the county instead of the town or township became the unit of representation in the colonial assembly. This practice has continued in many of the states even to the present day, for the counties are very often units of representation in the state assemblies. Thus while the township did not disappear entirely, and continued to be a very definite and important area, especially in its relation to the board of supervisors, the tendency was distinctly to cut down the functions of the township and enhance the power of the counties.

Counties in Pennsylvania.—Farther south, in Pennsylvania, the same tendency was carried still farther. Counties were created there about the same time they were created in New York, and a very definite move was made to center full control of local government affairs in the hands of county officers. The township appeared in Pennsylvania but it was not a unit of representation on the county board, it did not have as many functions to perform as the township in New York, and indeed instead of being an area for local self-government it was but little more than an administrative district for exercising county functions.

The Board of Commissioners.—The townships did not have the power of making by-laws, and local legislative powers, such as they were, were exercised by the county board of commissioners. The board of commissioners was a group of three men chosen at large from the county, and resembled the New York board of supervisors as regards power and functions. This board succeeded the county court in so far as administrative functions were concerned. It licensed innkeepers, even fixed the price of meals, had complete jurisdiction over finance matters through county assessors and collectors, kept records of land transfers, constructed highways, and in a word supervised the exercise of all the functions of local government.

Counties in the South.—Still farther south, as has already been pointed out, the township never appeared at all and the county always was the one and only significant unit for purposes of local government, the parish occupying a very unimportant position. The county in the South was a distinctly undemocratic institution. County courts were established in two of the principal cities and later in the smaller communities, the justices being appointed by the governor. These county justices served as the county board and had complete control over local government.*

* Howard, p. 393, calls attention to the fact that at one time it was pro-

Other county officers were a clerk, coroner, sheriff, surveyor, and a lieutenant,—all appointed. This organization made the county competent to handle all matters of local government. Of course the county in the South was also usually the unit of representation in the colonial legislature.

Four Types of Local Government.—The four principal types of local government organization which were established during the early history of the United States have now been examined. They are the bases, the roots out of which the present types have emerged. There were certain variations of the four types, but they were not important enough to call for any extended discussion or to justify a more extended classification. These four types were quite distinctive and were important determining factors in the development of modern institutions. Each is to be associated with a particular geographical portion of the country.

1. New England Type.—Thus, to summarize, in the New England group of colonies was to be found the town type of local government organization, the town being the principal unit for local government. But the county also existed there for some few purposes.

2. Southern Type.—In the southern group of colonies, principal among which was Virginia, was to be found the highly developed county exercising practically all of the functions of local government, in the absence of the township.

3. North-Central Type.—In the colonies that were between New England and Virginia—the Central colonies they may be called—were to be found two distinct types of local government involving a combination of the township and the county. In New York, a typical representative

vided that each parish might send a delegate to sit with the court for the purpose of making laws, but adds that it is doubtful if this was ever done.

of the North-Central group, the township was clearly defined, had certain important functions of local government which it exercised independently of the county, and served as a unit of representation on the county board of supervisors.

4. South-Central Type.—In Pennsylvania, a typical representative of the South-Central group was to be found the township and the county, but the township was distinctly a subordinate unit, had virtually no independent functions, was not a unit of representation on the county board and served principally as an administrative district for the county.

Counties and Townships in the West.—It would be a most interesting subject of study for the historian if he were to trace the development of local governmental institutions in each one of the four areas discussed. It would be still more interesting to follow out the steps in the establishment of governmental institutions as civilization pressed westward, finally embracing the whole continent. For many decades down into the nineteenth century there was a frontier area just as free of habitation as New England or Virginia had been when they were first settled and institutions of local government were created. What happened in Ohio, Kentucky, Tennessee, Illinois, Michigan and Indiana as civilization gradually embraced them one by one? Was the same old story worked out—did towns appear in some places, counties in other places, and varying combinations of the two in still other places?

Of course the question can be answered in the affirmative. Institutions emerged, always responsive to a complex composition of forces, aided now and then by artificial stimulus in the form of legislation, state or national. Just as in the early day, so on the western frontier, social, economic and other considerations led to the emergence of thriving towns in some places, to the strengthening of the county in other places, and to many variations of the two. But always the four great types on the Atlantic seaboard were the models, and sooner or later institutions of local government had struck root in every state, developed, and finally emerged into the situation which exists to-day.

State Law and Local Government.—It would be a very long, and not altogether profitable task to trace the influence of state constitutional and statutory provisions upon the development of institutions of local government. In many cases towns existed before the state itself, and the state legislatures merely recognized an existing situation when finally the state governments did come into being. Other times the state legislatures arbitrarily marked out a system of counties and townships, resorting to various devices in order to stimulate their growth.

Act of Congress of 1785.—But it is well worth while to touch upon certain acts of Congress which had a pronounced effect upon the development of institutions of local government in the West. In 1785 the Continental Congress provided for the survey and sale of public lands. The land was to be surveyed into areas six miles square which are known even to-day as the congressional townships. Each purchaser's land was recorded as located in a particular township, at first known by number only, but the inhabitants were urged to give their townships distinctive names. This was all intended to stimulate in the buyer an interest and a sense of loyalty to his particular township. The ordinance applied to the area north and west of a point at the intersection of the southern boundary of what then was Pennsylvania, and the Ohio River.

The Northwest Ordinance of 1787.—In 1787 the famous Northwest Ordinance was passed. It provided for a governor and judges for the Northwest Territory, and in some detail made provision for the carving out of new states from this territory. In 1790 the governor and judges mentioned in the ordinance of 1787 appointed a constable for each congressional township who was to function "specially" for his township and "generally" for the county in which his township was located. And finally, Congress set aside one square mile of land in each township for school purposes.

Significance of These Acts.—These acts are all significant in that they provided a sort of artificial stimulus calculated to induce the inhabitants to organize and govern themselves. Such legislation stimulated local allegiance and suggested certain functions which could properly be carried on through areas of local government, particularly functions in connection with such matters as maintenance of peace, land transfer records, and education. The inhabitants responded with more or less enthusiasm and in some places organized vigorous, thriving townships, while in other places the county was allowed to take the lead and assumed all the functions of local government.

Here the thread of history must be dropped. There are in the United States to-day over three thousand counties and of course the number of townships would be ever so much larger. All of these areas of government have grown out of the bases established on the Atlantic seaboard during the seventeenth century, and have been the product of forces similar to those which operated in the early day. Experience and forward-looking legislation played a large part in building up the counties and the townships in the West, but even so it will be found that the four characteristic types still exist very much as they did at first.

It is desirable now to take a hasty survey of the United States and get a picture of the situation as it is at present.

CHAPTER IV

PRESENT–DAY TYPES OF LOCAL GOVERNMENT ORGANIZATION

Types of Local Government may be Classified.—In the light of what has been said about the origins of local government in America it may reasonably be expected that all the states in the Union can be grouped in four classes, depending upon the variations in type of local government organization to be found within their borders. These four types as they exist to-day may conveniently be examined with a view to three significant considerations: first,—the relative importance of the township and the county; second,—the character of the principal unit of government; and third,—the degree of organic connection existing between the township and the county.

No attempt will be made at this time, however, to examine with any thoroughness the structure of local government in any given section of the country, nor to study in detail the functions of the local areas and the duties of local officers. The purpose for the moment is but to get a view of the whole United States and fix in mind if possible the outstanding facts about local government organization in each portion of the country. With these considerations in mind a classification of the states may be accomplished.

The New England Group.—The New England states even to-day, as might be expected, exploit the town as the more important unit than the county. They are:

| Maine | Vermont | Rhode Island |
| New Hampshire | Massachusetts | Connecticut |

Most of the functions of local government in New England are exercised through the town instead of through the county. Thus the town has charge of highways, poor relief, and schools. It is an area for the maintenance of peace and the administration of petty justice. It is through the town that taxes are assessed and collected. And the town is an election district. It furthermore should be remembered that in New England the town government embraces the urban community that may be within its borders and hence one would expect the town also to exercise those functions which, outside of New England, are exercised by petty municipalities such as villages. This is indeed the case, and thus in New England the town may embark upon public works such as street paving, water and sewer systems, electric lighting and other activities of a similar nature. The towns also are used as administrative districts for the administration of state business.

The most important purpose for which the county exists is the administration of justice. But in addition to the officers who are to be associated with the administration of justice, such as the judges, prosecutors, sheriffs and coroners, there are also to be found county officers who have duties in connection with the assessment and collection of taxes. The county thus serves some very important purposes, but the town is obviously the principal unit of local self-government.

The town meeting is the chief organ of government in the town and exercises all the powers of the town that are not specifically bestowed upon particular officers. These officers are the selectmen, a group in every way similar to the selectmen of three centuries ago, a town clerk, an assessor, a treasurer, an overseer of the poor, a highway commissioner, several constables, and justices of the peace, and a school board. In the more populous towns still other officers are found.

There is no organic connection between the county and the town, for there is no representative county board composed of members elected from the respective towns.

The South and Far West.—Outside of New England is to be found a group of twenty-five states where townships do not exist. They compose a great belt sweeping down from Maryland and Delaware, embracing all the southern states and some that are not quite far enough south to be considered strictly southern. This belt continues on including also the three Pacific coast states, the Rocky Mountain group and certain others of the Far West.

These twenty-five states are:

Delaware	Georgia	Louisiana	Utah
Maryland	Florida	Texas	Nevada *
West Virginia	Alabama	New Mexico	Idaho
Virginia	Tennessee	Arizona	Montana *
North Carolina *	Kentucky	Colorado	Washington
South Carolina *	Mississippi	Wyoming	Oregon
	California *		

As already has been pointed out the conditions in the South were not favorable to the development of towns or other small areas of government, and hence counties were organized which promptly assumed all of the functions of local government. This type of organization has been satisfactory to the people of this section and few attempts have been made to foist a system of townships upon such communities to which these small units of government would be quite unadapted.

Another factor, than the factors of social, economic and

---

* Townships exist in these states in name, but they are merely justice of the peace districts and do not possess the characteristic township organization.

climatic conditions, also explains the extension of the county type of government into the Far West. The portions of the country straight west from the southern Atlantic seaboard states was populated largely by men who went straight west, not by northerners coming south. And those who went west out of the southern Atlantic states carried with them the plan of government which had proved suitable in the states from which they came.

To say that the county is a more important unit of government than the township in this great section of the country is hardly accurate. The county here is the only significant unit of local government and performs all functions of local government, although the county may be divided into districts to facilitate administration.

Obviously there is no such problem as establishing organic connection between the county and township.

The Central Group.—The section of the country that remains is composed of seventeen states that are found clustering around the Great Lakes, and those immediately west of them as far as Wyoming and Montana. In these states are to be found townships as well as counties.

But the states in this area must be divided into two groups, for the states in each group are distinctively characterized by the relation existing between the county and the township. It has been customary to divide these seventeen so-called central states into the North-Central and the South-Central groups, respectively, even though the use of these terms is not at present altogether justified.

The North-Central Group.—In the so-called North-Central group are:

New York	Michigan	Wisconsin
New Jersey	Illinois	Nebraska

The type of local government organization to be found

in these states may be called the "township-county" or "supervisor" type. The distinguishing feature of this type of organization is that the county is controlled by a board of supervisors composed of one or more supervisors elected from each township in the county. The result is that the size of the county board varies from three to fifty, depending upon the number of townships in the county. This means of course that the county board is usually quite large, averaging about twenty. It further means that very definite organic connection is established between the two units of local government—the county and the township. The arrangement also emphasizes the importance of the township, for in reality it is township officers who manage county affairs.

The county is considerably more important than it is in New England, though not so important as it is farther south, many important functions of local government being left with the townships. On the other hand, the township is not so important as the town is in New England though of decidedly more importance than it is in the remaining eleven, or South-Central group.

Where both county and township exist there is a division of function between the two units of government,—some important functions being exercised through the township, such as the assessment of property for taxation,—while other important functions are exercised through the county. Until comparatively recent years the townships in the six states under discussion have been units of considerable importance. But the modern tendency is toward a steady decline of the township as an area of local self-government.

The South-Central Group.—In the South-Central group are to be found the remaining states.

They are:

TYPES OF LOCAL GOVERNMENT

Pennsylvania	Minnesota	Arkansas	Kansas
Ohio	Iowa	North Dakota	Oklahoma
Indiana	Missouri	South Dakota	

There has developed here a different combination of the township and the county and it may be called for convenience the "county-township" or "commissioner" type of local government. The distinguishing features are that there is no organic connection between the two units of government, the county is controlled by a board of commissioners of from three to seven, popularly elected, usually at large; and the township is a distinctly subordinate unit. Indeed, in this group of states the township is rapidly coming to be but little more than an administrative district existing in order to facilitate the administration of county business. Most of the important functions of local government are under the control of county officers, and while the township is still maintained as a distinct unit of government with its own organization, in order to perform such functions as caring for highways, extending poor relief and assessing property, it is greatly overshadowed by the county organization. This is looked upon by many as a very desirable situation and it is possible that the other six states in the Central group will adopt the commissioner plan sooner or later.

Merits of Each Type.—A word or two may well be said at this point about the relative merits and demerits of the four types of local government, though a study of the details of structure and function will later bring out the points more clearly.

In the first place the New England system is often hailed as being eminently democratic, and it appeals strongly to the imagination and prejudice of the person who thinks of forms rather than substance. It provides an opportunity for pure self-government if not for pure democracy. The modern student is not inclined to admit that local self-government, through the instrumentality of town organization, is essentially any more democratic than certain other forms of government; but it cannot well be denied that the town organization does afford an opportunity for direct self-government. Thus under the town system of local government organization small communities may be pictured establishing and maintaining schools in their own way, building roads and bridges to suit themselves, levying and collecting taxes as they choose, caring for their own poor and other dependents, maintaining the peace through their justices and constables, and passing local ordinances.

This is a very pretty picture, of which any American may well be proud, when it is conjured up as a vision of early day democracy. It provides a basis for a theoretical argument in favor of the town type of local government organization, which is indeed about the only argument which can be advanced. The objections that can be raised against the town system, and the other system most nearly analogous to it in which the township plays an important part, are so numerous and so well founded that nothing but a natural conservatism and reverence for past institutions protects the town system from breaking down.

Newer concepts of governmental functions cannot be worked out through such a decentralized system. State governments are expanding the field of their activities each succeeding decade, and the problem of exercising the newer functions in the way that modern public opinion demands that they be exercised is greatly complicated by the existence of a multitude of little towns or townships enjoying high prerogatives that cannot be invaded. Contemporary public opinion is demanding better school sytems, uniformity of standards is desired. This can only be attained through state action—which is necessarily impeded if each little local area is to have charge of its own school affairs. Public opinion is demanding better roads. They cannot be secured if the local units are to be relied upon to coöperate and build them. Public opinion is demanding more intelligent care of the poor and other dependents. It cannot be provided so long as local areas have complete supervision of the function. And so it goes, as the public is demanding better things of government, the town or township type of organization proves itself to be wholly inadequate to the newer problems.

Furthermore, the town and the township have lost their hold upon the imagination of the people, and township affairs no longer excite interest and enthusiasm. The individual is no longer so much interested in local self-government as he is in efficiency. He wants things done, and done well, and as economically as possible. He is very willing to sacrifice some of the opportunities for self-government in order to attain these ends. As this sentiment grows the township steadily declines, its government is apt to fall into incompetent hands, and it fails to perform well, even those functions which might properly be left to local officials.

Reasons for the absence of the town and the township type or organization in the South and Far West have already been discussed and it would be an idle task to discuss the merits and demerits of the county system in those states when there are so many fundamental obstacles to the establishment of any of the systems which obtain in the northern states. But it may be said that the county in these states never has been and is not now a particularly vigorous unit of self-government in the same sense that counties in the North have been, and would lend themselves readily to a programme of centralized control over functions of local government in the state administrative departments.

County Boards in Central Group.—The arguments to be advanced in favor of and against the types of local government organization to be found in the North-Central group of states where the combination of township and county is to be found, center largely around the merits and demerits of a large board of representative supervisors, or a small board of county commissioners. The division of function between the county and the township is not necessarily involved in a discussion of the character of the county board. It is quite possible to divide local government functions between township and county without changing their structure, and this process of dividing functions continues to go on, usually at the expense of the township. But regardless of the specific functions which the county has to perform, what can be said in favor of or against the practice of maintaining a county board of supervisors composed of one or more persons elected from each township in the county?

Merits of Large Board.—In the first place it is likely to mean that the county board will consist of about twenty members. Such an institution is quite in harmony with the principle of representative government, each man representing his constituency, which is one township. Such a board as this, it is said, is particularly well adapted to express the will of the people, being a truly representative assembly. The people of each locality feel that they have a personal representative on the county board through whom they can make their influence felt directly. Whether this is true or not, the thought at least exists in the minds of a great many people. Each individual feels that there is one member of the board who represents him and who is likely to be more sympathetic toward projects involving his own constituents, than he would be if he were elected at large and the whole county were his constituency.

Closely related to this point is the argument that members of such a board will be very conscious of their responsibility to a small, alert constituency, jealous of its own advantage and much inclined to bring pressure to bear upon its representative in order to induce him to carry through measures to the advantage of his community. Men elected at large it is said are not conscious of responsibility to any particular group, and on the other hand are not subjected to the scrutiny that is so often brought to bear upon a member by the residents of his township.

Furthermore, the large board of supervisors is necessarily deliberative in its methods, there is less chance of a large group being led into error, and less likelihood of embarking upon ill-advised projects. That the large body is slow there can be no doubt, and if delay and long deliberation are desirable in the administration of county affairs the large board of supervisors would certainly serve the purpose better than a small commission.

And finally there is invariably advanced the argument that it is more difficult to corrupt a large board than it is a small one.

Disadvantages of Large Board.—Most of these arguments continue to persist and are seriously advanced although there is some doubt as to whether they have much foundation in fact. But they are vigorously enlarged upon every time any move is made to do away with the township-county or supervisor type of local government organization. The disadvantages of this type—characterized as it is by the relatively large board of supervisors—are rather obvious. The large board is likely to be unwieldy and slow, and actually unresponsive to public opinion in spite of the fact that members are in a sense closer to their constituencies. The very fact that so many differing opinions find expression in the board meetings makes it exceedingly difficult to agree upon any one project. Deadlocks not infrequently occur and highly worthy projects are thrown into the discard or allowed to lie in abeyance simply because board members cannot agree upon some details which may be of distinctly minor importance.

Again, petty local interests will be advanced and occupy a great deal of time and attention when matters of greater importance to the county as a whole ought to be occupying the attention of the board. Members are likely to be so insistent upon carrying through programmes that will work to the particular advantage of their own townships that effective coöperation in the interests of all cannot be accomplished. Each member is likely to want roads in his township improved, to want the county institutions so placed as to suit his constituents, and to be constantly jealous of tax assessments. Such a conflict of interests is not likely to result in the best kind of administration. This situation is likely to promote the ever-present evil known as log-rolling, each member agreeing to support the programmes of his colleagues as a matter of reciprocity.

The large board of course results in the diffusion of responsibility. This is bound to be the case whenever a large group undertakes to exercise any function. The group, as a group, is responsible, and the individual member loses his identity—he cannot be held in any sense accountable for the acts of the group.

The large board as an institution of government is more expensive to maintain than a small board, and this argument might have some weight in the final balance. But the most potent argument of all against the large board of supervisors is that the functions of county boards come to be more and more each year pure administrative functions, rather than legislative, and it is an axiom of political science that the smaller the group the more efficient will be administration. Indeed administrative functions can be carried on best when responsibility is concentrated in the hands of a single individual. Small boards and commissions can also function successfully as administrative organs, but the large board is utterly unfitted to supervise administration.

If the county enjoyed any broad legislative powers it would be highly desirable to maintain a large, deliberative body to deliberate upon the legislative measures and determine policies. But each decade witnesses a decline in the number of legislative functions exercised through institutions of local government, and although a large measure of discretion is still reposed in county officers their functions are essentially administrative rather than legislative, and the situation demands institutions or organs of government that are fit to carry on administration rather than to legislate.

Merits of Small Board.—Arguments in favor of and against the type of organization existing in the South-Central group of states where the county-township or commissioner system prevails are but adaptations of the arguments advanced for and against the board of supervisors found in the North-Central group. The board of commissioners in the states where townships are not represented upon the board usually consists of from three to seven members elected at large. It is thus much better adapted to the handling of administrative work, and likely to be much more effective and efficient than the larger board. A small board can be called together frequently to dispose of pending business with dispatch. It is much more likely than the larger board to be adaptive to new circumstances, and inclined to embrace new and effective methods of administration. In the small board there is not the necessity for unsatisfactory compromising and log-rolling, as there are not so many divergent interests to be adjusted. And lastly, responsibility would be more nearly centralized in a small board of men.

The objections to the small board are largely theoretical. It is insisted that a small board of men elected at large cannot be so truly representative as a board of men coming from definite, small constituencies. The inhabitants of the various localities would have no personal representative on the board, too great power is vested in the hands of a few men, and a small group is easily corrupted.

Summary.—A survey has now been made of the four characteristic types of local government organization in the United States to-day, and the relative merits and demerits of each have briefly been discussed. The four types are in general to be associated with four more or less well-defined geographical areas: 1. Six states in the New England group where the town type exists and the county is relatively unimportant. 2. Twenty-five states in the Southern and Far Western group where there are no townships and the county is all-important. 3. Six states in the so-called North-Central group where a township-county combination exists which emphasises the importance of the township, and is characterized by a representative county board of supervisors. 4. Eleven states in the so-called South-Central group, where a county-township combination exists which minimizes the importance of the township and is characterized by a small board of county commissioners.

Types of Board Classified.—It is possible to go a few steps further in an attempt to generalize about county organization throughout the United States. Several distinct types of county board are to be found even among

TYPES OF LOCAL GOVERNMENT 71

states that all fall within one of the four areas enumerated above. These types of county board are well defined, but it is quite impossible to associate them with any distinct geographical areas, and no attempt will be made to do so.

1. In certain of the states a relatively large board of supervisors is to be found. They are the six states enumerated above as falling in the North-Central group, plus two more,—Delaware and Virginia. In these two states the county board is composed of a relatively large number of men chosen from districts; for there are no townships. Thus there are eight states with this type of board.*

2. There are four states where the county board is composed of the county judge plus the justices of the peace within the county. This frequently means that the board is relatively large.†

3. In three states the county board is composed of the county judge sitting with two or four popularly elected laymen.‡

4. In five of the states the county board is most irregular in its composition.§ In Connecticut it is composed of three commissioners appointed by the legislature. In Georgia special boards are created by the legislature for special purposes, such as Boards of Commissioners of Roads and Revenues. In Rhode Island there is no county board and the sheriffs, who are the principal county officers, are named by the legislature. In Vermont the county judge and two assistant judges compose the county board. And in Louisiana there are no counties at all; but in each parish there is a Police Jury composed of a police juror elected from each ward.

5. The remaining twenty-eight states, scattered from Maine to California and from Washington to Florida, have

* Del., Ill., Mich., Neb., N. J., N. Y., Va., Wis.   † Ark., Ky., Mo., Tenn.   ‡ Ala., Ore., Tex.   § Conn., Ga., La., R. I., Vt.

small boards of county commissioners of from three to seven members; and the smaller number is to be found most frequently.*

Tendencies Affecting Local Government.—In the light of this discussion of these types of local government organization it is pertinent to inquire if there is to be observed any marked tendency throughout the United States to adopt any one type. Are there any indications whatever that uniformity in type of organization may come about?

As a matter of fact it is natural to suppose that anything like uniformity never will be attained. Local conditions are likely to prevent that. But there are to be observed certain tendencies concerning local government that are practically universal, and a survey of them may give some intimation as to what the future may bring forth.

There is to be noted in the first place a very decided preference for the small board of county commissioners popularly elected at large. More than half of the states have this type of county board already, and many of the remaining states have small boards, but they are composed in irregular ways. The presence of a small board of county commissioners does not necessarily involve the abolition of the township; but on the other hand it seems to lead to a more or less complete assumption of control over most of the functions of local government on the part of county officers. Furthermore there is so much to be said in favor of having a small board to administer county affairs, instead of a large board, that the tendency is in favor of that system even where the township is still an important factor in local government.

Closely related with this tendency is what may be called

* Ariz., Calif., Colo., Fl., Idaho, Ind., Iowa, Kans., Maine, Md., Mass., Minn., Miss., Mont., Nev., N. H., N. Mex., N. C., N. D., Ohio, Okla., Penn., S. C., S. D., Utah, Wash., W. Va., Wyo.

the gradual degeneration of the township as an area for local self-government. Each decade witnesses a further decline in the importance of the township, and the taking away of control over various matters. In one state it may be that the township loses control over school affairs, in another it may be highways that are taken from its jurisdiction, and very rapidly the townships are losing control over the function of caring for the poor and other dependents. The process still goes on until it may be, within the course of a few decades, that the township will be nothing but an empty shell, with very little of importance left to do.

This situation of course grows out of another tendency, which is, that public interest in local affairs generally is falling to a rather low ebb. The population in these areas is no longer so homogeneous as it was. The inhabitants are not so much interested in the prerogatives of local self-government as they are in efficiency. They are not possessed of any very active desire to take part, personally, in the control of local affairs, but rather simply want things done and done well. The public no longer fears for democracy—although demagogues do their best to keep prejudice alive,—but is keenly interested in securing effective and businesslike methods of administration. This tendency of the public mind is sure to have a very profound effect upon the future of local government organization.

Another phase of this same tendency is that the public usually looks directly to the state government to launch broad progressive programmes in the interests of public welfare. The state is called upon to carry out programmes looking to the betterment of public health and sanitation methods. The state is called upon to build up a school system that will square with modern standards. High-grade cross-state roads are wanted, state institutions for the care of different types of dependents are springing up. In some states elaborate park systems and forest preserve projects are under way, or now in contemplation.

Each step in this general direction taken by the state government is likely to involve more or less an invasion of the prerogatives of the county and the township. But the tendency is very pronounced, and regularly each decade the state governments make heavy inroads. The public has become impatient with duplication of function in neighboring townships and counties, impatient with hand-to-mouth methods and ineffective policies administered through the instrumentality of local officials. There has been a lack of harmony and absence of common standards that has aroused public sentiment to thoroughgoing disgust. All this is bound to have a pronounced effect upon local government organization and functions of the future.

Another tendency is to develop county machinery to a point where the county is in a position to perform all of the functions lately carried on by the townships, and the manifest unwisdom of maintaining two systems of government adequate to carry on identical functions becomes more and more obvious. The proper solution of the problem is to give the county full control and allow the townships to continue to exist as mere administrative districts for the purpose of exercising county functions. This naturally involves a great decline in the importance of township government.

All of these tendencies grow out of a more fundamental tendency which lies at the base of all of them. There has been going on a gradual decay of the sense and spirit of unity that once upon a time was such a potent factor in molding the forms of local government. The sense of economic unity is gone; the people of a given small community no longer pretend to maintain anything like economic autonomy. Commercial and industrial intercourse have been developed to such a point through the instrumentality of new modes of transportation and wire communication that whole great areas are now economically interdependent. And this breaks down local autonomy. Thus the powerful economic tie that bound men together in local government areas has all but disappeared.

The sense of religious unity disappeared long ago. Geographic factors are no longer of much consequence because of the artificial means of overcoming the influence they might otherwise exert. With the stratification of society that comes with the development of industry and education, with foreign immigration and the rapid specialization and division of function as between groups of men, the social and cultural ties have been weakened greatly. All these factors were tremendously potent in the vast composition of forces which gave rise to institutions of local government and kept them intact throughout three centuries. Now they are breaking down, and the fact cannot but have a profound influence upon the future of local government.

A survey of these considerations leads to the belief that a certain degree of uniformity in type of local government organization may be expected, just as there is to be found a very decided uniformity in type of state governments. However, in this connection it should be added that institutions of local government are very much more susceptible to social and economic, and other such factors, than are the state governments. Thus while the state governments of Maine, Georgia, and Oregon might be substantially alike, it will not be at all surprising if institutions of local government in three such widely separated states always remain substantially different.

CHAPTER V

THE LEGAL STATUS OF THE COUNTY AND THE TOWNSHIP

Counties and Townships are Creatures of the State.— Notwithstanding the variations in type of township and county organization, the legal status of these two units is much the same everywhere. In a word they are both creatures of the state government in which they are found. Subject only to the state constitutional restrictions, the state legislature is everywhere competent to control the county and the township in every particular. They may be swept away entirely, or new ones may be created. Old ones may be consolidated and readjustments of county and township lines may be undertaken to any extent by the legislature, unless the state constitution forbids. Even in the older portions of the United States,—in New England indeed,—there are unorganized areas which from time to time are marked out into counties and towns quite at the will of the state legislature.

So it may be said that to-day, everywhere, the county and the township are created by, or exist on sufferance of, the state in which they are to be found. They do not have any claim to existence that can be defended in law, although there have been cases in which New England towns have attempted to defend themselves against encroachments by the state government upon what they have been pleased to call their inherent prerogatives.[*]

Furthermore, both the county and the township enjoy

[*] Eaton, "Right to Local Government," *Harvard Law Review*, XIII, 441.

only enumerated and delegated powers. Their power is specifically delegated to them through state law, either constitutional or statute, and the enumeration of powers is to be found in more or less detail in the law which bestows them. In this respect institutions of local self-government exhibit some degree of similarity to the federal government itself, in contrast to the state governments. The state governments in legal theory enjoy an unlimited residual and inherent power—namely, all political power which is not specifically denied to them by the federal constitution. The federal government, on the other hand, does not enjoy any such residuum of power but only those specific and enumerated powers which are delegated to it through the federal constitution. In this respect counties and townships resemble the federal government, enjoying only those specific powers delegated to them, usually by the state legislatures.

The state government is furthermore in a position to determine the character and structure of the government machinery in the counties and the townships. The various officers, their mode of selection and their duties are all determined by the state constitution or by acts of the state legislature. Offices may be abolished or created at the will of the state, and functions may be transferred from the hands of one officer to the hands of another. The fact that there is not greater variation in type, and more arbitrary juggling with local institutions is due partly to state constitutional limitations but more to the good sense of legislators and the strength of custom.

Limitations upon the State Legislature.—As a matter of fact, however, legislatures do not enjoy as extensive control over institutions of local government as these statements might suggest. It is the state as an entity that has the broad control, and this control may be exercised through two distinct channels: one is through constituent assemblies which write the constitutions, the other is through legislatures which enact the statutes. Years of experience have taught statesmen that it is wise to interpose certain restrictions on the power of legislatures to tamper with local government. Thus it is that there are to be found certain definite limitations of about the same character in most of the state constitutions.

1. May Not Alter County Lines.—It is customary for instance to forbid the legislature to alter county lines. This limitation was not found in early constitutions and indeed was not necessary or desirable in the early periods of settlement. When population was very sparse, and men could not foresee the flood of pioneers that came in later days to populate the western territories, it could not have been expected that territorial legislatures, or early state legislatures, would create counties small enough to suit the needs of later times. Large counties that might have been created in a state west of the Mississippi in the fifties for instance would not be quite suitable for the immensely larger population that appeared a few years later. It became desirable to cut the large, sparsely populated counties down and divide them up into smaller counties, and it would have been exceedingly inconvenient had the legislatures been tied by constitutional provisions that would have prevented the making of these changes as the growth of population made them desirable.

However, sooner or later each state established a system of counties of approximately equal area, though not of equal population, and it has been deemed altogether desirable that for the most part these counties should remain as they are, regardless of the shiftings of population. County lines might possibly be moved for political reasons, to promote party advantage, to hamper the activity of progressive officers in certain counties, or to remove certain areas from their jurisdiction. The temptations might be numerous and if it were a common practice to alter county lines through legislative act from time to time gross abuse could very well develop, which might lead to log-rolling and bargaining of a disgraceful sort. To permit legislatures to go further than merely to alter county lines, and actually to abolish counties or create new ones, would merely magnify the opportunities for abuse. So for these reasons it has been the almost universal practice in recent years to deny to the legislature the right freely to alter county lines.

But in order to obviate the necessity of amending the constitution whenever it does become desirable to change county lines the legislature may be permitted to do so through special procedure involving certain checks and safeguards. Thus in some of the states county lines may be altered only by a two-thirds vote of both houses of the legislature. Again, the legislature may make the alterations provided that they do not result in reducing the size of any county below a fixed minimum number of square miles, or provided that such alterations do not result in leaving any county with a population below a fixed minimum. Or the constitution may forbid the altering of county lines in such a way that any boundary of a county will be nearer than a fixed number of miles from the county seat. And it is also customary to require a referendum vote in the counties to be affected by the change before any alteration of boundaries can be made.

But there is a still more important point to be considered in this connection than any that has so far been mentioned. It is that counties are in many states the units of representation in the lower chamber of the state legislative assembly, and the opportunity to gerrymander the state from time to time, involving the dislocation of county lines, ought not to be left open to state legislatures.

But there is something to be said in general against this practice of permitting the counties to serve as representative districts. Such districts ought to be marked out according to population, just as are the congressional districts, and from one point of view it should be easily possible to alter the district lines appropriately after each census in order that the districts can be made to conform to the fluctuations of population. At present that can only be done by changing county lines.

In spite of the fact that counties are very frequently representative districts they are laid out with no regard to population, and since it is very undesirable that county lines should be changed frequently a compromise is often effected in order to obviate the grossest inequities when one county exceeds by a large margin the population in other counties. This is accomplished by giving the densely populated counties a certain measure of extra representation. But such a step is merely a compromise, not a real solution of the problem. Thus so long as county lines and representative district lines continue to be coterminous the problem of shifting either of them will be more or less complicated and it is thought well to prohibit the legislature from doing it. This means, of course, that any change in representative district lines must be secured through amendments to the state constitution, or by some such special process as has been described above.

Prohibition upon the legislature in the matter of changing county lines does not ordinarily extend to township lines. The same complications do not arise in this connection and it is not so serious a matter to upset township jurisdictions, particularly in those states where the township has come to occupy a relatively unimportant position. Oftentimes indeed county authorities have the right to alter township lines within their counties, and do so from time to time as the movement of population and the exigencies of the moment seem to require. Particularly is this true in counties that are still very sparsely populated. As the population does increase it becomes desirable to establish township government, and this is done on the motion of county authorities.

2. *Cannot Move County Seat.*—A second limitation upon legislatures in their power over institutions of local self-government is found in may constitutions, and forbids the legislature to change the county seat from one place to another. Whenever a county is created some certain city or village is denominated the county seat. At this place the courthouse is erected, in which sessions of the court are regularly held. The jail is also located at this place and all of the county officers are ordinarily expected to maintain their offices in the courthouse. However, it should be noted that county hospitals, poorhouses and other institutions need not be located at the county seat.

With the shiftings of population and the development of new centers of social and economic intercourse, it not infrequently seems desirable to change the county seat, in spite of the fact that such a move involves considerable expense and no little inconvenience to many people. In those states where legislatures have been free to make these changes at will there have been evidences of considerable chicanery and juggling for political advantage, prompted by ulterior motive. But whatever the cause, it will be found to-day that most state legislatures find themselves forbidden to change county seats arbitrarily. Sometimes it is made posisble to make the change following a referendum vote of the people in the county concerned. In a few counties, two county seats are to be found, the obvious result of compromise between opposing factions. But when this is the case it is found that one of the cities is the place where most of the county officers have their offices, while the other is merely another place for holding court; thus the court may divide its time in such counties between the two.

3. May Not Abolish Popular Election of Officers.—Another constitutional limitation upon state legislatures which has grown out of the experience of the past is that which forbids them to dispense with the popular election of local government officials. Such a prohibition as this is particularly significant in that it helps to protect the areas of local self-government from becoming pure administrative districts.

If it were possible for state legislatures, at one stroke, to do away with the popular election of local officials, and to fill offices with incumbents appointed by the governor, or by the legislature, the counties and townships would be very close to losing what semblance they still have of being areas for local self-government. The principal characteristics they still possess that serve to make them true areas for local self-government are: first, the right to elect their own officers—officers who are not to be accountable to superiors; and second, the right to determine policies and programmes and ways and means of executing them.

The tendency of the state to rob the townships and counties of this second prerogative has already been noted, and if local government officials were to be appointed by central authorities the last bare form of self-government would almost have disappeared and the counties and the townships would be nothing but pure administrative districts. So, although there has not been very much danger in the last few decades of state legislatures doing away with popular election of local officials, even if they had the power, the prohibition which is found in modern state constitutions does have considerable significance.

It must not be assumed, however, that all county officers are thus protected, or even that most of them are protected in a majority of the states. But the state constitution does frequently protect the more important county officers by providing in the body of the constitution itself that these officers shall be elected by the people. Members of the county board are thus protected in a large majority of the states, and the public prosecutor and the sheriff are also very likely to be made elective officers by the constitution itself. Many times the treasurer, the clerk, the recorder and some others are thus protected, but the practice is by no means so general as regards these less important officers. However, some limitation of this type is to be found in every constitution, and in so far as the constitution provides for the popular election of any county officers, just so far is the legislature prevented from making those officers appointive. If the constitution is silent the legislature is free to make an officer appointive.

There is more agitation at the present time than there has ever been before, for the reform of county government in such a way as to have the principal officers appointed and made responsible to central authorities. There is much to be said in favor of this, and the subject will be taken up at some length later in this volume, but it is doubtful if all of those who are behind the movement with such enthusiasm really appreciate the fact that it may mean the death knell of local self-government.

4. May not Abolish Offices or Reduce Salaries.—Another limitation which usually rests upon state legislatures in their dealings with institutions of local government is that which forbids them to abolish offices or to reduce salaries during the term of an officer involved. The purpose of this limitation is obvious. Should it not exist any state legislature would be in a position to work its will upon local officials by threatening to reduce their salaries or to abolish their offices altogether. Legislatures have been known to stoop to such devices, and it is highly desirable that a limitation should be imposed upon them in order to prevent it.

5. *May not Pass Special Legislation.*—Still another prohibition upon state legislatures is that which is intended to prevent the enactment of special legislation designed for the advantage or disadvantage of one or a few counties. Were this limitation not to be found in the constitution it would be possible for the legislature to discriminate unfairly and to confer upon certain counties various privileges, liberties, and powers that could be withheld from others. Certain counties might be allowed to build institutions such as hospitals or libraries or to carry on new activities that might seem desirable in the light of changing conditions, whereas other, less favored counties, might ask in vain to be permitted to enjoy the same privileges.

Again, the structure of county government might not be kept uniform if legislatures were free to alter conditions in those counties where they saw fit to change them. New forms of government might be permitted to some favored counties and not allowed to others. And if counties were made to suffer under such discrimination because of the party complexion of the county, the situation would become intolerable. So it is found that most constitutions forbid legislatures to pass special legislation for the benefit or disadvantage of particular counties.

The difficulties that give rise to the need of special legislation for counties are not so numerous or so acute as the difficulties that arise in connection with municipal legislation. State legislatures are usually forbidden to pass special legislation for cities, and this prohibition is designed to prevent favoritism in the matter of control over public utilities, the granting of franchises, and the engaging in new municipal undertakings.

But sometimes it is desirable to pass special legislation. All cities cannot be fitted into a single mold, particularly when variations in size are great. Large cities require certain powers that are not required by smaller cities, and it is desirable that certain cities be permitted to undertake new programmes that ought not to be allowed in others. Seemingly the only fair basis of discrimination, however, is size, and so it is that cities in most of the states are now grouped according to their population, into three or more classes. Then the legislature is permitted to pass general laws applying to all the cities within a group.

This device has served to prevent the worst abuses and the grosser sorts of discrimination are no longer possible in a majority of the states. But it should be mentioned that each year uncovers some new attempt upon the part of state legislatures to circumvent the obvious spirit of this constitutional limitation forbidding special acts. Legislatures are usually left free to determine the basis of classification and they sometimes do so in such a way that only the favored city will fall within a given class. Then legislation can be passed ostensibly applying to a group of cities within a given class when as a matter of fact there is only one.*

On the whole this constitutional limitation has worked very successfully, in spite of the attempts to circumvent it, and the idea has in many cases been adapted to the same problem in connection with the counties, and they too are now protected in exactly the same way against unfair

* F. E. Horack, "Special Municipal Legislation in Iowa," *American Political Science Review*, XIV, 423.

discrimination. Yet even where this protection does not exist there has not developed the tendency to discriminate as between counties to their disadvantage as was the case with cities. However, in recent years the more populous counties have sought permission to engage in activities that are not suitable for rural counties. Thus they have sought power to build and maintain general hospitals, to build and maintain elaborate parks, to carry out drainage projects and various large undertakings, and special power to do these things has been needed. The problem has been solved by classifying counties according to population and bestowing the necessary power upon those few which ought to have it. So, in many states even where the legislature is prevented by constitutional limitation from passing special legislation dealing with areas of local government, this special device has been exploited to very good advantage.

6. *Minor Limitations on Power of Legislature.*—These are about the only constitutional limitations resting upon the legislature which can be considered general, that is,—found in a large proportion of the states. Of course it is to be expected that in this period of political experimentation numerous idiosyncrasies affecting local government would crop out in the newer state constitutions. But they are for the most part of minor importance and an account of them would but promote confusion without serving any important end. The borrowing power of counties is often limited in the constitution just as the borrowing power of cities and the legislature is limited. Counties are forbidden to go into debt beyond a certain fixed sum, or the limit is fixed relative to the value of the property within the limits of the county. The tax rate which may be imposed by county boards is also fixed. The county is frequently forbidden to become a stockholder in any corporation, and there are various other limitations that need not be enumerated.

Viewed all together these limitations on the power of legislatures to deal with areas of local government may seem rather formidable. But when it is remembered that the legislature is still in a position to create offices, fix salaries, outline functions, bestow and withhold power to almost any extent, it will be seen that counties and townships are but creatures of the state and are controlled in the smallest matters through the principal state organ, the legislature.

Whether the limitations here discussed apply or not in a given state, it is universally the custom for state legislatures to defer to certain fundamental ideas that are deep rooted in the minds of American people. In the first place, legislatures defer to the sentiment which demands some measure of local self-government and this means that a large proportion of local officers, particularly the older ones, shall be elective; and furthermore that some discretion, some right to determine policies and to execute them, shall still be vested in the areas of local government.

Secondly, state legislatures usually defer to the American belief in the principle of administrative decentralization, which means that local officers, who are popularly elected, and not responsible to superior state officers, shall be left free to execute state law in whatever way they see fit. Constitutions do not present very many formidable obstacles to the radical reform of county government. Legislatures are for the most part very free to do what they please. But even in the absence of constitutional restrictions the state legislatures prefer to act upon these older principles that permit a very considerable measure of local self-government.

Bodies Corporate and Politic.—Pursuing further the general question of the legal status of the county and the township it will be found that they are usually referred to in the terminology of law as bodies corporate and politic, and as quasi-corporations. These terms need some explanation. A corporation is a legal entity, a juristic person, actually an individual in the eyes of the law, enjoying certain specified powers, exercising some specific functions, vested with certain privileges, and owing certain obligations. Corporations are created by the legislature. Most of them are known as private corporations and exist for the purpose of carrying on some business enterprise, though it is quite customary for clubs, societies and other groups of people to incorporate for purposes other than business activity. They are granted charters in which all the details of their organization, powers, and functions, are set forth; or else they may be incorporated by a general act of the state legislature.

Public and Private Corporations Contrasted.—Public corporations are to be clearly differentiated from private corporations. Private corporations have no governmental powers, do not exist for governmental purposes and are in no sense instrumentalities of the state. They exist for private purposes, and the act or charter by which the private corporation is created and its privileges and powers defined, constitutes a contract between the members of the corporation and the state itself.[*] So-called public service corporations are strictly private corporations, and are not to be confused with public corporations.[†]

Public corporations on the other hand do have governmental powers, they exist exclusively for governmental purposes and are instrumentalities of the state. But public corporations are of various grades. The municipal corporation is of the highest grade. Cities, towns, villages and boroughs are municipal corporations. They exist

[*] Dillon, J. F., *Municipal Corporations*, Fifth Edition (1911) I, 142.
[†] *Ibid.*, p. 146.

primarily for the satisfaction of local needs of a special nature. The municipal corporation is created at the behest of those persons who are to be within its jurisdiction, the character of its governmental powers and functions is intended to suit their convenience; and it is not ordinarily used as an area through which the state government itself shall function.*

An administrative district, such as a road or park district, may be a civil or a public corporation and serves as an area through which the state itself exercises just one function—the maintenance of roads or a park. And somewhere between the municipal corporation, which is of the highest grade, and such an area as the park district, which may be considered of the lowest grade, are to be found the county and the township.

Counties and Townships as Public Corporations.— Counties and townships are not municipal corporations for they do not exist primarily to satisfy the needs of the locality. They are further to be differentiated from municipal corporations in that they are created ordinarily to suit the convenience of the state and not at the behest of the persons who are to be included within the jurisdiction. Furthermore, they are used as instrumentalities of the state government in ways that municipal corporations are not. The state government functions through the county and the township. Even so they are to be found upon a higher plane than pure administrative districts and special districts such as park and drainage districts, in that they do afford some opportunities for local self-government. Thus they have governmental machinery through which they determine policies, their officers are popularly elected, and they enjoy the prerogatives that go with administrative decentralization.

* Dillon, J. F. *Municipal Corporations*, Fifth Edition (1911) I, 64.

They are called quasi-corporations. The word quasi means "similar to" or "like." Thus they are similar to the municipal corporations but they are not municipal corporations. They are similar to public corporations even when, as in some states, they do not actually have the status of public corporations. They are like corporations in many particulars, enjoying certain corporate powers. Hence they are known as bodies corporate. As bodies corporate they have a status in law very similar to that of an individual in many respects. They may sue in the courts, and suits may be brought against them by individuals or other corporations, and they can be compelled to pay damages if circumstances warrant. They may buy and sell property, both real and personal. They may enter into business contracts which are enforcible in the courts, and they can hire and dismiss employees, just as can true private corporations. These are the powers and privileges that are implied when the county or township is referred to as a body corporate.

Their Corporate Powers are Limited.—But there is a distinct limitation upon their privileges as bodies corporate. They may exercise the corporate powers only in the furtherance of governmental functions. Thus they can buy land, but only in order to use it as the site for a public institution or for some other public purpose. Thus they can enter into contracts and employ persons to do work, but only in the furtherance of political functions. And the courts by proper process will block any attempt on the part of public corporations to exercise corporate powers for any other purposes. Thus is emphasized the fact that counties and townships are bodies politic as well as bodies corporate. They exercise their corporate powers in the furtherance of their political functions.

Legal Status and Extent of Power.—In this chapter

have been discussed the essential aspects of the legal status of the county and the township. It should be observed that this status is not necessarily affected by the importance or unimportance of the area in question. Thus a township may be a body corporate and politic and be properly referred to as a quasi-corporation whether it has very few and unimportant functions to perform, as in Pennsylvania, or has relatively many and important functions to perform, as in the state of Michigan. And the legal relation of the county to the state in New England, where the county is of relatively slight importance, is much the same as the legal relation between the county and the state in California, where it is of distinctly greater importance.

The legal status of the county and the township is furthermore not affected by the character of the governmental structure within the area in question. Thus it makes no difference whether there be a large board of county supervisors or a small board of commissioners, or what other officers there may or may not be, the legal status of the corporate entity is not affected by the wide variations in character of governmental structure.

But these variations in governmental structure must be examined. The governmental structure, that is,—the offices, organs, and institutions through which functions are exercised in the counties and the townships—are hardly just the same in any two states. The character of these institutions, organs, and offices, their functions and methods of operation must be the subject of succeeding chapters.

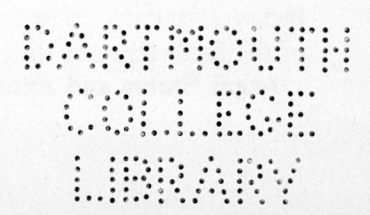

CHAPTER VI

FUNCTIONS OF THE COUNTY AND THE TOWNSHIP

Functions of Local Government Enumerated.—Before turning to an examination of the various officers of local government, their duties and methods of operation, it will be profitable to take a preliminary survey of the governmental functions that are ordinarily exercised through the county or the township, even though they will be discussed at greater length in the chapters that follow. No attempt will be made for the present to classify the functions and assign certain of them to the county and others to the township. The practice in this regard differs widely in the various states. But it is possible at least to enumerate a number of very important and clearly defined governmental functions that are in most cases exercised through the areas of local self-government, though in certain cases it may be through the county and in other cases through the township. The problem for the moment is to discover those things which people in small districts do for themselves through officers and institutions of their own, and which they can control. There lies the essence of local self-government. If a community of people can determine policies of their own, provide ways and means of executing them, and see that they are executed through officers locally chosen, and who are not responsible to superior authorities outside the district—there is a manifestation of local self-government.

1. *Maintenance of Peace*.—Maintenance of peace may

be considered a function of local self-government. The maintenance of peace may be considered the most elementary function of government in any time or place. Peace is a relative term of course, and a band of disorderly and tumultuous aborigines might be considered relatively peaceable if they submitted to the dictates of any recognized authority. Maintenance of peace is necessary before any other functions of government can possibly be exercised. Indeed the exercise of other functions of government always is contingent upon a condition of peace.

Peace may very well be maintained by some external authority and very frequently it is. Thus a government may send its soldiers to maintain peace in dependent colonies. Thus the federal government might maintain an elaborate organization of federal police to maintain peace throughout the United States, were it not for the limitations of the constitution. Thus each of the state governments might maintain police forces to patrol the entire state and maintain peace in the cities and the counties. Each is an illustration of the maintenance of peace by external authority.

But the practice in colonial America and the United States to-day has been quite the contrary. The colonial governments never maintained police forces. The federal government has never maintained a police force, and very few of the state governments have anything in the nature of a police force. For three hundred years on American soil it has been the practice for the people in each small community to maintain the peace through officers of their own selection. These officers have been the sheriffs and the constables. They have been locally elected and are not under the authority of state or federal officers. Contrary to the impression that is quite general county sheriffs are not under the authority of state governors.*

Except for the cities which have police forces of their own, the maintenance of peace throughout the whole United States is in the hands of county sheriffs and township constables. And so far as area is concerned the cities are but dots upon the map in spite of the fact that half the national population is concentrated in them. The sheriffs and the constables are general peace officers. This means that it is their duty to do more than simply to enforce certain specific laws and to arrest persons who violate specific acts,—they are expected to assume the very general and much more comprehensive function of maintaining peace with all that it implies.

Federal officers may be appointed to enforce certain federal laws which are related to the maintenance of peace. Thus federal officers run down counterfeiters, they seek out smugglers, they suppress disloyalists and they carry on an elaborate campaign against violators of the federal prohibition laws. In doing this they are in a sense peace officers; but it is not their function in a general sense to maintain the peace, for that remains to local officers.

State agents may also be appointed to execute certain laws and exercise specific functions closely related to the maintenance of peace, and yet not be general peace officers. Only in very recent years have state officers, exercising general peace functions, appeared. These state police organizations will be considered at a later time; suffice it for the present to say that the general maintenance of peace throughout the United States is in the hands of local officers. They are obliged by law specifically to enforce state and local legislation, and usually are very ready to assist

* This fact was vividly illustrated in Illinois (1921) when the Governor of the state was arrested by a county sheriff.

federal officers in the enforcement of federal acts, though it may be questioned if they are required to do so.

The question may arise as to which is the more important officer in the exercise of this function: the county sheriff or the township constable. This depends somewhat upon the type of local government organization which obtains. In those states where the townships have declined to a very unimportant position the constable's chief function is to serve as an attaché of a justice court. And in some counties, particularly in New England and in those counties which contain cities of considerable size, the sheriff also has little to do except to act as the executive officer for the court. But even so he continues to be the principal peace officer in every section of the United States.

In many sections of the country, although he continues to exist, the township constable has gone almost into total eclipse. The advent of the automobile in the twentieth century, however, has been instrumental in drawing him out of retirement, momentarily at least, while at the same time it has greatly complicated the problem of maintaining the peace in rural districts. Not only have rural peace officers been sporadically active, and in a vacillating way attempted to prevent violation of the speed laws; but they have been faced with the problem of suppressing general crime in rural sections. The automobile, and the highly developed interurban railway systems have greatly facilitated criminal activity in rural districts, for city criminals are now able to launch their exploits far out in the country and get back to the city again in a very short time. And as said above, this situation has served to bring rural peace officers out of growing obscurity, and the results have not been to their credit. But while blame should not be attached to the officers themselves they have proved to be unable to cope with the new situation, and the inevitable demand has come for state police. Many counties have employed special officers, equipped with motorcycles, to work under the direction of the county sheriff, particularly in an effort to prevent speeding. But such a move does not solve the greater problems of peace maintenance that have loomed in recent years.

The general function of maintaining the peace involves also certain other functions. If the county and the township are to be responsible for the maintenance of peace they must provide institutions for the restraint and possible reformation of lawbreakers. Each local area must have its prison, and thus the county jails have become familiar the country over. The maintenance of reform schools for juvenile offenders of both sexes is a proper function to exercise in connection with the maintenance of peace. But local institutions of this sort are few and far between. Those reform schools which do exist are usually state institutions. Houses of correction where adult offenders sentenced for a year or less can be sent to learn some trade or mechanic art during their period of incarceration are a distinct improvement upon old time county jails, and might well be supported by the more populous and wealthy counties in their exercise of the peace function. But such institutions are very scarce. The county penal farm idea is being developed in certain states where petty offenders are sent to farms where they are kept under some restraint but are given an opportunity to do outdoor work to their own advantage and that of the whole community.

These functions are merely mentioned in passing at this time in order to give some idea of the problems involved in the general function of maintaining peace, which still remains one of the fundamental governmental functions exercised through the areas of local self-government.

2. *Administration of Justice.*—A second function of

government very closely related to that of maintaining peace is the administration of justice. This function is almost as elementary as the function of maintaining peace, though not quite. Peace may well be maintained without justice and frequently is, but of course enlightened public opinion always demands free access to systematic machinery for the administration of justice. This machinery may be provided by and controlled by external authority, or again it may be created and controlled by local authorities. The latter practice has always prevailed on the American continent to a greater or less extent. The general tendency has been to permit the people of each local community to set up their own structure of judicial machinery and to administer justice in their own community through officers of their own selection.

This practice has not been carried out quite so consistently as it might have been, for many times judges of the county courts were appointed by superior colonial officers and thus were not in any sense controlled by the inhabitants of their respective jurisdictions. However, outside the southern states judges sooner or later came to be popularly elected, each county had a judicial structure of its own, and most of the other functionaries connected with the court were popularly elected as well as the judges.

At the very basis of the judicial system have been the justices of the peace, functioning for their respective townships. They had in the early day, and still possess, jurisdiction over petty criminal and civil cases. They have final jurisdiction over criminal cases which involve very small fines or short prison sentences, and over civil cases involving small amounts. It has always been possible to carry appeals by certain prescribed steps to the supreme tribunal in the colony or state. But the significant thing is that justice has been for the most part administered through local machinery, through judges elected by the inhabitants of their jurisdiction, through public prosecutors elected by the people whom they are to prosecute, and through machinery that is maintained by the taxes which the inhabitants have imposed upon themselves for the purpose. That is a manifestation of democracy, and of self-government.

"Not a very happy one," the reformer of the present time will say. Justice of the peace courts have been immortalized with the ridicule which has been heaped upon them since the days of Shakespeare. Elected judges in the county courts have not always maintained the standards that could be desired; and these facts together with the example of the federal judiciary which is highly centralized and not controlled through popular suffrage, have led to a lack of faith in local machinery of justice.

To a considerable degree state centralized control has been accomplished by the establishment of judicial districts larger than the counties, each district embracing two or more of them. The judges are still elected for the most part, but they hold court in the various counties of the jurisdiction and virtually have ceased to be "county" judges. Other court functionaries, however, clerks, sheriffs and prosecutors, are still county officers just as much as they ever were.

The administration of justice involves the selection of public prosecutors, clerks, and other court attendants. It involves the maintenance of a courthouse and all the equipment necessary to court procedure. Every county must do these things as part of the function of administering justice, for it is still administered through areas of local government.

3. Probate.—A third function of local government, which is but one aspect of the judicial function, has to do with the probation of wills, and other *ex parte* proceedings. With the appearance of the state district court it often happened that a county court would be retained for certain purposes, chief among which would be the probation of wills and the disposition of the property of those who died intestate. These county courts are now also very frequently intrusted with other judicial functions that can be exercised without a jury and all the processes necessary to the trial of cases in the state district courts. These functions ordinarily are the disposition of insanity cases, the commitment of orphans or other dependents to county or state institutions; and sometimes the handling of juvenile cases when these are not handled through the regular courts.

Altogether these functions make quite a mass of judicial business that can very well be removed from the dockets of the regular courts, and each county in many of the states maintains a separate special county court for the sole purpose of handling this business. The clerk of this court is likely to be charged with keeping vital statistics,—records of births, deaths and marriages.

It not infrequently happens too that such county courts enjoy control over certain administrative functions. Thus the special county court may have some authority in the management of local charitable institutions, some powers in connection with the maintenance of highways; and also may possess a very considerable power of appointment to minor administrative positions. This is not altogether a satisfactory situation for it means a division of administrative authority between the court and the county board. It were much better that courts be confined to strictly judicial business and that administrative authority be centralized in the county board.

But at any rate, whenever a special county court does

not exist, it means that the county must provide itself with a judge, through popular election, with a clerk, and all the other officers necessary to the handling of this work. It may be, however, that the same clerk and staff which attends the sessions of the regular district court also attends this special county court.

4. Poor Relief.—A fourth function of government that has been exercised since earliest times through local areas is that of poor relief and the care of dependents generally. It is only in recent years that the state governments have undertaken to care for dependents on any extensive scale. Ever since small settlements were established in America each community has been expected to care for its own dependents in its own way, to build institutions, to employ managers for them, to dictate the methods of control, to collect taxes and to provide for the maintenance of the institutions. Thus the care of dependents has been a function of local government in every sense of the word.

In its larger aspects this has involved the building and maintenance of poorhouses, institutions that have been notorious in the United States for generations; and in later years the maintenance of county farms where the poor of the community can be cared for more intelligently. For many years dependents of all types, the poor, the diseased, the insane, both aged and infant and of both sexes have been indiscriminately herded together into one institution denominated the poorhouse; but at the present time there is a decided tendency to create various types of institutions to care more effectively for the various types of dependents. This can be done of course only in those more populous counties that have the wealth to do it, though several counties may coöperate in the matter; other communities, which do not possess the wealth to do this, have no alternative but to await state action in this direction.

But in its newer and bigger aspects it can readily be seen that the function of caring for dependents has some very broad implications, and if it is to remain a function of local government the machinery must be built up and maintained in order to do it in a manner that accords with modern thought on these lines.

5. *Maintenance of Schools.*—Another and fifth function of local government is the maintenance of schools and all that it implies. In the earliest times this was strictly a town or township function wherever townships existed; and to-day they exercise control to a greater or a less degree. While the exercise of this function is not so necessary to the maintenance of political existence as are some of the other functions that have been enumerated, it is nevertheless a duty which was promptly assumed by small communities everywhere, and fulfilled with considerable success.

It has already been noted that the national government did a little something in the interests of public education, but it was rather by way of encouraging the inhabitants of the respective townships to do something for themselves.* They seized upon the parcels of land that were given to them for the purpose, built schools, provided for their maintenance and have been inclined to want to exercise control over them ever since. The maintenance of schools involves the erection of school buildings, the selection of a school board or group of trustees to have direct charge, the employment of teachers, the fixing of standards and the levying of taxes to cover the expense. Each local area that enjoys this function must have the machinery to do all these things.

The practice very early was established of creating systems of school districts more or less independent of the

* Through the Northwest Ordinance of 1787.

county and township authorities. Furthermore, present day dissatisfaction with the standards maintained by local district schools is leading very rapidly to a curtailment of the power of local authorities over the local schools, and they are gradually being brought into a centralized system. The first step usually is to organize all the rural schools into a county system, and the next obvious step is to bring all the public schools of the state under the control of state authorities. But for the present at least the local areas have a very large measure of control over their own schools, particularly in the matter of providing funds for equipment and salaries for teachers.

6. *Care of Highways.*—A sixth function of local self-government is the care of highways with all that it implies. Until very recent years state governments have not concerned themselves to any great extent with highways. If new roads were cut through it was the local authorities who were obliged to do it, if bridges were build it was necessary for the people of the locality to build them, if highways were improved each community carried on the improvement in the way that seemed best to it. Such is the situation to-day in a very large measure. Each locality must provide itself with the necessary political machinery and equipment for exercising this function. It means the existence of some group of locally elected men to determine highway policy and to impose taxes for the purpose of executing it. It implies the existence of highway commissioners or overseers, or engineers, or some persons of that description to take direct charge of road building. Road building and maintenance is in every sense a function of local self-government.

That the building and maintenance of highways has been in every sense of the word a function of local government is illustrated most vividly in the custom which still prevails in many quarters, of the farmers working on the roads themselves. It was not many years ago that the men of each local community literally went out and built their own roads with their own hands in just the way they chose. This eminently democratic custom was largely displaced by the imposition of a small tax on each man of the community, and each man was allowed the alternative of paying the tax for road improvement or doing a certain number of days' work upon the road himself. It is no uncommon thing, however, to discover farmers in certain rural sections out working on the roads today, rather than pay a tax. This practice is the very essence of self-government, but in the present day is distinctly undesirable. The work is likely to be done in a haphazard way, inconsistently and without order. And at best the work done in this way is likely to be poorly done, even if it does not do more harm than good.

Although counties and townships now have almost complete control over highways there have been certain very significant developments in the twentieth century that are calculated to break down this control and carry the function over to state authorities. The development of the automobile, both for pleasure and business purposes, led to an ever-growing demand for better highways than local authorities were ready to provide. The improvements made in concrete and other materials have made possible much more extensive road improvement. The inadequacy of the railroads has led to the demand for truck lines, and the steady development of national industry and national markets makes it ever more desirable to bind all portions of the country with fine highways. This may mean ultimate control by the state and even some participation by the federal government.

7. *Administration of Taxes.*—A seventh function of

local government is the function of administering the tax machinery. This has been a function always jealously guarded. Probably no public official in all history has been so universally disliked as the collector of taxes, particularly if the exercise of his function involves any personal contacts. And when the tax collector comes into a community as the emissary of some external authority his popularity is at a very low ebb indeed. Tax-gatherers sent out upon the evil business of mediæval kings have been hated of all men, and live in history and fiction as arch-tyrants. It is no wonder then that in the relatively democratic atmosphere of colonial America the principle of administrative decentralization should have been applied to the process of tax collection, and it is no wonder that the function of administering the tax machinery still remains a function of local government.

The people of each community select officers by popular election, who are not responsible to higher authorities, and who have full charge of the assessment and collection of general taxes both state and local, and the fixing of the tax rate for local purposes. Sometimes they are county officers, but where townships exist they are more likely to be township officers. This practice illustrates the contemporary application of the principle of administrative decentralization to the function of tax administration.

Had it not been for the application of this principle the function might to-day be exercised by state officers operating under the direction of state authorities and responsible to them. Indeed this change may come about in the future for there is great dissatisfaction with the administration of tax laws, and bills have already been introduced in certain of the state legislatures looking toward such centralization. It would mean the abandonment of township and county assessors throughout the state and the substitution of state officials, in no direct way controlled by the people whose property they would assess, and whose taxes they would receive.

For this very reason they might do better work and bring order out of chaos; but it cannot be expected that such a move can be made without arousing vigorous opposition—opposition sometimes based on prejudice and ignorance, to say nothing of ulterior motive, and also based on a firm belief in the older concept of democracy in which is cherished a firm belief in local self-government. These concepts of democracy have their roots down deep in the political experience of Americans and are not to be carelessly thrown aside at the behest of reforming enthusiasts.

The exercise of the function of tax assessment and collection involves the existence of some body competent to fix a tax rate for local purposes. Machinery must also be provided for the assessment of property and the collection of taxes. Each local area must have its officers to carry on this work, properly equipped with books and other materials that are necessary. The business of tax assessment and collection grows more elaborate and complicated each succeeding decade, and areas of local government should be prepared to do it well if they can expect to retain control over such a very important function.

8. Administration of Elections.—Another, and an eighth political function that is carried on under the direction of local authorities and subject to their exclusive control, is the management of elections. Naturally local officials would supervise the election of local officers, but it is also invariably the practice for the same local authorities to conduct elections for all public officials, national, state, district and local. This practice is but a further development of the principle of administrative decentralization and local self-government. The inhabitants of each locality have been jealous of their privilege of conducting elections themselves without intrusion on the part of external authority. In the past this has meant that local authorities even fixed the days on which elections were to be held, just to suit themselves. Polling places were set up in a most informal way, voters came to the tables that were provided, voted by word of mouth, openly and without possibility of secrecy, the votes were recorded by local officers, and final returns were made by them. Thus each little community engineered its own elections in its own way,—it was a manifestation of local self-government.

To-day of course state laws are so elaborate and detailed that the right to control the election machinery has but very little significance. The law is usually very precise as to the days on which voting shall take place, details concerning the polling booths, and elaborate provisions guaranteeing secrecy through the Australian ballot, leave the officials in charge but very slight discretion. Yet nevertheless it is the local officials who have full charge of the machinery of elections, and these local officials are not in any sense accountable to superior officers. They conduct elections according to the letter of the law as they see it, and make their returns as they think they should be made. Disgruntled candidates or other citizens may always appeal to the courts of proper jurisdiction if there is reason to believe that the local authorities have acted illegally.

The conduct of elections involves the appointment of numerous officials: Judges of election, clerks, tellers, watchers, etc., and they are all local officials chosen through local machinery. It involves the preparation of ballots, the maintenance of polling places, the actual conduct of the voting on election day, the counting of the ballots and the publication of the final returns. It is all done by local officials, and the counties and the townships must see to it that the process is carried out according to the law.

Furthermore, and this is very significant, the counties and townships are invariably the basic units in the political party structure. It is in the townships that party caucuses are held, and these caucuses are the very foundation of party machinery through which the people of any democratic state operate their government. Political parties are but groups of people organized for the purpose of running their institutions of government, and the party caucus, in the past at least, has been the starting point of all party activity. Out of township or precinct caucuses go delegates to county conventions. From the county conventions, or from the caucuses directly, go delegates to all the district conventions and to the state conventions; and thus it clearly can be seen how important are the townships and the counties in this party structure.

Direct primaries have largely done away with old-time party caucuses and conventions, but in so far as the great parties maintain any organization whatever they make use of the townships and counties as basic areas. Thus committeemen are selected for each precinct or township, chairmen and county committees are chosen to function for the county, and every detail of party organization is based upon these political areas. Political parties have really ceased to be private organizations, if indeed they ever were such, and it is of importance to note that their present elaborate organization is very closely related to the governmental structure.

9. *Recording Land Titles.*—The remaining functions of local self-government are not so important as those which already have been enumerated, but there are at least two more which ought to be mentioned. One of them, the ninth, as they have been presented here, is the function of

recording land titles. In early times it was the duty of town clerks to keep a record of land transfers, and the work frequently was not at all well done. It is necessary that some public officer should keep an accurate record of every transfer of land that takes place, in order that when occasion may arise it will be possible to trace the title to a particular piece of land straight back to the day when it was owned by the government itself. Although it is a purely clerical function and might as well be performed by a state officer under central control, it has been intrusted invariably to local officers locally elected. It thus becomes a function of local government and the local areas must make provision for its exercise.

10. Militia Organization.—A tenth function arises in connection with the state militia organization. Counties, or even townships, have served as the units in this military structure. One of the earliest purposes of county organization was to serve as units in the colonial military system. They are still recognized as the units for militia organization, but the fact has had very trifling significance because of the absence of compulsory military training. Had it been the policy in the past to maintain a system of compulsory training there certainly would have been a vigorous manifestation of the old spirit of democracy, and the people of local areas undoubtedly would have insisted upon the privilege of training and disciplining their own men through officers of their own choosing, in each county. However, it is altogether probable that such a decentralized system would have broken down sooner or later in the interests of military efficiency.

But in the absence of compulsory training public opinion has not been greatly concerned with the problem of military organization. The counties simply serve as units for the very imperfect organization that exists in most of the

FUNCTIONS OF COUNTY AND TOWNSHIP

states, although all military officers are responsible to central authorities,—specifically the state governor. It also may be added that it is customary for assessors to keep in their assessment books a complete list of all men eligible for military service. But this is a perfunctory task, and the records are of very small value.

11. State Administration.—To this list of ten functions which areas of local government must be prepared to exercise should be added the general and rather ill-defined function of serving as pure administrative districts for the purpose of executing state governmental programmes. New activities are being undertaken by state governments every decade —activities that were never thought of before and which the local areas do not, and ought not, to claim as being part of their functions. But it is necessary for the state government to divide the state into districts and sub-districts in order to facilitate the administration of the work in hand. Rather than divide the state into arbitrary and artificial districts for these purposes state authorities prefer to accept the counties just as they are and let them serve as administrative districts for the purposes they have in mind. Special state officers responsible to central authorities may be appointed in each county to carry on the state administrative programme under the supervision of their superiors; or again the existing organization may be accepted to a still further degree, and the regular county officials may be called upon to exercise the new state function. Local government machinery must always be available for state government purposes. The administration of health laws and pure food laws are cases in point. State officers are frequently appointed in the counties to administer this legislation, and such officers not being locally elected are directly responsible to the state officials who appoint them.

Special districts such as park, drainage or sanitary districts may be created independently of the counties and the townships, or else the functions involved may be carried on directly through county and township officers. Thus in some states township trustees devote a very large proportion of their time to drainage projects.

12. Minor Functions.—Finally, it may be said that as the public is demanding greater service from governmental agencies, counties are found exercising a variety of minor functions: the maintenance of playgrounds, hospitals, parks, libraries, and such like institutions, that may be classed as miscellaneous.

It is apparent that the line between strictly local functions and state functions is exceedingly difficult to draw, and some authorities insist that there is no such thing as a strictly local function as differentiated from a state function. Even so, students of administration and the law of public officers strive to make a working classification on this basis.

But before examining this problem an attempt might be made to classify all these functions that have been enumerated into two groups: on the one hand those that are township functions, and on the other hand those that are county functions. The other basis of classification, as already stated, would lead to a grouping of certain of these functions as purely local, and the others as more properly state functions.

Summary.—The governmental functions that have been enumerated here as being the functions of the county and the township are as follows:

1. Maintenance of peace.
2. Administration of justice.
3. Administration of probate, and other specialized judicial work; and keeping of vital statistics.

4. Poor relief.
5. Maintenance of schools.
6. Care of highways.
7. Administration of tax machinery.
8. Administration of election machinery.
9. Recording of land titles.
10. Militia organization.
11. Serving as an administrative district for purposes of the state government.
12. Miscellaneous minor functions.

Classification of Functions.—If an attempt were to be made to classify these functions by calling some of them township functions and some of them county functions it would be necessary to make a special classification for each of the forty-eight states. It is even impossible to generalize in this matter. In some states the county has jurisdiction over poor relief and the township over highways, in other states the situation is reversed, and in still others both the areas coöperate in both matters. All these functions are carried on through the county or the township or through both together, and no good purpose would be served by an attempt to analyze the situation in each and every state.

The county always has its peace officer and so does the township. The township has its justice court, and on the other hand the county is a vital unit in the state judicial system. Probation of wills is done by the county or district court, but vital statistics may be kept by county or township officers. Poor relief is extended through both areas, the county usually maintaining institutions, while the township may extend what is known as "outdoor" relief. Both areas are likely to have something to do with schools. Care of highways may be vested in either one, or the principal highways may be consigned to the county and the less important ones to the township. As to taxation, each area may be permitted to fix a rate for local purposes. There is likely to be a county collector; but assessors are usually township officers. Both areas play a part in elections. County officials are likely to have charge of recording land titles. The county is the militia unit. Either may serve as a unit for the administration of state functions although the township is seldom so used. And obviously miscellaneous minor functions may be carried on through either area.

Turning to the other basis of classification that has been suggested above, it would be necessary to list some of these functions as purely local functions and others as more properly state functions carried on through local areas. Such a basis of classification may be quite untenable, at least from one point of view: inasmuch as the local areas have no inherent or residual power it may be said none of their functions are purely local, but all are state functions exercised through local areas on the principle of administrative decentralization. However, in so far as local authorities are vested with real discretion, exercised through organs of government that are fully competent to deliberate upon and determine policies, they may, in one sense, be said to be exercising purely local functions. Poor relief, and the care of highways and schools, are clearly such functions, for in these fields of activity the local area is largely free to determine whether much or little shall be done, and how it shall be done. As regards maintenance of peace, and the administration of tax and election machinery the case is not so clear, but a very considerable measure of discretion is permitted in the exercise even of those functions.

But whether the functions discussed in this chapter be county or township, whether they be purely local, or state, the county and the township must be prepared to exercise them. It is necessary to have a structure of government in each area, officers must be selected, institutions established, and powers and duties clearly defined.

CHAPTER VII

THE COUNTY BOARD AT WORK

The County Board.—The principal organ of government in the county structure is the county board. It may be a very large board of supervisors representing the various townships within the county, or it may be a very small board of not more than three commissioners elected at large or from districts, by the voters of the county. In any event, whether the board be large or small, whether it consists of men elected in the various townships or at large, or even if it be composed of appointed justices as has been the case in certain of the southern states, the county board is the very heart of the county government. And it is to be found exercising practically the same functions, in much the same manner, in all of the states in the Union. The county board is usually created by the state legislature in a general law, and its functions and duties are prescribed by the legislature subject only to constitutional limitations.

Meetings.—The legislature determines the frequency of meetings. It is possible and customary for very small boards to meet as often as every two weeks. The larger and more cumbersome boards of supervisors may not meet oftener than twice a year. Meetings are held in the courthouse at the county seat and ordinarily are open to the public. The meetings of the very small boards are apt to be rather brief and perfunctory, held simply because the law requires it, and in order to satisfy the legal requirements by getting the business transactions into a formal record. Meetings of small boards are perfunctory because it is possible for three or five men to determine policies beforehand in a very informal manner. Important matters can be decided on the courthouse steps, in a hotel lobby, or on the street corner, by a little group of three or five men; and they go into formal session merely to legalize decisions which in effect have already been made.

This is not necessarily an undesirable practice. Such a group, talking things over privately and informally, may very likely arrive at wiser decisions than would be possible in a formal public session. But the practice does serve to shut the public out from the real discussion of county problems. One result is that the meetings of small boards are not generally attended by the public.

Meetings of the large boards are decidedly more formal. It is not so easy for twenty or thirty men to get their business cut and dried before the meeting, and therefore it is necessary to debate issues in full assembly quite at some length. While this involves more publicity, and provides an opportunity for interested citizens to hear matters discussed more or less at length, it does make it very much more difficult to effect those compromises which are so necessary to the quick dispatch of business.

Organization and Procedure.—The board selects one of its own members to serve as chairman. He does not have any special prerogatives and is in no sense a chief executive. He is merely a presiding officer at the meetings of the board. The board does not choose its own secretary. The county clerk, or the county auditor, himself an elective officer, serves as secretary for the board. He must of course be present at the meetings and fulfills all the functions of a secretary. This completes the organization of the board meeting and obviously it is very simple. Committees are appointed as occasions arise, and other problems of procedure do not present any special difficulties. A quorum of the board is usually fixed by law at a majority of the membership, and a majority of a quorum is sufficient to do ordinary business. In order to pass certain more important measures it is often required that a majority of the entire membership vote favorably. This rule is likely to apply to such measures as those which are intended to alter township lines, to appropriate sums of money above a certain amount, or to award large contracts.

Comparing the governmental organization of the county with that of the city, state, or nation, it is rather easy to think of the county board as the county legislature. This is hardly proper. In so far as the county enjoys any legislative powers they are indeed exercised through the county board. In other words, if any legislating is done the board does it. But the board actually has very little legislative work to do. It does make appropriations and that is pure legislation. It also determines policies in the matter of county undertakings, such as road making, the building of charitable institutions, and schools, perhaps; that too is legislation. But the principal work of the board is administrative, rather than legislative, as will be seen.

Legislative Functions.—Legislation in its broad aspects involves the determination of civil and legal relationships. The legislative power is the law-making power, and the law fixes the responsibilities, duties, rights, privileges, obligations, claims and penalties that grow out of the social or economic relationships and contacts between individuals, or between individuals and the government. This in its essence is the law-making power, and the county has very little of it. The county does not define crimes and fix penalties. The county does not determine the rights and duties of one citizen to another and fix the conditions under which they may engage in business relations. The county exists largely for administrative purposes and the board is primarily responsible for the proper discharge of the administrative functions. Hence it is not quite proper to speak of the board as the county legislature. Other analogies to city and state are just as difficult to make, for there is no distinct county judiciary or county executive.

In legal contemplation the board is the county and has the residuum of power, so far as the county is concerned. This means that the board exercises all powers granted to it specifically, and it also exercises all powers granted to the county and not specifically bestowed upon any other county officers. It should be remembered always of course that a county board must find definite sanction in the statutes or the constitution for every act it undertakes to perform. This means that its powers are enumerated and delegated, and in no sense residual or inherent.

Functions of the Board.—The statutes usually confer upon the board the function of exercising general supervision over all the activities of the county and county officers. This would seem to be a fairly broad grant of powers and ought to put the county board very definitely at the head of the county government. But upon closer analysis it will be discovered that "general supervision" does not mean very much unless the supervising authority has power to remove, or at least to control in some measure, the officers under supervision.

1. General Supervision.—This power the board is not likely to have. The board may investigate, examine, demand reports from, and criticise most of the county officers, but seldom is it able to give authoritative orders. The clerk, or the auditor, the sheriff, the attorney, and various other county officers are popularly elected and look to the statutes to find their duties enumerated. This illustrates the application of the practice of administrative decentralization. Such officers will not take kindly to attempts at authoritative control on the part of the county board, and the board has no means of enforcing its demands. Hence the function of general supervision is apt to be exercised in a most perfunctory manner. The function of supervision ought to involve the power to investigate thoroughly, to criticise, to outline changes in method that seem desirable, and most important of all—to give authoritative orders to the persons being supervised. Since this cannot be done effectively in the case of popularly elected officers, supervision over them and their activities usually involves nothing more than acceptance of the formal reports which they are obliged by law to submit to the board.

On the other hand, the county board is in a position to exercise very real supervision over the various county institutions such as poor farms, and hospitals, if they are managed by superintendents selected by the board itself. The board is also able to supervise very effectively the work of such county officers as are not popularly elected. Thus the road commissioner, or highway engineer, if he is not popularly elected, does his work under the constant and authoritative supervision of the board. General supervision ought to mean a great deal and it does mean a great deal when power is centralized in the board; but it never can mean very much under the present decentralized system, which is found in nearly every state.

2. *Keeping of Records.*—The board is responsible for the keeping of various county records. Most important of these are the records of its own proceedings. These should always be up to date and properly authenticated. Records of land transfers, and records of various legal documents are usually kept by the recorder, while the

clerk of the court is responsible for the court records. But there are certain other records for which the board should be directly responsible. There should be something in the nature of a claim register in which all claims against the county are recorded, and there should be a warrant book in which could be found a record of all warrants authorized. There ought to be also a very complete highway record in which could be found a record of all highway improvements undertaken, their cost, the bridges erected, and all other significant facts bearing upon the location and condition of public highways.

Such records as these enumerated constitute a minimum. They should be available in any county courthouse and the board should be directly responsible for their proper condition. But there are other significant records which the board may well be required to keep, at the discretion of the legislature. With the development of state control over county administration, more complete records are being demanded—records showing the location of electric wires, pipe lines, drainage systems and parks, railroad and interurban lines, cemeteries, schoolhouses, and other places of interest. Such records may be kept in a uniform way in books supplied by the state, and as years go on they afford a mass of well-organized information of value to public officers and citizens alike.

3. Determining Policies.—Upon assembling for its first meeting a county board is under the necessity of facing certain problems of policy. The field of free action and discretion for county boards is rapidly being narrowed by the expansion of state activity, but there still remain very important problems for the board to solve in its own discretion. The board must determine what undertakings shall be launched, what buildings and institutions shall be erected, what roads shall be cut through, what roads improved and how, what bridges built, what machinery and equipment purchased and what supplies shall be provided for the various offices and institutions of the county. It is in the exercise of this discretion that the county board functions primarily as an organ of local self-government, even though many of the board's functions are purely ministerial and call for the exercise of no discretion.

4. Awarding Contracts.—Having decided upon these various undertakings, it becomes the duty of the board to award contracts to the various corporations and business firms which desire to undertake the work. Letting of contracts is one of the most important tasks the board has to do. It is usually the business in which the members themselves are chiefly interested; it is of interest of course to business men who are seeking county contracts; and the taxpayer is also vitally interested in the size and number of county contracts. Obviously these contracts cover a great variety of subjects; they cover everything from lead pencils to be used in the school superintendent's office to the building of a million dollar courthouse. Contracts must be let for the erection of new buildings, for the repair and decoration of old buildings, for road work, for the building of bridges, for printing, stationery, office supplies of all sorts, and for food and provisions to supply all the county institutions. Even in small counties these contracts amount to thousands of dollars each year, and in thickly populated counties they amount to millions of dollars. It is not surprising, therefore, that the function of awarding contracts should attract so much attention. To contractors they mean good business deals; to board members they mean patronage, power and prestige; to the taxpayer they mean economy or extravagance.

A history of county contracts would be filled with many disgraceful episodes. Contracts for public work, be they granted by the federal authorities, states, or cities, are always considered by many unscrupulous business men as proper spoils; and by certain public officers as unparalleled opportunities for graft. Temptations are numerous and improper dealings are easily covered up. Probably county contracts are susceptible of greater abuse even than city contracts. The county board is more obscure than the city council and its dealings are not so much in the public eye. For this reason as well as others, the spoilsmen and the corrupt politician are usually very much in evidence when county contracts are to be awarded.

County contracts do many times exhibit gross extravagance, incompetence, and lack of business sense on the part of board members, to say nothing of fraud and favoritism. This unfortunate situation can be explained in ways that are not altogether to the discredit of the board members. It is not infrequently a plain fact that the members do not know enough about the work in hand to interpret a good or bad contract. A contract for building a hard surfaced road involving deep cuts and much grading can easily be padded in such a way as to deceive the untrained eyes of board members. Contracts for printing and building afford many opportunities for exploiting men who are unfamiliar with such work.

But of more significance is the fact that no single member of the board, and no other county officer, assumes personal responsibility for seeing that programmes of work, and the purchase of supplies, are being planned in the most economical way. Several building projects, repairing operations, painting and decorating programmes might all be included in one single contract in order to effect great economies. The printing of election ballots, and the stationery for all county offices could often be embraced in one contract. Supplies of food for all county institutions could be provided under the terms of a single contract; and through careful planning, such as always must be done by successful business firms, county contracts could be greatly improved. But there is nobody to assume responsibility for this and the result is that perfectly legitimate and unimpeachable contracts may still be very uneconomical when viewed all together.

Added to this ineptitude on the part of county boards is the fact that great pressure is brought to bear upon them to award these contracts in a liberal way. Contractors and the representatives of business firms are constantly seeking to bring political pressure upon various members in order to secure contracts. Members themselves always have their friends and favorites whom they hope to see legitimately benefited in one way or another. And when the county board is a large one there is always more or less log-rolling among the different members in order that each may gain the advantages he is seeking. Board members can always make a great many friends by awarding numerous and liberal contracts, and they are not likely to make any enemies by doing so. On the other hand, a close-fisted board invariably makes a great many enemies who are often very powerful. Virtue must be its own reward in this connection. A parsimonious and economical board has small chance of permanence in office, whereas the liberal and free-handed board quickly builds up a large following to sing its praises and send the members back again to office. All these factors combined are apt to have a demoralizing effect and are largely responsible for extravagance and wastefulness.

State legislatures have been keenly aware of this situation and have done about all that can be done through law to prevent the abuses that are most obvious. Thus it is usually required that county boards must advertise for bids or county work if it is to cost more than a certain fixed minimum, such as one or two thousand dollars. This requirement serves two very important purposes. In the first place it brings the project into the light, it makes it impossible for the board to engage more or less secretly in expensive undertakings. Secondly, it gives every contractor or business firm an equal opportunity to figure on the contract, for any person who desires it must be supplied with data and specifications on which he can base an intelligent bid.

It is further required that all bids must be sent in to the board sealed, before a certain day; unsealed bids cannot be accepted. These bids are opened in regular meeting, the day and hour having been fixed. It is expected of course that all interested persons will be present. The board is then expected to award the contract to the lowest responsible bidder. However, it would not be wise to bind the board too closely in this regard for many factors may enter into a situation of which a hard and fast law could take no account. A bid might be so low as justly to arouse suspicion, though on its face nothing would appear to be wrong. There might be good reason to doubt the competence of the lowest bidder though his integrity be unquestioned. Paving and roadbuilding contracts have been awarded frequently to woefully incompetent contractors with deplorable results. Thus to put the county board in a strait-jacket in this matter of awarding contracts might do more harm than good. Boards may therefore reject a bid on the ground that the bidder is irresponsible, or they may reject all bids and advertise again for new ones. This is very frequently done, and need not prejudice the interests of any reliable bidder. In practice, boards sometimes ignore the spirit of the law and deliberately award the contract to a favorite whether or not his bid is low.

These legal safeguards have done much to eradicate the grosser abuses that have enveloped county contracts, but there are many ways of circumventing them. The simplest and most difficult to remedy is collusion on the part of bidders. There may be only two or three firms competent to handle the work in question. A clear understanding among them may result in their passing around the county work at their own figures. This is notoriously true of printing contracts, and where the law does not forbid, indignant county boards have sometimes gone outside their own states to find trustworthy contractors.

Other times responsibility for defeating the spirit of the law lies very definitely with the board itself. It may deliberately refuse to award the contract to the bidder who is entitled to receive it by declaring him to be irresponsible, and he is tacitly defied to take his case before the courts in order to oblige the board to award him the contract. Through bitter experience contractors have learned that it does not pay to secure contracts by such disagreeable methods. Even if he wins out, a contractor is likely to find the details of the contract enforced upon him rigorously by county authorities, his work may be rejected on frivolous grounds as being unsatisfactory; during the progress of his work he may be tormented by inspectors, and finally his pay may be held up on various pretenses for a very long time. Thus it is that boards are rarely challenged in the courts for the awards that they have made; and thus it is that frequently the best, most reliable and trustworthy contractors and business firms will have nothing to do with county work, they do not even care to enter bids and have no desire to do work for the county.

5. *Purchasing Land.*—It is sometimes necessary for the county board to purchase land, which of course it has power to do for certain purposes. It is necessary to acquire land

for the various county institutions such as the poorhouse and schools; and it is frequently desirable to cut through new roads or alter the course of old ones. This may involve the purchase of large tracts of land and frequently leads to condemnation proceedings and long, expensive litigation.

6. *Making Rules and Regulations.*—It is the duty of the county board to make all needful rules and regulations for the management of county institutions. There is always the courthouse, the jail and the poorhouse, and there may be other institutions such as hospitals or even county libraries. Each of these institutions is under the personal direction of some particular officer, but the county board prescribes in considerable detail such rules and regulations as may be necessary. The board ought to have power to appoint these officials, for then they can be controlled. But if they are elected, the rules and regulations of the county board are not taken very seriously and the members of the board give but scant attention to the matter.

7. *Appointing Minor Officers.*—With the expansion of the administrative activities of the state and county more officers are needed to carry on the work, and each decade witnesses a lengthening of the list of minor officers whom the county board is empowered to appoint. Thus stewards of the poor farms, superintendents for other institutions, health officers, surveyors and engineers, to say nothing of an array of deputies to the older county officers, compose a very respectable amount of patronage that rests in the hands of the county board. The law often permits the board to appoint assistants and deputies as they are needed; and as for the newer officers, short ballot agitation has at least been effective in that it results in making most of them appointive rather than elective.

Probably county boards are no worse than similar appointing authorities in the abuse of their patronage; but county government is more or less in the dark, does not attract the same public attention that city government does for instance, and it is rather easy for county boards to overload the pay roll with needless assistants and deputies unless the law guards against it. The civil service merit system seldom applies to county appointments, although it is sufficiently obvious that it is needed as much in connection with county appointments as it is needed anywhere. Assistants in the auditor's office, the treasurer's or the collector's office, and all the workers about the courthouse might well be under some sort of merit system of appointment.

8. *Extending Poor Relief.*—Usually the members of the county board individually have power to commit persons to the poorhouse or to other county charitable institutions, while the board as a whole authorizes the use of funds for outdoor relief. But the functions of the various county officers in this connection will be discussed later, under the subject of local charities.

9. *Providing Supplies.*—The county board must provide all the county officers and institutions with necessary supplies and equipment. This gives the board an opportunity to control these officers and institutions to a certain extent even when the board does not have direct and positive authority over them. The activities of an officer or an institution may be greatly hampered or developed through the granting or withholding of supplies and equipment. The finance officers need adequate books and modern equipment for the proper discharge of their duties. The register of deeds needs suitable office equipment. The highway officials need proper machinery and equipment to do their work. The school officers need supplies to do

their work in the most approved way. And it is obvious that the usefulness of such institutions as the poorhouse and farm is greatly affected by the liberality of the board in providing equipment, furnishings, and supplies.

In order to provide supplies intelligently someone must do a great deal of careful investigating, or else the matter is likely to be handled in a most unbusinesslike and extravagant manner. There is of course the temptation to allow unnecessary supplies in order to make large contracts for political purposes; but dismissing this consideration it can be said that the chief trouble grows out of diffused responsibility. There is seldom any one officer, who might be called a purchasing agent, whose business it is to purchase supplies for all the county offices and institutions. Ordinarily each official makes his requisition upon the board individually, and each request is judged upon its own merits. There ought to be one responsible officer whose business it would be to purchase supplies for all offices and institutions. By a system of centralized purchasing great economies could be effected and supplies could be provided much more intelligently.

This is particularly true in the large and more populous counties when there are many offices to be supplied with a variety of materials, and numerous institutions to be kept supplied with food, fuel and other things. If the purchasing is all done through one responsible person the entire purchasing power of the county is concentrated; hence goods can be purchased in large quantities at the best prices. The individual who has the work in charge will develop skill in bargaining and will learn of the best markets and the character of competing firms. Such a centralized method of purchasing would encourage the best firms to enter competition. Responsibility for purchases would be clearly located. And such a method would permit of standardization of different types of supplies. Great strides in the direction of centralized purchasing are being made in the various state governments and there is no reason why great economies cannot be made in county governments if county boards would but adopt the principle.

Also, it may be added, the budget principle as worked out in many municipalities and in a few state governments might well be applied to counties. In the past it has been the universal practice for state legislatures to handle appropriation measures one at a time, judging each upon its merits and without regard to what other expenditures it might become necessary to make, and with small regard to available revenue. The same policy has been followed by city councils and for the most part is still followed by county boards. They are likely to take up each proposed expenditure, be it for road purposes, the maintenance of the poorhouse or supplies for the treasurer's office, examine it carefully, pass it, and go on to the next. There may be many weeks between the passsage of these various appropriation measures, and thus expenditures are made, each without regard to the other, until gradually they accumulate to unexpected proportions and it is found that the tax rate must be raised to a point which the board members never intended.

If, however, a budget were prepared early in the fiscal year and presented to the board, much of this embarrassment could be overcome, and appropriations could be made much more intelligently. The county clerk or auditor could have the preparation of such a budget personally in hand, though of course it would necessarily be subjected to the scrutiny of the board. Each county officer, and the person in charge of each county institution or activity could present to the budget officer an estimate of what the cost of carrying on his work for the coming year would be.

These estimates should be in considerable detail. The budget officer could then combine them into one orderly statement, and add to it such other information as might be desirable. There would be a statement of the amount spent through each office the preceding year, and if a larger sum were asked for some explanation should be included in the statement. The budget officer should make his own recommendations in the light of the various amounts that were requested; and finally he should add a statement of the exact financial condition of the county, in order to show just what tax rate it would be necessary to apply in order to cover all the estimates.

Such a document would be a budget. It should be laid before the county board and studied thoroughly. The members would thus have before them a complete survey of proposed appropriations and revenues and could cut and trim here and there with confidence and intelligence, knowing just how they were going to come out at the end of the year. The budget principle is very simple, logical, clear and in every way sensible and businesslike. Its practical application might entail certain difficulties, but would always make for improvement, be it ever so slight.

10. Passing Upon Claims.—It is the function of the county board to pass on all claims against the county. Every claim for compensation, be it for service rendered, supplies provided, or contract fulfilled, are entered in a proper record and come before the county board at a regular meeting. No claim may be paid unless it has been approved by the board. Most of them are based on contracts previously entered into, and the only question involved is whether or not the provisions of the contract have been fulfilled. Other claims are usually for minor amounts and are passed as matters of routine business.

Unfortunately it seldom happens that any one individual

takes responsibility for examining into the merits of these claims. They may be laid before the board by the auditor or clerk without any comment whatever, the board members are apt to be more or less indifferent and to pass them in a perfunctory way, assuming that the claims are perfectly legitimate. As a result of this careless way of handling such business it has happened that county boards have approved the same claim two or even three times, and thus some unscrupulous person has been paid twice for his work or his goods. Such carelessness makes it possible for unreasonable and padded claims to slip through and thus opens the door to petty graft which in the long run mounts up to very large sums.

There ought to be some individual, preferably someone strictly accountable to the board, who would have the function of examining carefully into the merits of all claims, and the making of recommendations to the board on each one. The members of the board naturally would hesitate to repudiate the recommendations of such an officer unless they had examined into the case very thoroughly themselves.

After a claim has been passed by the board a record is made of the fact, and a warrant is issued by the proper officer and sent to the claimant. This warrant when presented to the treasurer entitles the holder to the sum named in the warrant. In case a claim is not allowed by the board the only recourse of the claimant is to bring civil action against the county. The county must appear in the court, through its attorney, and answer to the charges made. If the decision goes against the county the board has no alternative but to allow the claim.

11. Administering Tax Machinery.—The county is an important unit for the administration of the tax machinery, and the board has certain duties in this connection. In the first place the board determines the tax rate which it will be necessary to apply in order to raise the money which the board itself has decided to spend. It has been frequently pointed out in this connection that here is involved a most undesirable combination of financial powers in the hands of a single authority. In the first place, the board decides what enterprises are to be launched, then it makes the necessary appropriation, then it levies a tax in order to raise the money, and finally the money is collected and spent under the board's supervision. There is no other authority competent to check or restrict the board at any point in this procedure, for there is no independent executive in the county organization as there is in city, state or federal government.

The general property tax is the principal source of public revenue in every one of the states, and in order to apply it the county board must have at hand a complete record of all the real and personal property owned within the county, with an assessed valuation placed against it. Then after the county board has determined the amount of money in dollars and cents that will be needed to carry on county activities for the ensuing year this sum is divided by the total assessed valuation of all the taxable property within the county. This operation will produce a fraction which can be interpreted as a tax rate, expressed in terms of per cent, or mills—a mill being one-tenth of one per cent. This rate, if applied to all the property in the county, will produce the necessary revenue.

The rate is authorized by the county board. But the determination of a rate necessary to raise money for county expenses is not the only function of the board in connection with tax administration. The county ordinarily is the channel through which all taxes are collected.

Therefore it is necessary for the board to apply a rate in order to raise revenue for every other taxing area. The state authorities determine the rate which must be applied in order to raise money for the state—and this is added to the rate fixed by the county board. If there be any cities within the county they usually certify to the county board the amount which they will need, and a rate is applied for them. So too the townships and minor areas, such as school, park or drainage districts which are privileged to levy taxes, certify to the board the amount which they will require. However, the law imposes a certain limit above which tax rates may not go; thus it is forbidden that the rate for a certain purpose shall exceed a certain percentage of assessed values.

The county board directs the preparation of tax statements for each property owner, and taxes are then collected through the proper officers, under the general supervision of the board. It is then necessary to distribute the funds among the various taxing areas, the county retaining that portion to which it is entitled. As a matter of fact the members of the county board do not have very much to do with the actual administration of the tax machinery. There is a vast amount of clerical work to be done, and very few opportunities for the exercise of discretion, so the board has but little more to do than to provide the necessary staff and see that the work is properly done.

12. *Serving as a Board of Review.*—A much more significant function for the board to perform is that of serving as a board of review for the equalization of assessments as between individual property owners or as between townships. In those states where assessments are made by township assessors the township board of trustees, or some other township authorities, sit as a board of review to hear complaints from individuals who may protest

that their property has been assessed at too high a figure relative to the value at which other property has been assessed. And when this is the case, the county board, or a committee thereof, sits as a board of review only to equalize assessed values as between townships. Thus if the assessor in one township has consistently placed values on the property within his jurisdiction at too low a figure, compared to the values assessed in neighboring townships, the county board, as a board of review, is competent to raise them.

13. Approving Bonds.—Another duty of the county board is to approve the bonds of county officers. Certain of the county officers, particularly those who have the handling of public funds, are obliged to supply bonds intended to protect the county in case the officer should defalcate. Public officers formerly were put to the necessity of finding personal friends or relatives who would "go their bond," but to-day there are many responsible bonding firms which will supply bonds at a fixed premium in very much the same way that insurance is provided. Hence the function of the county board has come to be quite perfunctory and bonds are provided strictly on a business basis, the officer no longer being obliged to seek friends willing to vouch for his honesty with their pocketbooks.

14. Supervising Elections.—The county is the principal unit for the conduct of elections, and the county board has certain important duties in this connection. The board usually makes up the official ballot, indicates the polling places, and provides each polling place with all the physical equipment necessary, such as ballot boxes, and poll books. The board appoints the judges of election, unless the law provides for their appointment in some other way; and has general supervision over the elections. The board must canvass the returns, issue certificates of election to those who have been elected to county offices, and certify the results of the election in the case of other officers to the proper authorities, state or city.

15. *Minor Functions.*—In addition to these duties of the county board which have been discussed in more or less detail, there is a great variety of petty functions which it would be impossible to enumerate. The board makes up jury lists, fills vacancies that occur in county offices, orders land surveys, may change township lines, and perform a multitude of other miscellaneous and unrelated functions. The ordinance-making power of the board has come to be of very small importance, but in the absence of state legislation a county board is usually competent to pass petty ordinances dealing with such matters as the suppression of nuisances, the removal of obstructions from the highway, the cutting of noxious weeds, the restraint of stray animals, pollution of streams, and the preservation of public health. However, it is usually quite unnecessary for the county board to concern itself with these matters because the state legislature is likely to have enacted sufficient law to cover such cases, and county ordinances would be superfluous.

Finally, the county board may be authorized to issue licenses for pool rooms, dance halls and amusement resorts which are established outside the limits of any municipality. Before the eighteenth amendment to the federal constitution was passed, the granting of licenses to sell liquor was frequently no small part of the duties of the county board.

This completes a general survey of the organization and functions of a typical county board. It must be remembered, however, that there are some three thousand county boards in the United States operating under the laws of forty-eight different commonwealths, and that there are wide divergencies in the character of these boards. It would be impossible to go more into detail in a consideration of their functions without presenting endless variations.

CHAPTER VIII

THE CLERICAL OFFICES

There is no County Executive.—Inasmuch as the county is not a major area of government it does not necessarily require a complete structure of governmental machinery. In a major area of government a chief executive is virtually indispensable; and in certain of the minor areas also, chief executives are to be found. Thus there are the mayors of cities, and the village presidents. But it has not been the practice in the United States to establish chief executive officers in the counties or the townships; although it is believed by many that county government would be greatly improved if there were a chief executive.

Executive Functions:

1. To Represent a Government.—It is the business of a chief executive to represent his area of government in its political and corporate character. He, as an individual, speaks for the political entity of which he is the executive. He announces the policies of his government. He conducts diplomatic relations. He promulgates the law; and in a word he is the voice of his government. The President of the United States, the governors of the various states, and the mayors of cities, are all chief executives in this sense. They are the individuals who personally represent their governments, and it is through them that these governments hold communication with the rest of the world.

2. To Execute the Law.—Another elementary function of a chief executive is to see to it that the people within his jurisdiction obey the law. He executes the law. Thus he is expected to see to it that the will of the law-making power is fulfilled. Obviously this is a most elementary function, be it exercised by an aboriginal chieftain or the President of the United States; and in the fundamental aspects their duties are no different. The one enforces the law upon his subjects through force and violence, the other does the same through elaborate governmental machinery devised for the purpose.

3. To Supervise Administration.—A third primary function of an executive, closely related to the function just mentioned, is that of supervising and directing the administration. Whenever a government undertakes to do things, to erect buildings, to collect taxes, to build a navy, to manage a railroad, or to build a one-room schoolhouse, some individuals must undertake personal responsibility for doing the work. The people who do this are known collectively as "the administration," although it is customary to use the phrase when referring only to the principal officers. The executive is chief of the administration. It may be the case that the executive has little actual control over the administrative officers, but in political theory at least the executive is at the head of the administration, and sees to it that those things which the legislature wants done by the government are done through the administrative officers.

It is unnecessary to go further into the functions of an executive; those mentioned are basic, elementary and fundamental. He personally represents his government and speaks for it, he enforces the law, and he directs the administration.

The question now arises: is there to be found, or should there be, an officer to perform these elementary governmental functions for the county?

County Executive not Needed.—It is seldom necessary that the county should have an individual to speak for, or to represent it. The county does not carry on diplomatic negotiations, there is little correspondence with other areas of government, and a board of commissioners or supervisors with the aid of a clerical officer is entirely competent to exercise the executive function of speaking for the county. As for the function of enforcing the law upon individuals, it will be remembered that the county exercises no extensive law-making power. There is no real county legislature and hence no need for any county executive to execute county laws. As for the state law, that is enforced within the county by various independent officers such as the public prosecutor and the sheriff.

There are, however, certain administrative officers in the county, and they might well be under the control of a county executive if there were one. But such is not the practice. These administrative officers are largely independent, and when they are not entirely so they are made responsible to state officers or to the county board.

County Board is the County Executive.—It is to be observed, then, that in so far as executive functions are performed in behalf of the county it is the county board which performs them. If these functions were very numerous or important it would be quite necessary to have an independent chief executive for the county; but the situation being as it is, the county board is able to function as an executive in a reasonably satisfactory manner.

Clerks and Auditors.—But a clerical officer is needed in this connection as well as for other purposes. He is found in the person of the county clerk or county auditor. In about one-half of the states he is known as the county clerk, in the others he is called the auditor, though the functions performed in either case are virtually the same.

In less than a dozen states both officers are found, and in these states the auditor confines his attention exclusively to finance matters, while the clerk performs all the typically clerical and secretarial functions discussed below.

The terms clerk and auditor are each suggestive of certain distinct functions. A clerk is one who keeps the records and does the secretarial work for a deliberative body such as a legislature, a council, or a board; or he is one who keeps the records of a court. Thus it might be expected that the county clerk would be secretary of the board, and possibly keep the records of the court. He does almost invariably serve as secretary of the county board, and in a few states also keeps the records of the county or district court. However, in a majority of states there is to be found a clerk of court known sometimes as the county clerk or circuit clerk, but who performs this latter function, and who is in no sense a secretary for the board. Confusion is apt to arise when both officers are referred to as the county clerk. The county clerk is primarily secretary of the board and may or may not also serve as clerk of court. The clerk of court simply keeps court records, does secretarial work for the court and has no relations with the county board. And when he is known as county clerk, the officer who functions as secretary of the board is usually known as county auditor.*

The term auditor is suggestive of finance operations. Primarily an auditor is one who inspects finance accounts of other officers, and authorizes payments from the treasury. But in a large number of states where a county auditor is found he does not confine himself to finance matters but performs all of the functions of a county clerk, except that he does not serve as clerk of court.*

* The situation is illustrated in the neighboring states of Iowa and Illinois. In Iowa the county clerk is simply a clerk of court, while a county auditor

The duties of all three of these officers must be performed in every county, but there are only two states where all three officers are found. In the other states the functions are so combined that one or two of the officers perform all three of the functions. The function of clerk of court, or circuit clerk, is highly specialized and is not closely related to other county activities. It can be left for later discussion, although it should be remembered that in a few states it is performed by the county clerk. The functions of the county clerk and the county auditor are exactly the same except in those few states where both officers are found. In those states the auditor is primarily a finance officer, as already indicated. The functions of county clerk or auditor, as the case may be, should now be examined. This officer will be spoken of as the county clerk, though it must be remembered that in a number of the states the same functionary is known as the county auditor, while the county clerk is merely a clerk of court.

THE COUNTY CLERK

The County Clerk.—The county clerk is popularly elected. This fact makes him largely independent of all other officers, including even the county board. Inasmuch as many of his more important duties are performed on behalf of the county board and in the furtherance of the board's programmes, greater harmony might prevail in his relations with the board if he were appointed by the members thereof. His work is purely ministerial and does not involve the exercise of independent discretion, so little or nothing is gained by making him free of the board.

performs all the clerical, secretarial, and administrative duties. In Illinois the county clerk performs virtually all the functions performed in Iowa by the county auditor, while a circuit clerk serves as clerk of court, performing the functions exercised by the county clerk in Iowa.

Secretary to the Board.—One of the clerk's most important duties is to act as secretary of the board. He prepares the business for their meetings, gets all the papers and records which they will require into proper shape, sees to it that the meetings are properly announced and the place of meeting in readiness. He must then attend the sessions and keep a detailed record of all the proceedings. He is not a member of the board, he does not have a vote and does not have a legal right to participate in deliberations. However, inasmuch as he is in closer touch with county affairs than any other officer, and is likely to have more knowledge of county business than board members themselves, perhaps, the county clerk's suggestions and comments are of considerable weight in board meetings.

Minutes of Meetings.—The minutes of these meetings are permanent records in the office of the clerk and are open to public inspection. All decisions made and all business transacted is found recorded in these minutes. These records in some cases have been kept in very bad condition. County clerks are sometimes unskilled and careless. The clerk's records are seldom used, they are not subject to the inspection of a superior officer, and the board members themselves are apt to be indifferent, particularly in view of the fact that they are not in a position really to control the clerk. This is merely one of the examples of inefficiency that grow out of the system of administrative decentralization. If the clerk were responsible to a superior he would be more likely to keep his records in good shape. Yet of course in most cases the county records are in quite acceptable condition, and it must be said that modern office equipment and typewriting devices leave little excuse for their being in any other condition.

Secretarial Duties.—After the meeting is over the clerk is expected to carry out instructions that may have been given to him. He immediately engages in any correspondence which the board may desire, he sends notices such as may have been ordered, and in a word does all the secretarial work which is necessary. In a populous county this is no small task and the clerk is supported with a very considerable staff of assistants, stenographers and bookkeepers. The functions of the clerk as secretary of the board occupy a large proportion of his time and are among his most important duties.

Superintendent of Courthouse.—On the other hand, the clerk has many things to do quite independently of the board. In the first place he is what may be called the superintendent of the courthouse. His own offices are in that building and he is responsible for it in very much the same way that the superintendent of any institution is responsible. Such matters as heating, decorating, cleaning and maintenance are all his problems. He attends to these things subject to the approval of the board when expense is involved.

Correspondence.—His own office in the courthouse is the very center of county activities. He is expected to give full time to his duties and he or his deputies are always in his office to serve the people in their relations with the county. He is the channel of communication through whom the public must deal with the county as a corporate entity. In this connection his office must handle a very considerable correspondence. Most inquiries and communications of a trivial nature can be answered at once, others must be referred to the board, while still other communications are turned over to other county officers who may have the matter in charge.

Receiving Claims.—All claims against the county for

services rendered or for materials and supplies provided must be filed with the clerk. Claims that amount to more than a few hundred dollars are usually based on contracts that have been previously entered into. Other claims, for smaller amounts, grow out of verbal agreements with the various county officers who are permitted to employ help and purchase supplies on their own account.

Of course all of these claims must be laid before the board and approved by it before the person who makes the claim can get his money. The board either passes or rejects the claim. The clerk assumes no responsibility in this connection. However, as said before, the claims are originally filed with the clerk. He in turn has them ready to lay before the board at its next meeting, and he should be in a position to advise the board as to the legitimacy of the claims, and to make trustworthy recommendations concerning them.

If a claim is based on a contract it is only necessary to determine whether or not the terms of the contract have been fulfilled. The contract may have been for the improvement of a highway. The county highway official is in a position to say if the terms of the contract have been fulfilled. The contract may have been for the erection of a building. A committee of the board would no doubt have the matter in hand. It may have been for supplies to the county hospital. The superintendent of that institution is the person who can say if the terms have been fulfilled. It may have been for equipment in the treasurer's office. Obviously these contracts are of great variety. The board, meeting as it does only at intervals, and composed of men from different parts of the county, cannot always be responsible for knowing whether or not the terms of the contract have been fulfilled. In reviewing claims based upon these contracts the board must rely upon the advice of the highway officer, the hospital superintendent, the treasurer, the superintendent of schools, the recorder, the sheriff, or any one of a number of other officers as the case may be.

This practice is reasonably satisfactory so long as officers are intelligent, capable and trustworthy. But for the most part these officers are not conscious of any responsibility to the board, many times they are careless or indifferent, frequently they are not businesslike even though they may be highly capable in their official capacities, and it is not unusual for them to be imposed upon by unscrupulous contractors and business firms. The situation might well be greatly improved if some person representing the county board were to investigate personally, with a keen sense of responsibility, every claim that might be based upon a contract. This person could then make very definite and trustworthy reports to the board on every claim. The clerk at present does not and cannot be expected to do this. He merely lays the claim before the board, together usually with a statement of perfunctory approval from the officer involved.

In addition to the claims based on contracts there is the great mass of minor claims for petty services, day labor and the like, or small quantities of material or supplies for the various officers and institutions. These too are laid before the board by the clerk, possibly with a brief statement of approval from the officer who has received the service or supplies. There is no person whose business it is to investigate or scrutinize every claim with a view to discovering overcharges, poor work, and bad materials. Responsibility for such investigation is now so widely scattered that it is difficult to tell just what economies could be effected. Yet it is clear to the most casual observer that a higher degree of business efficiency would be attained if responsibility for recommending that claims be passed or rejected were centralized in some individual.

In the absence of a county purchasing agent the county clerk could do much in the matter of checking up on claims that are too high; and by refusing to give favorable recommendation to the claims that come from their offices he could enforce much greater care in business activities on the part of other county officers. But he cannot be expected to assume such a function very seriously so long as he is an independent, popularly elected officer. He can have nothing authoritative to say as to allowing or rejecting a claim, and cannot be expected to incur the displeasure of fellow officials by investigating their business dealings when no possible advantage can accrue to him by doing so. He probably would accomplish little but to make many enemies for himself and no friends, and could be used as a scapegoat for the board.

However, if he were appointed by the board, and was in every sense of the word responsible to it, the situation would be altogether different. He would have no other concern than to satisfy the members of the board and to convince them of his efficiency and trustworthiness. This would lead to much more thorough and intelligent supervision of the business operations of the county.

The method of selecting a public official and the degree of responsibility established between him and other officers has a very great deal to do with the attitude which he will take toward his work and the manner in which he will discharge his duties. An official who is popularly elected is not likely to assume an aggressive manner that is calculated to impair his popularity. An official who is not responsible to some alert superior is not likely to be overscrupulous in the attention he gives to the more disagreeable details of his function. This is why county clerks cannot be expected to do much toward improving county business methods. They wash their hands of the business, and county boards must get along as best they can without the aid that could be rendered by such an officer as the clerk.

Warrants.—After claims have been passed upon and allowed by the board, the clerk must fill out warrants signed by himself. These are handed to the claimants and when presented to the treasurer will be honored. All too frequently it happens that there is not enough money in the treasury to meet these warrants and ordinarily the law provides that in such contingencies the warrant shall be signed by the treasurer and draw interest for the holder from the day on which it was presented.

The clerk has no discretion in the matter of signing warrants. He must prepare warrants at once for every claim that has been properly allowed by the board in the manner prescribed by law. The warrant, signed by the clerk, is, furthermore, protection for the treasurer. The clerk's signature is enough for him, he is not expected to examine into the legitimacy of the claim and is not even expected to discover if the claim was properly allowed. He honors every warrant bearing the clerk's signature and there ends his responsibility.

Records.—The clerk must keep a permanent record of all claims and all warrants. The fact that claims are presented, and rejected, or passed, is of course all a matter of record in the minutes of the board meetings kept by the clerk. But in addition to this record there is what usually is called a claim register in which all claims are entered in order as they are presented, whether they are legitimate or illegitimate and whether they are allowed or rejected.

In addition there is a warrant book in which a record is kept of all warrants signed by the clerk. These records together with the minutes of the board meetings provide complete information concerning all financial transactions of the county. It seems needless to say that these records ought always to be up to date, legible and accurate, open to the public, and kept on standard forms. Yet occasional investigations on the part of irate citizens, or professional accountants who examine the records of defaulting county officers, sometimes uncover records that are well-nigh undecipherable, slack methods, carelessness and general disregard of the first principles of business efficiency.

This is due partly to the fact that incompetent men are elected to office, but in the case of the clerk it is due more to the fact that there is no one to whom he is responsible. The indifference of board members and the general apathy of the public, the fact that the clerk's records are seldom consulted by the public, and not inspected and criticised by a superior authority, all conspire to tempt him to carelessness and indifference himself. Improved methods of bookkeeping, and systems of state inspection have done much in recent years to improve this bad situation in some of the states. When a state officer is given authority to prescribe methods of keeping records, and is given authority to inspect the books of county officers, very marked improvement in the character of these records is the immediate result.

The Clerk and Tax Administration.—The county clerk has a great deal to do in connection with the administration of the tax machinery. It will be remembered that the county is the unit through which most of the taxes are collected. Thus it is necessary that county officers should be prepared to do the work. The clerk is responsible for all the clerical work that must be done. Each taxing area, the state, the city, and the minor areas, determines the tax rate which is to be applied in its behalf, subject to the limitations of the law; and the clerk with his assistants must go through the arithmetical processes that are necessary in order to determine the total rate that is to be applied against the property of each individual.

Preparing Tax Books.—A separate account between the county and each person who owns taxable property must be kept by the clerk. From the assessor's books he discovers the value of each piece of property. All the tax rates are then applied and it is possible to prepare a detailed statement of the amount due from each individual. It is not always the practice to send statements of taxes to each individual, but it is a very great convenience to the taxpayer when this is done. Yet in any event the clerk must have in his books an account with each and every taxpayer. The preparation of these accounts involves an immense amount of clerical work, and the burden of it is not evenly distributed throughout the year. Thus it is the custom for county clerks to augment their staffs temporarily during the rush period. The work is not particularly difficult but it must be done accurately. The tax records are voluminous, they are being consulted constantly by taxpayers, and must be used by other public officials than the clerk. They cannot be permitted to fall into arrears, they must be up to date, and no matter how obscure the other records kept by the clerk may be, his tax books are always in the light of day and he is likely to spend a good share of his time over them.

Collecting Taxes.—The clerk usually has nothing to do with the collection of the taxes. After his books are in shape they are turned over to the collector, or the treasurer who may also be the collector, and a period is announced during which taxpayers must go to pay their taxes. In case a person does not pay his taxes within a specified time a penalty is added to the amount due; and sooner or later, if the individual is still delinquent, his property is sold for taxes. This simply means that some other person pays the taxes, and thereby establishes a claim against the property which must be satisfied by the owner before his title can again be clear.

From this discussion of the clerk's duties in connection with the administration of the tax machinery it can be seen that there are several very distinct steps in the process of taxation. First, every piece of taxable property must be assessed, and a value fixed upon it. This is usually done by township officers in those states where townships exist. Second, each taxing area must determine the amount of money which will be required for its purposes, and a rate is fixed which will raise this sum. Legislatures, county boards, and city councils fix these rates subject to the limitations of the law. Third, the county clerk goes through the detailed process of preparing an account of the taxes due from each taxpayer in the county. Fourth, the taxes are collected through the office of a collector or the treasurer and the proper amounts turned over to the state, the city, and the various other areas. All this work is supposed to be done under the supervision of the county board, but in practice the various officers involved are quite independent.

The Conduct of Elections.—The conduct of elections brings many duties and responsibilities upon the county clerk. One of the principal features of the Australian ballot, used almost universally in the United States, is that all ballots shall be prepared by public officials and remain in charge of public officials at all times. This means a great deal of work and responsibility for someone, and it usually falls upon the clerk. Candidates for county offices must file their papers with him in accordance with the procedure stipulated in the law. Names of candidates for other than county offices are certified to him by the proper authorities. He must then make up the official ballot, placing the names of the respective party candidates for national, state, county, township and district offices all on a single sheet.* The county board approves the official ballot prepared by the clerk and authorizes the printing of a sufficient quantity of them.

Administrative decentralization in this connection begets some curious results. One might expect to find the official ballots in every county of a given state very much alike. Indeed the state law does usually describe in general terms the form of the official ballot. But each clerk interprets the law as he sees fit, and no superior officer is in a position to overrule him so long as he stays within the general terms of the law. Hence the official ballots in neighboring counties may present great variations in size and character.

An examination of the official ballots from a considerable number of counties in any given state is quite likely to illustrate this fact. Some of the ballots would be found to be four or five times as large as others, although there would of course be just the same number of names printed on every ballot. On the large ballots the type might be exceedingly large, broad spaces will have been left between the names and many square inches of space will not have been utilized at all. Other ballots will be found printed in rather small type and the ballot made as small as it conveniently could be. All the ballots are usually printed on white paper—the law requires this in most states—but the quality need not necessarily be uniform. In some cases very high-grade book paper may be used, in others very inferior print paper. Thus, due to the discretion vested in county clerks and county boards it could easily

* City elections are usually held separately at another time of the year.

happen that the printing bill for a given number of ballots for the same election might be from two to ten times as much in one county as in another.

Probably there is no very good and sufficient reason why the official ballots should be exactly uniform in each and every county; but the situation described above does illustrate very clearly the way in which extravagance and even corruption can be practiced under such a system. There would appear to be no reason why such matters as the preparation of ballots could not be handled as efficiently and economically through independent local officers as through state officers. But when carelessness and extravagance do appear, reform can be accomplished best through state control.

Distributing Ballots.—After the ballots have been printed and deposited with the clerk it is his duty to supply them to the various polling places. These polling places are indicated by the county board, and the area served by one polling place is known as a precinct. In many states townships are also precincts, but obviously where the population is dense the precincts must be very much smaller than the average township.

Election officials are appointed for each polling place and they conduct the election under the general supervision of the clerk who gives them instructions and provides them with all the equipment needed. The registration books, in which every voter must register his name and place of residence before he is permitted to vote, are in charge of the clerk. And from these records he prepares the voting lists which are mere alphabetical lists of registered voters.* These lists he provides for each precinct, and as voters appear on election day it is a simple matter

* These records are also the basis of jury lists which the clerk ordinarily must prepare.

to find their names and check them off as they cast their ballots.

Final Returns.—When the polls are closed the ballots are immediately counted in the various precincts, the results tabulated, and all the records brought to the clerk's office. There the final returns are made up. Reports are sent to state officers, and the clerk prepares certificates of election to be given to those who have been elected to local offices. All of the records, including the actual ballots that have been cast at the election, are then stored away in charge of the clerk. The law usually requires that he must keep the ballots for a period of years, after which they may be destroyed.

Other Records of Clerk.—It will be seen that the clerk's office becomes a veritable storehouse of information, a depository of records and documents concerning all the various governmental operations carried on through the county. In addition to the records already mentioned, such as the minutes of board meetings, the claim register, the warrant book, the tax books and the election records, he has charge of other records of less importance. There are various maps showing all the roads and bridges, the drainage ditches, the various streams and lakes, railroad and interurban lines, electric wires, pipe lines, the location of cemeteries, school buildings, and other things which may be required by state law or the county board. These records and maps are all open to the public and the clerk is ready to assist any person seeking information from them. Written transcripts of the records may usually be had from the clerk on payment of a small fee.

Issuing Licenses.—The clerk also issues licenses for various purposes. Hunting licenses, dog licenses, licenses to operate dance halls, resorts and pool rooms that are conducted outside of city limits, are often issued through the clerk's office. However, if any discretion is to be exercised in the matter of issuing any of these licenses it is exercised by the county board rather than the clerk. Marriage licenses are issued by the county clerk in those counties where he also functions as clerk of court, but where there is a clerk of court that functionary usually issues the marriage licenses.

Reports.—In many states an annual report dealing with the county offices, county business and affairs generally is published. When this is done it is published under the supervision of the clerk. He prepares his own report which includes a statement concerning any funds handled through his office, it includes a condensed statement of all the pertinent facts shown by his various records. It also includes statements based on the reports of other officers; thus it provides information as to the number of inmates in the various institutions, such as almshouses, hospitals orphanages and the jail, the number of commitments and releases. There is likely to be a county census in his report, showing the number of deaf, blind, orphans, and men of military age. There may be included agricultural statistics concerning livestock and crops. And his report also includes a county directory stating the names of all county and township officers, their salaries and terms of office.

Added to the clerk's report are the reports of all the other county officers. They are simply appended to his own and printed in the same folder. Thus the sheriff, the treasurer and other officers hand their annual reports to the clerk for publication. And there are also reports from the persons in charge of the various institutions.

All these reports are, in form, reports to the county board. However, under existing circumstances it is not possible for these reports to serve the purpose they ought to serve.

A report ought to show a superior authority what his subordinates are doing, and it ought to be the basis of authoritative and constructive criticism. But since county officers are not the subordinates of the county board the reports are apt to be mere perfunctory and formal statements, condensed to a point that makes them useless, or extended with unimportant detail until they become almost unintelligible. Members of the board are not likely to spend much time examining these reports when they are fully aware that they are not in a position to make authoritative criticism. On the other hand, county officers cannot be expected to prepare very thorough reports when they realize that no one is in a position to make authoritative criticism, and that very few people are likely even to read the reports. Thus the reports of county officers often degenerate into nothing but a few general statements of fact and a mass of petty detail that very few people will read and still fewer can interpret to any purpose.

This is an eloquent illustration of the point made so many times before in these pages, that the whole county organization is so loosely bound as to promote, or at least to permit, the grossest kind of extravagance, inefficiency and irresponsibility. When the law requires the making of such perfunctory reports to superiors who are superiors in name only and who cannot control their subordinates, it merely recognizes the need of enforcing responsibility, but does little toward accomplishing it.

Reform of Clerk's Office.—Other functions of the clerk might be enumerated, but they are hardly of enough significance to deserve any comment. But before leaving the office of county clerk it is well to review briefly the possibilities of reform in that office which have been suggested.

The clerk is popularly elected and yet he is an administrative and ministerial officer for the county board. It has been pointed out in this connection that he is thus in an anomalous position, that he ought either to be a truly independent executive and continue to be popularly elected, or else that he ought to be nothing more than an instrument of the county board and be appointed by the board. The first suggestion is hardly tenable for reasons that already have been pointed out. There is no need of an independent county executive. The other suggestion does, however, seem to have considerable merit.

If the clerk were appointed by the board he could still continue to perform every function that he now performs, except that of clerk of court. There could be a clerk of court appointed by the court itself. The county clerk would then continue with the same functions that he now exercises, but his new relationship to the board ought to bring about certain desirable changes. He could be made very strictly accountable to the board for the performance of certain duties which now rest upon the board itself. He could negotiate contracts subject to the approval of the board, he would examine claims and make recommendations to the board with a keen sense of responsibility. He could be a purchasing agent for all the county institutions and thereby effect great economies. He could do all the inspecting and supervising which the board is vaguely expected to do, and make reports to the board. In other words, he would be a true administrative agent of the board, a functionary sadly needed; and this he will not be so long as he is popularly elected.

Such a change would inspire the clerk with a new sense of responsibility and would in no way interfere with the performance of those duties which he now performs as an independent elective officer. It would give the board a much firmer grip on the affairs of the county and might well result in substantial improvement in county government generally. The change as suggested here is a simple one, but it is suggestive of the much more radical reforms involved in the county manager plan which is being worked out in certain quarters.

THE CLERK OF COURT

Various Kinds of Courts.—While it has already been pointed out that in many states the county clerk serves also as clerk of court, it is well to consider the functions of a clerk of court as if he were a separate officer. It is necessary that there be some well-trained officer to keep all the records and do all the voluminous clerical work in connection with the proceedings of any court. There may be a court of general jurisdiction in each county. Again, the state may be divided into several judicial districts, each embracing several counties. In this case there may be several judges or only one for each district. In any event sessions of the court are held in each county even though every county does not have a judge or a court of its own. These are courts of general jurisdiction. They may be known as the county courts, the district courts, or circuit courts.

Separate County Courts.—In a few states there is in addition another court, one for each county, which is not a court of general jurisdiction but is intended to relieve the district or circuit courts of certain special types of judicial business. The probation of wills, the disposal of estates, and the appointment of conservators, are types of judicial business that frequently are left in the jurisdiction of a separate county court. Juvenile cases, cases involving the insane or feeble-minded, commitments to public institutions and the appointment of guardians, often fall to the county court. Election cases and cases involving the condemnation of property for public use may lie within the jurisdiction of the county court. And the county court may have general civil and criminal jurisdiction up to a fixed minimum, and entertain appeals from the justice courts. This relieves the district or circuit courts of a great deal of routine work and leaves them free to handle the major criminal and civil cases.

Each county must therefore be provided with clerks of court who will keep the records of the various courts which hold their sessions in the county. The county clerk himself may serve as clerk for the county court, while the district or circuit courts have special clerks of court. All these clerks are elective officers in nearly all the states even when the office is not combined with that of county clerk.

Functions of a Clerk of Court.—The duties of a clerk of court are technical and exacting, and the details of his work are not of interest to the ordinary citizen. He must make a permanent record of all suits entered in the court for which he is functioning. He must send formal notices to all persons involved. He makes out subpœnas for witnesses and summonses for jurors, which are delivered by the sheriff. When the court is in session the clerk, or a subordinate, must keep a complete stenographic record of the proceedings. He prepares all papers and documents required by the court. He makes a record of decisions rendered and judgments pronounced. He prepares all orders of the court and all the notices that grow out of the case in hand. Thus in his office there must be a complete record of every case from beginning to end.

In addition to this he is usually required to keep vital statistics of births, deaths and marriages, and he issues burial certificates and marriage licenses. All these duties are purely ministerial and require a well-trained and competent individual.

There would seem to be no reason why this officer should not be appointed by the court instead of elected by the people.

THE RECORDER

Functions of the Recorder.—In every county there must be some official whose duty it is to keep a record of land titles and documents of different kinds. He may be known as the register of deeds, or simply as the recorder. Sometimes there is no such independent officer as this but the duties of a recorder are performed by some other officer, such as the county clerk. But in a great majority of cases there is an independent officer known as the recorder even though he may devote but a small portion of his time to the work, and his salary may be very small.

Original Land Titles.—His principal duty is to keep a record of land titles. The keeping of accurate records of land titles has been an exceedingly difficult problem since earliest times. There are two ways in which land may originally come into the possession of private persons. One way is for the individual to seize and occupy a piece of land over which no government has jurisdiction. Obviously this can be done ordinarily only along the frontiers of civilization. Presently, as time goes on, a government is established embracing the land occupied by the frontiersman, and he must then seek recognition of his title to the land from the government. The fact of his ownership is then recorded by some public official.

Patents.—The other, and the usual way, is for the individual to purchase land from the government, or to receive it gratuitously under the terms of a homestead law. In either case, the original private owner of the land secures what is known as a "patent" to his piece of land. This patent is a legal recognition of his title to the land and must be recorded in some public office. Where towns were established town clerks usually kept these records, but outside New England it became the practice ultimately to turn the function over to a county officer.

Deeds.—When an original private owner sells his piece of land or any part of it, the new owner or purchaser receives what is known as a "deed" to the piece of land which he has purchased. This deed contains a description of the land and a statement of its exact boundaries, together with other pertinent information. A record of this deed should be made in the recorder's office. And every time that title to a parcel of land changes hands a deed is given and should be recorded.

Land Transfers.—But the buying and selling of land is not always a simple process. Mortgages are given, liens are established against property, attachments are made, owners fail to pay taxes, legal actions are instituted challenging the title to the land, and orders and judgments of the court are entered which impair titles. In the course of time, during which a piece of land changes hands many times these legal complications multiply until only a skillful lawyer is able to uncover all the facts and point the way to clearing up a title. But every time legal action is started, or a transaction takes place affecting the title to land, written documents are made setting forth the nature of the transaction, and records of these transactions should be made in the recorder's office.

Thus in his office there should be found a complete record of all the papers and documents ever executed that could affect the title to a given piece of land. As regards most land there would be nothing but the original patent and a few deeds, leaving the title perfectly clear and obvious. In other cases, transactions may have been so numerous, and the owners and public officials so careless that it becomes literally impossible to clear up the title to a given piece, and the title always remains clouded as it were, for it is impossible to clear it up.

Abstracts of Title.—These records affecting titles to land have piled up in such confusion that the business of tracing down titles has become a profession. Lawyers and companies do this work and prepare for purchasers "abstracts of title" which are nothing more nor less than records of all the transactions affecting the title to land. Most of the information of course is to be found in the recorder's office.

Confusion of Land Titles.—It may well be imagined that records to land titles fall into great disorder. Sometimes the officer who is responsible for keeping the records is to blame, but very frequently the ignorance and carelessness of landowners themselves is the factor involved. Men sell land to each other without securing deeds or going near the public officials. They enter into contracts between themselves which affect the title to land but which are not recorded. Measurements are carelessly and inaccurately made. Fences and landmarks are erected and stand for decades as the accepted boundaries when in fact they are not correctly placed. Even paved streets are laid and huge buildings erected on lines that later are found to be wrong. In the great cities there are vast sky-scrapers erected on lines many feet out of square with official records. Of course in such cases owners must simply make the best of the situation. But nevertheless, carelessness, ignorance and inaccurate records give rise to an immense amount of litigation affecting the title to land.

A well-managed recorder's office would have records as complete as possible, of all manner of documents, deeds, mortgages, liens, court orders and decrees. They should be kept by modern methods and be well indexed.

Recorders are Elected.—County recorders are usually elected like other county officers, or else the office is combined with that of county clerk. There would seem to be no very good reason why the recorder should be elected, as his work is purely ministerial.

The Surveyor.—Another officer who works in close touch with the recorder is the county surveyor. He is usually elected and stands ready to survey land at the behest of the county board, the recorder, the clerk, or private individuals. His surveys are presumed to be authoritative and are the basis of the records in the recorder's office. Other functions of the surveyor, or engineer, are exercised in connection with the maintenance of highways and will be discussed below.

Reorganization of Clerical Offices.—The clerical offices of the county have now been discussed and the possibilities of reform have been suggested. To summarize briefly these clerical officers are known as county clerks, auditors, clerks of court, circuit clerks, clerks of probate,* registers of deeds, and recorders. It has been suggested that there is no very good reason why any of these officers should be elected. The judges of the courts might well appoint the clerks of court or circuit clerks and probate clerks. County boards might well appoint the county clerks or auditors, and a subordinate in the clerk's office might well perform the function of a recorder.

* In some states there are special county probate courts.

CHAPTER IX

COUNTY POLICE FUNCTIONS

Origin of Sheriff's Office.—The sheriff is the oldest of all the county officers. The history of this office can be traced back into mediæval England, and throughout the centuries the fundamental aspects of the sheriff's functions have not greatly changed. The origin of his office and its development are to be associated with the nationalizing tendencies which began to operate in England about the time of the Norman Conquest. In the years that followed England gradually became a unified state under the control of a central government. The sheriff is intimately associated with this process. He was an instrument of the central government and was a potent influence in binding the nation into a unified whole.

Before the Norman Conquest England was ruled by feudal lords who for the most part recognized no superior authority. They owed a certain allegiance to the king, who was not much more than the chief feudal lord, and rendered this allegiance so long as the king was strong enough to command it. But there was no well-organized central government embracing the entire realm.

The domain of a lord, an earl, was known as a shire. He ruled supreme within his shire. In order to bring about unification and the establishment of a centralized government it was necessary to break down the power of these feudal lords. This was done through representatives of the king who went into the far corners of the realm demanding allegiance to the monarch. These officers of the crown came to be known as sheriffs. An earlier term was shire-reeve.

Early Functions.—The sheriff collected taxes, enlisted men into the military service of the king, maintained the peace, enforced the king's decrees, and served as the executive functionary of the king's court, sometimes holding court himself. He had the character of a personal representative of the monarch. His presence was a constant challenge to the earls and other feudal lords. They were forced to become vassals of the king themselves or else to flee. And the aggressive activity of the sheriffs together with numerous other forces tending to the decay of feudalism gradually led to the strengthening of the central government, dominated by the king.

The shires, and the descendants of the feudal lords are still to be found in England to-day. But English shires are not areas of government, they are not civil divisions, except in those cases where the boundaries of a civil county happen to coincide with the boundaries of an ancient shire, for the whole realm was later divided into civil counties. The lords of England of course have long since lost all trace of personal governmental power. And an earl to-day, or a lord of any other rank, has no more civil authority over the land that he may possess than any other owner.

While these great changes were being wrought in the character of the British constitution the sheriff continued to function as an instrument of the crown. The area of his operations became the civil county. Yet while he remained the principal county officer certain of his functions fell away. Other machinery was developed for the collection of taxes. He ceased to be a military leader. But he remained primarily a peace officer, and never at any time has it ceased to be his primary function to maintain the peace in the name of the sovereign. This function involved the duty of taking charge of prisoners and acting as an executive officer of the court.

The Sheriff in American Colonies.—When counties were created in America it was natural that sheriffs should appear. In some cases they were appointed, in earliest times particularly, in the sparsely settled territories, and in the less democratic South. But it soon came to be the almost universal practice to elect the sheriff, and that is the custom to-day in every state but one, Rhode Island. His term of office is usually four years, and often he is not permitted to succeed himself but must go out of office for a term before he can again become sheriff.

The jurisdiction of the sheriff is the county. In the exercise of his functions he is not responsible to the county board or to any county officer, unless it be the county judge. One of his functions is to execute the orders of the court and thus in a sense he is accountable to the judge. Contrary to the general impression he is not ordinarily under the authoritative control of the state governor, or any other state officer. Obviously in most cases a county sheriff would be ready to give heed to the requests of a state governor and to coöperate with state officers in every way. But, in the absence of special statutory provisions, the sheriff is entirely free to administer the functions of his office as he sees fit. Thus he enjoys a large measure of independence and this is particularly significant in view of the fact that he is free to exercise his own judgment and discretion on most important matters affecting the safety of the people.

Modern Functions.—The function of the sheriff everywhere in the United States to-day is just what it always has been down through the centuries—to maintain the peace. Revolution, war and turmoil that wrecked empires and gave birth to republics, disorders and constitutional changes that affected parliaments and altered the whole structure of national governments left this humble office of the sheriff untouched and unchanged. It persevered through colonial times in New England, in the South, and traveled west with civilization. It prevailed through the War for Independence without change and is now a monument to local government. The sheriff's function is to maintain the peace as a general peace officer, and this involves having custody of prisoners, and acting as an executive officer for the courts.

Is Sheriff a State Officer?—It is maintained by many students of political science, and they are well supported by judicial decisions, that the sheriff is a state officer rather than a local officer. He is indeed a state officer in that he enforces state law. And furthermore, in a certain sense the sheriff is not a part of the county organization as are most of the other county officials; and this fact lends color to the contention that he is in reality a state officer. The county board, the clerk, the treasurer, the auditor, the assessor, the highway official, the poor-master, and the superintendents of the various county institutions compose a group of officers primarily concerned with county problems and county business. The board determines county policies and with these other officers carries on business and administrative activities for the county primarily; and these individuals are unquestionably to be considered county officers.

The sheriff is not one of this group. The sheriff concerns himself with the enforcement of the state law, his prisoners are prisoners of the state, and he executes the orders of the court in the name of the people of the state. He has virtually nothing to do with the county organization except that the county board has general supervision of the jail where he keeps his prisoners and is able to control him indirectly by granting or withholding funds with which he may discharge his duties in this connection.

However, the contention than the sheriff is a state officer would be greatly strengthened if he were appointed by, or at least were under the control of, some state authority. This is not the case, except in one state. Hence there is no organic relation between his office and the state government. And despite the theory that he represents the people of the state as a whole, he is elected by the people of a county, he has been identified with the county for many centuries, and what is of greater significance his policies in the matter of interpreting and enforcing state law are largely dictated by the county electorate. Thus it is entirely proper to look upon the sheriff as a county officer. But even so it must not be forgotten that he is somewhat apart from the county organization and is a representative of the state in a sense that most of the other county officers are not. His functions should now be examined in some detail.

Functions of Sheriff:

1. To Maintain Peace.—It has been said that he maintains the peace as a general peace officer. This means that he is responsible on his own authority for the suppression of all kinds of disorder and crime, he may make arrests on sight, and is expected to seek out and hold all criminals until they are released by a court. There is no other peace officer to be found in the United States with as broad jurisdiction as he. The federal government maintains marshals who are executive officers for the federal courts, and detectives who assist federal agents in the enforcement of particular federal laws such as the liquor law. State governments have only recently provided for peace officers at all, and the city police have a very limited area as their jurisdiction. But county sheriffs collectively embrace the whole United States, and it is upon them that responsibility rests for preservation of the peace and the suppression of crime.

This is an elementary function of government. Nowhere is that more evident than in pioneer communities and along the frontiers of civilization. In early days, and always in the Far West as settlements pushed forward, the sheriff was a conspicuous, powerful, dominant representative of governmental power. His office was the most important of all and not infrequently he even exceeded the broad powers which he legally possessed. Sheriffs were disproportionately powerful and important because governmental machinery was still in its rudimentary stage and the function of preserving peace was all important. As civilization develops the sheriff naturally retires from the front of the stage. But the picturesque sheriff of pioneer days was an interesting forerunner of his modern prototype. He has been preserved with a few embellishments by the moving picture industry.

The powers of the sheriff are elastic and can be extended to very great proportions. In order to preserve the peace it may be necessary that he command the services of a great many of the able-bodied men in his county. This he may do when emergency exists, and he is the judge of the emergency. This power is called the power to call the *posse comitatus*. He may summon any able-bodied citizen, on sight and without formality, to go with him and assist him in the preservation of the peace. It happens occasionally even to-day, when labor disorders occur, that business men are suddenly required to do police duty in emergencies. Refusal to respond is attended with definite penalties. The citizen thus called has no recourse unless he is able to show, afterwards, that the sheriff has acted without justification; and only the most flagrant abuse of discretionary power on the part of the sheriff would be discountenanced by the courts. In emergencies with which the sheriff cannot cope he may call upon the governor for the state militia; but of course the governor is competent to send the militia to suppress disorder or to enforce the law anywhere within the state whether the sheriff desires it or not.

Curious conflicts of authority sometimes arise between sheriffs and city police. In any such conflict of authority the presumption is in favor of the sheriff, for as in ancient days the sheriff's "bailiwick" is his county, regardless of the cities, towns and villages it may include. But in practice the sheriff is usually very willing, indeed eager, to leave the matter of law enforcement to the highly organized city police whenever he can, and confine his own attention to the other aspects of his function.

2. To Serve as an Executive Officer of the Court.—One of these is to serve as an executive officer for the courts. He must attend all sessions of the district or county court and perform certain duties preliminary to, during, and after these sessions. He summons the juries, the names of those who are to serve having been selected by lot from among the registered voters. He serves warrants on persons who have been indicted and sees to it that they are in court when they are wanted. He is responsible for summoning all the witnesses who will be required at the trial and if need be arrests them and brings them in as prisoners.

In all these matters he must work in close coöperation with the clerk of court who prepares all the documents which must be served upon the persons involved. The days preceding the session of a court thus are busy ones for the sheriff, and he and his deputies are fully occupied in serving all the papers, bringing in all the persons, and in general getting things ready for the session.

During a session the sheriff is at the service of the court. He and the bailiffs maintain order in the court room. He has charge of the jury at all times. He is responsible for the prisoners and witnesses and must perform services required of him by the court as the trial proceeds. He may be sent to bring in more witnesses, to serve documents, or to bring in exhibits required by the court.

After the session is over the sheriff must execute the judgment of the court whether it be to hang a murderer or to carry an infant to the orphanage. In some states, however, capital punishment is inflicted by state authorities at the state penitentiary. The sheriff must serve all papers involved in the execution of judgment. He may be obliged to seize property for the satisfaction of judgment. He turns convicted men over to the state penitentiaries, and those convicted of lesser crimes he takes back to the county jail to serve their sentences. He is thus the executive officer of the court. It is an ancient function which he has always exercised.

In populous counties where the courts are in session most of the time he is provided with a number of deputies, and with clerical help. In such counties this aspect of his function occupies his time to the exclusion of his other duties. The city police relieve him of his responsibility for maintaining peace, and they also take charge of prisoners. This leaves the sheriff in these counties primarily an executive officer of the court.

It has been the custom for the sheriff to retain certain fees in addition to, or instead of, a fixed salary. He receives a fee for every document served and for nearly every act performed in and about the court room, before and after sessions of the court. These fees individually are small, but in the aggregate they sometimes mount to huge sums. The practice began in the days when the sheriff had little to do but to hold himself in readiness to pursue an occasional criminal, and to attend the infrequent sessions of the court. His duties as sheriff did not interfere with his private business and it seemed fair that he should only receive fees which were supposed to represent reasonable compensation for work actually done. The practice might be defended in rural communities to-day; but in populous counties, and particularly where the sheriff devotes his whole time to the duties of his office, this practice is quite indefensible. The fees accumulate to a sum far in excess of that received by most other county officers.

It is unnecessary to discuss the evils of this situation. A sheriff who devotes his whole time to the work of his office should be paid a salary commensurate with that of other county officers. If the duties of his office do not occupy his whole time his salary could be adjusted proportionately. Fees, when they are charged, should go into the public treasury. The evils of the fee system are of course most obvious in those populous counties where the principal duty of the sheriff is to serve as an executive officer of the courts.

3. To have Custody of Prisoners.—The sheriff has one other distinct function which must be touched upon. He is expected to have charge of prisoners, and to keep them in the county jail. Here the sheriff comes in contact with the county board. The board is expected to appropriate money for the maintenance of the jail and the support of the prisoners. Whether the board is generous or niggardly has much to do with the condition of the jail. The board is expected to exercise general supervision over the jail as well as other county institutions and does annually, or semi-annually, conduct a perfunctory inspection; but in practice the sheriff is left in full charge of the institution himself.

It is the general practice for county boards to allow the sheriff a certain sum of money per prisoner, for board and maintenance. Needless to say the county board is likely to appropriate money for only modest fare, and the sheriff not infrequently finds it possible to keep his prisoners alive on even less than has been allowed by the county board. This practice operates to the disadvantage of the prisoners; but when the sheriff is permitted to support them as he sees fit, and then present his bill to the county board, whatever it may be, the door is opened to gross extravagance and wastefulness.

But there are other problems that arise in connection with the care of prisoners than providing them with food, that are just as difficult to solve. County jails are notoriously insanitary and unwholesome. The sheriff is not always to blame for this condition, especially when the county board refuses to make the necessary appropriation for improving the conditions. Jails are often very old and frequently not large enough. They are not equipped with proper sanitary facilities, they are ill-ventilated and poorly lighted. There usually is no way of segregating prisoners as they should be segregated, and no way of giving them the exercise and useful work they ought to have. Some jails degenerate into unspeakable pens that do incalculable harm in the influence they exert upon those who are placed in them for any length of time. Fortunately most prisoners are kept in the county jail only a short time. Those awaiting trial are not usually there very long, and those serving sentence would be sent to the state penitentiary if their sentences exceeded a certain minimum length of time. But this in no way justifies the deplorable conditions that have been uncovered.

Social workers, and the influence of enlightened public opinion, has led to great improvement in recent years.

There have always been certain provisions in state law intended to compel the maintenance of proper standards, but they are more or less futile when left to the administration of irresponsible local officers. No law can guarantee decent cleanliness, or even decent standards of morality, and any legislation which attempts to go into the details of such matters must necessarily be useless or even worse than useless. A system of state inspection backed with authority might bring improvement, but it would involve a very serious invasion of local prerogatives.

The proper segregation of prisoners in the county jail is an ideal that probably never will be attained. In the first place there are men, women and children to be segregated. There are comparatively few women, but since many jails have no separate quarters for them at all it is not unusual for the sheriff to hold women prisoners temporarily in his own home. There are very likely to be some young boys in the jail and they are usually turned in with the vicious adult prisoners and thus subjected to influences that tend to make them hardened criminals. There are also the sick and the well who ought to be segregated, but as a rule a prisoner must be very ill indeed before he can hope to be removed from his cell. Very few counties maintain hospitals, and the county boards are not inclined to pay for the care of prisoners in private hospitals.

But there is another sort of segregation that might be effected, too, but is seldom even considered. The status of prisoners is not always the same. Some are in the jail awaiting trial. According to the theory of the law they are innocent, and the law provides opportunity for them to gain their freedom until the time of trial by paying bail or giving bond. If a person cannot pay he must wait in jail. Other prisoners are serving short sentences of a few days or months. But the presumably innocent prisoner awaiting trial is thrown in with the convicted criminal serving sentence. Then too there may be some witnesses held as prisoners because the sheriff fears that if he does not hold them they will escape his jurisdiction before the trial.

Hence it may easily happen that men and boys, sick and well, vicious, hardened criminals serving sentence, innocent persons awaiting trial, and even some witnesses, will all be herded together in identical cells in a building that is old and inadequate, dark, ill-ventilated and insanitary. Still the fact must be recognized that few counties could afford to provide ideal accommodations for their prisoners, and furthermore there is not much sentiment in favor of it.

The most hopeful sign for the improvement of conditions is the move on the part of some states to establish state district jails, each district embracing several counties. Sometimes several counties will coöperate on their own initiative to maintain a jail at the common expense; but the state district idea is much better in that it insures state inspection and the probable maintenance of better standards.

Office of the Sheriff is Undergoing Change.—The office of sheriff is undergoing change. Probably the last twenty years have witnessed greater changes in the character of this office than were to be noted in the previous hundred years. More and more the sheriff proves to be a failure as a general peace officer. Only in the last four years more than a dozen states have found it desirable to establish for the first time a force of state police to assist the sheriffs as peace officers. More and more the sheriff fails to coöperate effectively, not only with the attorney-general's office but with the public prosecutor in his own county, and public prosecutors are demanding that they be provided with detectives whom they can control in order to conduct their prosecutions and investigate violations of the law independently of sheriffs. More and more the sheriff tends to become a mere executive officer of the courts, content to remain in his office and execute the orders and decrees of the courts through his deputies, serve papers and execute judgments. These tendencies would seem to herald some rather fundamental changes in the sheriff's office, but it may be expected that many years will pass before the changes will finally have been accomplished.

Sheriff's Failure as a Peace Officer.—The fact that the sheriff is failing as a general peace officer is not necessarily a reflection upon him. Nor is it a sign that crime is on the increase. It indicates rather that the criminal is finding new ways in which to express his individuality, and the sheriff's office is not properly organized to cope with him. The rapid development of good roads has given criminals certain opportunities that they never had before. Good roads have bound the rural districts to the cities, and along with the advantages that have come with this there has come some evil also. In effect the city criminal is much nearer to the country than he used to be, and thus the sheriff comes in contact with a much larger group of criminals than ever before.

Crime in Rural Districts.—Naturally the automobile is the instrument which facilitates the operations of the criminal in the rural areas. In recent years the area within a hundred miles of the great urban centers has been combed by bands of criminals who a short decade ago would have been obliged to confine their depredations to the cities. Country banks, village stores, rural post offices, and railroad stations without number have been the objects of midnight raids. The bandits come in one or two machines, perpetrate their villainy in a moment's time and are off in a cloud of dust.

While the automobile has contributed more than any other single factor to make such things possible, the ever-growing network of railroads, interurban electric lines, and even telephones have assisted the criminals very materially. These city criminals are of a type never before known in the rural districts, and county sheriffs are singularly helpless in dealing with them.

There are other new developments that are overtaxing the power of sheriffs to keep the peace. Labor disorders frequently reach proportions that find both sheriff and city police overwhelmed. Race riots have been numerous even in the northern communities, and sheriffs have not been able to deal with them efficiently. For years sheriffs have been unable to prevent lynchings in the South. A few disorders of a similar nature have been precipitated by various types of radicals, I. W. W. agitators and so-called reds and bolshevists; and those who have been over-eager in their efforts to suppress them. All of these developments serve to emphasize the fact that county sheriffs are not fitted to act alone as general peace officers.

Sheriff's Deputies.—Some feeble efforts have been made by counties to strengthen the sheriff's arm. In some cases he is provided with a number of deputies, but nowhere has any thoroughly well-organized county police force been established. This is not surprising for the rural communities do not feel that they can afford to maintain highly organized police forces. Indeed each individual county does not need such a force. A well-organized unit could operate over an area much larger than a single county.

In some counties the authorities have made vigorous and more or less effective efforts to prevent automobile speeding by the appointment of deputy sheriffs, and the county "speed cop" on his motorcycle is coming to be a familiar figure on the long stretches of cement highway.

But speeding is not the sort of offense that contains great menace to peace and security.

STATE POLICE

State Police and the Sheriff.—The solution of the problem would seem to be the establishment of some kind of state police organization. Such an organization may include the sheriff, giving him a prominent position in the organization; or it may involve the retirement of the sheriff altogether as a peace officer, leaving him simply as a functionary of a court; or it may be established by the side of the sheriff, leaving him free to exercise his police functions as he chooses.

State Police in Other Countries.—Examples of state police organizations are to be found all over the world.* There are to be found the gendarmes of France, the Royal Irish Constabulary, the Australian Trooper Police, the famous Canadian Northwest Mounted Police, and our own police forces organized in the Philippines and Porto Rico. A few experiments have been tried out in the United States, but only very recently has the step met with any enthusiasm on the part of the public generally. It means the breakdown of local autonomy and smacks of a militaristic system that is execrated throughout the land. But the very rapid developments in recent years seem to indicate a change in attitude on the part of the public.

State Police in the United States.—State officers exercising some police functions have been known in the United States ever since 1865 when Massachusetts established a state district police primarily for detective work. Between

---

* A splendid summary of state legislation dealing with state police is to be found in the *American Political Science Review*, Vol. XV, p. 82, "Legislative Notes and Reviews," edited by W. F. Dodd.

that time and 1901 several other states created state police. But in no case were they given general police power, they did not have the broad function of maintaining the peace as the sheriff has it. They usually were organized for one of two purposes. Either it was to be their function to help enforce some particular law that was causing trouble, such as the liquor laws, the anti-gambling legislation, or the measures designed to protect state forest preserves; or else they were merely to do detective work out of the attorney-general's office. Obviously these were very rudimentary state police organizations.

The Texas Rangers.—In 1901, however, the Texas Rangers were established. They were an organization of mounted men whose specific duty it was to patrol the Mexican border and prevent trouble there. They were highly efficient, well organized, inspired great confidence and attracted nation-wide attention. The possibilities of such an organization for general police work were at once appreciated. In 1903 and 1905 Arizona and New Mexico organized similar forces.

The Pennsylvania State Constabulary.—In 1905 there was created the Pennsylvania State Constabulary. It was a small group of highly organized, well-trained men, and their specific function was to suppress disorder, particularly in the vicinity of the great coal mining regions. They were at once the objects of much praise and admiration on the one hand, and violent condemnation on the other. Public opinion was distinctly divided and still remains so.

The New York State Troopers.—The most significant step was taken, however, in 1917 when the New York State Troopers were organized. The creation of this force was particularly significant because, while it was understood that they would be especially useful in labor troubles and mob disorders, they were to have general police functions. It was necessary to compromise on this point, however, to this extent,—they were not to operate within the limits of any city without the consent of the mayor. These troopers have the same power to arrest criminals and maintain the peace that a sheriff has, and they are free to go to any part of the state.

The troopers are organized into four units each headed by a captain. In all there are about two hundred men. The entire force is under the absolute control of a superintendent who is appointed by the governor. The value of such a force, when mounted, lies in the fact that it is very mobile, can be used in any part of the state, and possesses the advantages that go with a highly centralized military form of organization. A few men can patrol a very broad rural area and by constant and regular telephone communication can keep in touch with any developments requiring their prompt attention. For the most part they command the respect and good will of the countryside and are a potent influence in the suppression of crime in rural districts. When mobilized in a single unit for some particular purpose they make a very formidable body.

Compromises with the Sheriff.—Even so, a group of two hundred state police officers is not likely to cause the immediate retirement of all the county sheriffs in a large state, and that is not intended. But the possibilities of the future are most significant. If state police forces prove to be satisfactory they are sure to be developed to greater size and assume more responsibility. A clash with the sheriff sooner or later is inevitable. There are at present fifteen states that have some kind of a state police force, and nine of them have been created since 1917. It can thus be seen how recent the movement is. None of the others are as yet so highly developed as the New York

State Troopers and the Pennsylvania State Constabulary; but all of the organizations are highly centralized, of military type, mobile, and capable of quick, effective action.

The compromises that have been made with the sheriff's office are most interesting. In one state the act creating the state police bestows upon them general police power, but specifically stipulates that "their authority shall not be superior to the powers and authority of the sheriff as the principal officer of the peace in his county." In another state the resident sheriff is to have command of the state police when they are operating in his county. In yet another state the sheriffs and constables are themselves to constitute the state police, under the command of the governor. In no case has the sheriff been displaced or made subordinate to the state police. The usual form of compromise is to ignore the sheriff, to permit him to retain all his powers and functions, but to give the state police officers the same power so far as the maintenance of peace is concerned. These compromises indicate the reluctance on the part of legislatures to invade the prerogatives of county sheriffs. And even though the logic of the situation may demand the ultimate retirement of the sheriff as a general peace officer this will only be accomplished by slow degrees.

Situation in Illinois.—One of the latest developments in this connection occurred in the Illinois legislature in the winter of 1921. A bill was introduced providing for a state police force and was hotly contested. The bill was ultimately defeated, and the arguments against it were characteristic. It was said the principle involved was autocratic and militaristic. It was believed the state police would break down local autonomy, and would give state authorities too great power in the cities. It was said the state police would become brutal and arrogant, and worst of all they would constitute a weapon in the hands of Capital to be used against Labor, a club in the hands of reactionaries to be used to suppress liberals. Whether there is any truth in these contentions or not they are the basis of opposition to state police.

Opposition to State Police:

1. From Labor.—Indeed opposition comes from three well-defined sources. The principal source of opposition is organized labor. The labor unions are convinced that state police will always be used to break strikes and to promote the cause of employers in their conflicts with labor. In so far as the state police are used to prevent violence on the part of strikers, and to protect others in their legal right to work, this contention is no doubt true.

2. From Socialists.—Another source of opposition is the Socialist Party and those who are still more radical than the socialists. They believe the state police strengthen the hands of the propertied class in the mass struggle with the proletariat. In so far as the state police protect property this contention is no doubt true.

3. From Cities.—Another source of opposition is the cities. City authorities generally are unwilling that state police officers should operate within city limits. But this opposition can easily be met as in New York where the troopers may operate within city limits only with the consent of the mayor.

State Police Desired by Certain Groups.—State police forces are wanted on the whole by those who are primarily interested in law and order. Naturally this includes those who are inclined to be conservative in their political views, the employing class generally, and those who own property. State police are also wanted by the people of the rural districts who see in them a measure of protection that can never be afforded by the county sheriffs.

Possibility of Appointing Sheriffs.—Suggestions for the reorganization of county government seldom include any recommendations concerning the sheriff. It seems to be tacitly assumed that he must remain an elective officer and continue to exercise the same functions which he now exercises. There are, however, certain possibilities of change that are worthy of consideration. If a state department of justice were created, similar to the federal department, under the attorney-general of the state, the sheriffs might possibly be appointed by the head of this department and work under his supervision. This step should be taken, however, only if the public prosecutors also are brought under the control of the state department of justice. Such steps would mean very radical change and can hardly be expected in the near future.

Another possibility is that the sheriff might become merely an executive officer for the courts, and perhaps be appointed by the court along with the clerk. Police functions would then be exercised by some kind of a state police force. This may gradually come to pass. In the cities that are coterminous with counties, or nearly so, this is already the situation. The city police exercise the police functions, while the sheriff in practice is nothing but a functionary of the court, even though he continues to be an elective officer. With the development of state police the same fate may be in store for sheriffs in the rural areas.

Most proposals for the reform of county government look toward concentration of power in the hands of a small board which would appoint practically all county officers. But there is no very good reason for giving the board such a measure of control over the sheriff. His activities are much more closely related to the state, although he is elected for, and functions in, the county. To leave the prosecutor and sheriff out of any reorganized county machinery would not seriously impede the reforms ordinarily anticipated. But the county board might well have more effective control over the jail if that institution is not to come under the supervision of state authorities.

As a matter of fact the office of sheriff is no doubt destined to remain very much as it is for many years to come, except for the gradual changes that may be wrought in urban counties, and in those states where a state police force is highly developed.

THE CORONER

Origin of Coroner's Office.—The coroner is very closely related to the sheriff. The history of this office is almost as old as that of the sheriff and the coroner, too, is to be identified with nationalizing tendencies in England. He was in early days a representative of the crown, and throughout a checkered career has exercised a variety of functions. At one time he appeared almost as a rival of the sheriff, seeking to curb and curtail the powers and ambitions of sheriffs who were near to breaking away from royal authority.

Coroner has One Primary Function.—But there has been one important function held by the coroner throughout all the years and it is the one which he to-day exercises, that is, the function of investigating deaths that occur under unusual and more or less mysterious circumstances.

The coroner is popularly elected for the same period as the sheriff and acts as a substitute for that officer when for any reason he is incapacitated. The coroner is entirely independent of any authority, state or local, and in the exercise of his functions uses his own discretion at all times. He is to be found in virtually every county of the United

States, although programmes for reform of county government usually leave no place for him.

Whenever information of a death that has occurred under unusual or more or less mysterious circumstances comes to his attention the coroner is expected to begin an investigation immediately. The statutes which impose this duty upon him are rather vague and leave much to his discretion. They cannot be otherwise. Personal judgment must be exercised in nearly every case, and the coroner alone determines whether or not an investigation is necessary. The statutes contain wordy provisions that can do no more than serve as suggestions. They require him, for instance, to conduct an investigation "when it is thought death has occurred due to violence," or "when foul play is suspected," or "in case of accident," or "when a physician was not in attendance." Always it is the coroner who must exercise his discretion. The sheriff, the city police, the public prosecutor, may all urge him to begin an investigation but they have no authority to compel him. As a matter of fact, however, coroners are likely to conduct numerous unnecessary investigations rather than to neglect cases which ought to be investigated. Coroners are expected to be on the alert themselves, but cases are regularly brought to their attention by sheriffs, the police, the prosecutor, physicians, the newspaper men, and other private citizens.

Inquests.—After a very brief and cursory investigation the coroner decides whether or not to hold an inquest. If he decides to do so he is expected to do it at once. He proceeds to the scene of the death and impanels a coroner's jury. In most cases it is found more convenient, and it is quite permissible, to conduct the inquest at an undertaking establishment, or in the coroner's office.

Coroner's Juries.—A coroner's jury is ordinarily very

small, in some states it consists of three members, more often it is six. The coroner selects the jury on his own authority, often from among bystanders. Impaneling a coroner's jury is thus a very informal proceeding; but of more significance is the fact that jurors chosen in this way are very likely to be guided entirely by the judgment of the coroner. He is thus often in a position to dictate verdicts, and through collusion with jurors their fees may constitute a prolific source of petty graft.

Proceedings Informal.—It is the duty of the jury to view the remains and listen to the testimony presented to them. The coroner presides, though he is not a member of the jury. He summons witnesses and interrogates them before the jury. The public prosecutor may also be in attendance. Proceedings are usually very informal. The testimony of police officers and those who discovered the victim is usually of most value. The coroner cannot compel witnesses to testify if they do not choose to do so. There is nothing in the nature of a prosecution or defense, the whole purpose of the proceeding being to discover how the victim came to his death. A stenographic record of the proceedings may be kept and it may not. It is seldom of much value even if it is kept.

Three Types of Verdicts:

1. Natural Death, Accident, or Suicide.—After hearing all the testimony which the coroner permits them to hear, the jurymen deliberate briefly and arrive at a verdict. In general there are three kinds of verdicts. The first kind is rendered when the jury believes that all mystery and suspicion has been cleared up, that the victim came to his death under circumstances for which no one is criminally responsible; and in the opinion of the jury the case may be considered closed as far as public officials are concerned. Such verdicts are rendered in cases of natural death, or pure accident, or suicide. This sort of a verdict usually does end a case.

2. Murderer Unknown.—The second type of verdict is rendered when the jury has reason to believe that the victim came to his death by foul play, due to violence, or poison, or something else, but are unable or unwilling to fix suspicion upon anyone. In such cases they render a verdict declaring the opinion of the jury that the victim came to his death at the hands of some person or persons unknown to the jury. This sort of a verdict is a tacit urge to the police officers and the public prosecutor to seek out the murderer as soon as possible; if indeed they are not already upon the quest.

3. Responsibility Fixed.—The third type of verdict is rendered when the jury believes it is justified in fixing responsibility for the death upon some person or persons. Coroner's juries are reluctant to do this upon the basis of their very superficial investigations, but if the case is obvious they do so and render a verdict which names the person whom they believe responsible. Such a verdict should be followed by the immediate arrest of the persons named, the coroner is competent to issue the warrant, and it is expected that the public prosecutor will proceed at once with his prosecution.

Inquests Unnecessary.—At first thought all these proceedings would appear to be quite regular, altogether desirable and necessary. However, such an inquest is too hasty, too informal, and too largely controlled by one man, to be relied upon as conclusive in any particular. If murder is suspected the police and the public prosecutor are expected to leave no stone unturned in their efforts to apprehend and convict the murderer, and none of their responsibility can be shifted to the coroner. Even though the coroner's jury were to declare the fatality a pure accident the police and prosecutor would not be justified in abandoning the case if they thought otherwise. The coroner's verdict cannot legally exonerate anybody, although press reports of inquests sometimes lend color to the belief that they do in effect exempt a suspect from prosecution. Yet it must be said that in practice a prosecutor is less inclined to prosecute if the coroner's jury has not cast suspicion upon anybody.

On the other hand, if the coroner's jury does cast suspicion upon some person, full responsibility rests upon the police and the prosecutor for obtaining a conviction. The prosecutor must conduct his own investigation, and while he has access to the records of the inquest they are of little value to him for he must make a very much more thorough investigation himself. In a word, nothing whatever of importance is done by the coroner that must not be done over again by the prosecutor and his aides. Nothing that the coroner has done can be relied upon, and indeed the prosecutor is fortunate if the coroner's activities have not actually impeded his own movements as prosecutor.

Prosecutor Should Perform This Function.—The coroner's inquest thus appears as a clumsy, inconclusive and unnecessary preliminary investigation on the part of an independent officer who bears no responsibility whatever. If such an investigation is to be conducted at all it ought to be under the supervision of the official who is responsible for the apprehension and conviction of the criminal. For this the coroner is in no sense responsible, and there would seem to be no reason why his functions should be performed independently of the prosecutor's office.

The Coroner Should Be Eliminated.—The services of a physician are nearly always required at an inquest. Sometimes the coroner himself is a physician, if he is not an undertaker; but in any event there could be a county physician ready at the call of the prosecutor to make any investigations that might be necessary. And if the prosecutor were permitted to employ detectives when needed he would be in a position to do everything that the coroner does, do it much more effectively, and do it with a much keener sense of responsibility. The coroner and his machinery could then be eliminated altogether.

Abuses in Coroner's Office.—Numerous abuses have developed in the coroner's office, as would in any office the functions of which might come to be superfluous. The possibility of petty graft has already been mentioned. In the more populous counties the fees of coroner's jurymen, witnesses and other attendants mount up to large sums that can be divided as party spoils. And furthermore indolent prosecutors can often hide behind a coroner's jury and fail to make the investigations that ought to be made simply because a hasty, careless inquest has resulted in a verdict of pure accident.

Another abuse grows out of the insidious influence that is sometimes brought to bear upon coroner's juries by public service and other corporations seeking to be exonerated from responsibility in connection with the death of employees or other citizens. Lawyers representing these corporations can be present at the inquest. It is sometimes easy to "fix" juries chosen in such an informal way, witnesses are corrupted very much more easily than in regular trials, testimony is badly garbled beyond the ability of coroners to straighten it out; and it has even happened that coroners have permitted the stenographers of private corporations to prepare the official reports of the inquests.

Thus by corruption and insidious influence coroner's juries can be brought to return verdicts that cast no blame upon the corporation. This is done so skillfully as sometimes to escape the knowledge of coroners and jurymen themselves. Such verdicts do not of course protect a corporation in the slightest degree from prosecution by relatives of the victim. But they do at least establish a presumption in favor of the corporation and constitute an initial advantage that is of very distinct value.

CHAPTER X

THE LAW OFFICERS

The Public Prosecutor.—There is in every one of the states a local officer known variously as the state's attorney, the prosecuting attorney, the county attorney, or the public prosecutor. Probably the last of these terms is the best one to use, though any of them is satisfactory. This officer has the same functions in each of the states, he is popularly elected in nearly all of them, and except in Oregon, Massachusetts, and some of the southern states he is a county officer. In those states where this exception is the rule he is elected for a district larger than a county—a judicial district.

It is maintained by some that a public prosecutor is not properly speaking an officer of local government but rather is an officer of state government. As regards this matter he is in just the same position as the sheriff, and the same line of reasoning applies to his case as applies to the case of the sheriff. From one point of view it may be said the public prosecutor is not a local officer for he is not to be identified with that group of officers centering around the county board, and who are concerned primarily with county business and the administration of county affairs. He is not part of the county organization in the same sense that they are. Furthermore, his chief function is to represent the people of the state in the prosecution of criminals, and that certainly gives him the appearance of being an officer of the state government. But on the other hand, as in the case of the sheriff, he is absolutely independent, he is not responsible to any state authority, he is not controlled by any state officer, he is elected by the people of a county, he is paid by them, and in so far as he is controlled by anybody at all he is controlled by the county electorate. It is therefore quite proper to speak of him as a county officer, bearing in mind, however, the theory that as a public prosecutor he represents the people of the state.

The Prosecutor as Legal Adviser.—He usually has other functions than that of a prosecutor, and these may be examined briefly before his duties as prosecutor are considered. In the first place he is usually the official legal adviser to all other county officers—the county board, and the other officers individually. Questions are arising constantly as to the legal powers of the various officers, their liabilities and their legal obligations. The law is often obscure and officials want authoritative interpretation of it. The public prosecutor is expected to give this legal advice and to interpret the law when requested to do so by any of the county officers.

That some trained lawyer ought to be at hand to give such advice there can be no doubt; but that the public prosecutor should be the one to give it there is considerable doubt. It is not at all infrequently the case that he is more or less at odds with other county officers. There are several reasons for this. In view of the fact that all the county officers are popularly elected a great deal of campaigning must be done. Many bitter clashes occur among aspirants for the different offices, animosities are developed to a rather high pitch, and they may not quickly be forgotten. This is true particularly in view of the fact that the office of public prosecutor is usually one of the most hotly contested positions in the county. Furthermore, whenever it is alleged that a corrupt ring of county officials exists, the prosecutor's office is the point on which attack is made. Reform campaigns are launched many times, and if a reform candidate goes into the office of the prosecutor he is likely to find his relations with the other officers not altogether friendly. Open hostility is rare, but latent distrust is very frequently to be discovered.

Under such circumstances, and others of a similar nature, the public prosecutor is not the best person to render legal advice to his colleagues. One should have implicit confidence in a legal adviser, and especially is this true of public officers who may be handling large sums of money and who may not be quite sure of their liabilities in certain contingencies. The county treasurer particularly is at times more or less embarrassed by legal problems that arise in his office. He cannot rely upon the advice of an attorney who is a political enemy. The only alternative for an officer who finds himself in such a predicament is to employ private counsel at his own expense, and this is sometimes done.

Other circumstances also combine to render the prosecutor more or less unfit to serve as legal adviser. Being quite independent of any other officer he does not have the same sense of responsibility that he would have if he were employed by the person who might be seeking his advice. He may be impatient or indifferent toward requests for advice that would involve considerable investigation on his part; and on the other hand he may be annoyed with constant inquiries concerning small matters that need not have been submitted to him. Furthermore, he is perfectly aware of the fact that none of those whom he is advising are in a position to discharge him or even to subject him to authoritative criticism.

It should be understood that advice given by the public prosecutor to another county officer concerning his official duty in no way absolves the officer from responsibility for any subsequent action he may take based on this advice. The public prosecutor might advise the treasurer with great confidence that it is proper for him to retain the interest on public funds. But if the treasurer acts upon this advice and it is discovered later in the courts that he is not entitled to the interest money, the treasurer cannot set up as a defense the fact that he acted upon the advice of the public prosecutor.

Public Prosecutor Should be Relieved of This Function.—All these considerations lead to the conclusion that it would be for the best to relieve public prosecutors of the function of rendering legal advice to other local officers. As already has been pointed out the prosecutor is not closely associated with county activities. His office seldom is in the courthouse, and he has comparatively few contacts with other county officers. He has been given this function of rendering legal advice without any account having been taken of the political aspects of his position. Potent influences, insidious pressure, temptations, prejudices, and a variety of other factors always grow out of extra-legal relationships and political situations that may not even be suspected when considering the mere formal organization of an office or an institution of government. Examining the mere formal structure of the President's cabinet, for instance, an observer might not suspect that all the members must be of one political party if it is to function successfully. And yet political, or extra-legal conditions, make it absolutely imperative that this should be the case. Just so it is that political conditions tend to render a public prosecutor more or less unfit to give legal advice to his colleagues.

Need of County Counsel.—The legal adviser to a public official ought to be subject to the control of the one whom he is expected to advise. Only thus can real confidence and a keen sense of responsibility be developed. It is therefore suggested that the county board might well be permitted to appoint a legal adviser, who could be known as county counsel. This officer could be employed on a salary at full time, or part time, or he could be paid only for the specific services he might be called upon to perform. These matters could be determined as circumstances might dictate.

If such an arrangement as this were made the prosecutor would be entirely relieved of his function of rendering legal advice. The principal objection to the proposal for establishing the office of county counsel is that it would involve a considerable increase in expense. Furthermore, it should be observed that very little benefit would result unless the county board were also to exercise authoritative control over other county officers as well.

The Prosecutor as Attorney in Litigation.—Another usual function of the public prosecutor is that of representing the county in its corporate capacity, and county officials in their official capacities. It will be recalled that the county is a body corporate. As a body corporate it may sue and be sued in the courts, it may buy and sell property, enter into contracts and employ persons to do work. Thus it is obvious that a county may frequently be involved in litigation either as plaintiff or defendant. Cases sometimes grow out of contracts, the contractor failing to fulfill his obligation; or it may be that the contractor must sue in order to get his money. Litigation frequently grows out of real estate transactions engaged in by the county; and when condemnation proceedings are necessary there is a great deal of litigation. Whenever the county as a corporation enters an appearance in a court the public prosecutor serves as counsel for the county. In the same way he appears as counsel for other county officers in their official capacities.

This function of representing the county in all litigation may occupy a good share of the prosecutor's time, particularly in those populous counties where many business relationships are entered into by the county board. And if it is necessary to employ additional help in the prosecutor's office, a subordinate may be assigned exclusively to this phase of the work.

Exactly the same arguments that were presented in favor of relieving the prosecutor of his function of giving legal advice apply with equal force as regards the function now under consideration. It is the county board which negotiates contracts. It is the members of the board and the other officers who suffer the consequences if their legal representative is incompetent. It is therefore not proper that they should be represented in litigation by an attorney whom they cannot control, who is absolutely independent, and who is conscious of no responsibility to the parties whom he may be representing. The absurdity of this situation is constantly illustrated by county officers who employ private counsel to represent them.

It may be suggested, therefore, that county counsel appointed by the board for the purpose of rendering legal advice might also exercise the function of representing the county and county officers in litigation. The public prosecutor could then be entirely relieved of this function.

In those rural counties where the public prosecutor does not have enough public business to keep him busy anyway, it would seem to be rather unnecessary to relieve him of the function of acting as legal adviser, and of serving as attorney in litigation. But certainly whenever his duties as public prosecutor reach such a point that his entire time can be occupied as prosecutor, then he might well be relieved of his other functions, to the distinct advantage of all concerned.

The Prosecutor as Prosecutor.—We now come to a consideration of the functions of this officer as a public prosecutor. Serving in this capacity is by far the most important duty that he has to perform. In a word, he is expected to prosecute all persons in his county whom he believes have violated the law. The criminal who commits robbery or murder, the autoist who speeds upon the highway, the corporation which employs children under age, the pool-room owner who operates gambling devices, the public official who absconds with public funds,—all must be sought out by the public prosecutor and the machinery of justice must be set in motion by him.

It should be clearly understood that the public prosecutor has nothing to do with civil suits between private individuals. A criminal act may give rise to civil action, but that is no concern of the public prosecutor. He is interested only in seeing the criminal punished according to the law; the person who has been injured as a result of the crime may seek damages on his own account if he chooses to do so, and has any hope of success.

Theory Underlying this Function.—The theory on which the public prosecutor performs this function is an old one. It is based upon the assumption that a criminal who violates the law of the state has committed an offense against the state itself, and that the sovereign power of the state which has ordained the law will punish him no matter how long it takes, how much it costs, or where he goes, so long as he can be found within the boundaries of the state. The public prosecutor is the agent of the sovereign for this purpose. When the sovereign is a king the prosecutor acts in the name of the king. When, as in the commonwealths of the United States, the people are sovereign, he conducts his prosecution in the name of the people of his state. Thus the punishment of crime is the primary concern of the sovereign who has ordained the law. The person who has been injured as a result of the crime may assist the prosecutor in his work of prosecution, he may be quite indifferent toward the matter, or he may even attempt to obstruct prosecution. But in any event it is the duty of the prosecutor to proceed with his case, in the name of the sovereign people.

Relation to Chief Executive.—It will occur to anyone at once that the chief executive of the state is responsible for the enforcement of the law. This of course is true. And it might well be expected that the public prosecutors would be subordinates of the chief executive and do all their work under his direction. This would be a logical arrangement, and so far as the United States federal government is concerned the theory is put in practice. The President of the United States as chief executive is responsible for the enforcement of law and the prosecution of those who violate it. The function is exercised by an attorney-general appointed by the President and responsible to him. And below the attorney-general are a great many district attorneys working under his direction. Thus all the federal agencies of justice and law enforcement are highly centralized under the chief executive.

Independence of the Prosecutor.—But in the several states the doctrine of administrative decentralization has led to quite a different situation. The governor ordinarily does not appoint the attorney-general of the state, and the public prosecutors in the various counties are not controlled by the state authorities. Each public prosecutor in his own county is free to interpret the law as he sees it, and to prosecute or not as he sees fit. Neither the governor nor the attorney-general of the state are in a position to compel the local prosecutor to institute proceedings if he does not desire to do so. But the attorney-general himself, however, may institute proceedings in any county if he chooses to do so, regardless of the wishes of the local prosecutor. It should be remembered, too, that there is usually adequate means of bringing pressure to bear upon a prosecutor, or any other officer, who manifestly refuses to exercise the functions of his office or to abide by the law himself.

Evils of this Situation.—There are at least two distinct evils growing out of this decentralization. One is that local prosecutors are exempt from authoritative supervision of any sort. This means that local prosecutors may be indolent, careless, venal, indifferent and altogether unsatisfactory; and yet there is no one in a position to stimulate them to better efforts or to force them to do better work on pain of dismissal. It means that hundreds of young, incompetent, ill-trained lawyers blunder along as public prosecutors through a period of four years or more, permitting the state's business to fall into hopeless confusion, permitting lawbreakers to slip through their fingers day after day, while no one is at hand to render assistance, give advice, or to exercise even unauthoritative supervision. Here is to be found administrative decentralization at its very worst.

The other evil growing out of the situation is that it often results in the law being interpreted differently and enforced differently in the various counties. Laws that deal with gambling, and the laws that dealt with the liquor traffic, are of the sort that lend themselves to different interpretations, and of course there are many others of a somewhat less conspicuous nature. In some counties the prosecutors will enforce them literally and vigorously, in other counties the prosecutors may interpret them liberally and be very negligent about enforcing them. There is no central authority competent to give the law official interpretation and to compel consistent enforcement of it throughout the state. Each prosecutor interprets the law and enforces it to suit himself, or to suit the wishes of the voters in his county. This is administrative decentralization, it is a species of self-government, it is a peculiarly American manifestation of democracy.

Responsibilities of Prosecutors.—It will be seen that vast responsibilities weigh upon the local prosecutors. If they are careless, indifferent or venal, crime may become rampant within their jurisdictions. The best of laws may virtually be nullified in certain counties. A local prosecutor should be on the alert constantly to detect violations of the law on his own initiative, to investigate rumors and suggestions that come to his office from other officers and from private citizens. A very large part of his work indeed should be investigation accompanied with warnings to those whom he finds violating the law. A prosecutor who can build a reputation for alertness and persistence is able to make his county a law-abiding community with a minimum of actual prosecution. On the other hand, a prosecutor who is indolent and inconsistent, who conducts spectacular raids, seeks notoriety for himself, starts many sensational trials and presently drops them when he finds it convenient to do so, brings the law, his county, and himself, into contempt and ill repute.

Local prosecutors may be very seriously hampered in their work by lack of funds. While the county board has no direct control over the prosecutor it is the county board which must allow the appropriations for the maintenance of his office. The prosecutor's salary is fixed by the state legislature and the board is unable to change it, but the board may refuse to allow him an assistant even though he needs one badly, it may refuse to employ detectives and investigators for him when it may be very necessary that he have such aid in order to secure evidence and conduct investigations.

In those counties where large cities are to be found the public prosecutor is likely to have a relatively large staff of assistants who are assigned to various types of work. Not only does the prosecutor have legal aides, but it is becoming more and more the practice to permit him to employ special investigators and detectives to work under his direct supervision. The purpose of this is to make him more or less independent of the sheriff, and the city police as well. The sheriff is often quite unable to apprehend the criminals whom the prosecutor is seeking, and many times the city police are not willing to coöperate with him whole-heartedly. Indeed clashes between the public prosecutor and city administrations are not at all uncommon.

On the whole it would seem to be the part of wisdom to strengthen the arm of the prosecutor in every possible way. It is he who is responsible ultimately for the conviction of lawbreakers and it is not altogether fair to him that he should be made too greatly dependent upon incompetent or unfriendly officials whom he cannot control. Yet frequently that is just his predicament.

Disorganization of Law Enforcement Agencies.—Governmental agencies for the investigation of crime and the apprehension of criminals are woefully disorganized. The sheriff, the city police, the prosecutor and the coroner may all be trying to do the same thing at the same time; each is independent of the other and each officer is apt to be jealous of his own prerogatives. They get in each other's way, they challenge each other's authority, they cast blame on each other for blunders, and altogether they often present a most unedifying spectacle of inefficiency.

Radical Changes Proposed.—Effective reorganization of the agencies of law enforcement would involve some very radical departures from the present situation. It would involve the appointment of public prosecutors by the attorney-general of the state, the retirement of the sheriff as a peace officer, and the substitution of state police officers, and the abolition of the coroner's office altogether. Radical as such a proposal may seem it merely contemplates the establishment of a system in every way similar to that already established in the federal government.

Steps in Prosecution.—The actual steps ordinarily taken by a public prosecutor against a lawbreaker may be very briefly outlined. Criminals are arrested on sight by officers of the law if apprehended in the act, or they may be arrested later upon warrants, issued at the behest of the prosecutor or any other citizen who is willing to assume responsibility for charging a person with crime. An immediate hearing before a justice of the peace or a city magistrate may be demanded in order to discover if there is sufficient cause to hold the accused. This question is decided by the magistrate, and in case he believes there is sufficient evidence to justify the action he orders the accused bound over to the grand jury, bail is fixed according to the law, and the accused must then await further action by the grand jury and the prosecutor.

Procedure in civil offenses is slightly different. The prosecutor merely starts suit against the offender who is then required to appear in court upon a certain day and answer to the charges.

The Grand Jury.—Very frequently the first step in the procedure against a lawbreaker is indictment by a grand jury. A grand jury may be composed of anywhere from five to twenty-three members selected by lot from among the registered voters of the county. It is called and meets at stated intervals, fixed by law. Special grand juries may be called in the discretion of the court on request of the prosecutor. The jury assembles and gives attention to the cases which the prosecutor lays before it. His object is to induce the grand jury to bring indictments against the persons whom he thinks ought to be prosecuted. The jury listens to all the prosecutor has to say, and examines all the evidence he thinks it necessary to lay before it. This proceeding is in no sense a trial, for the accused is not present nor is he even represented. It is the business of the jury merely to consider the prosecutor's evidence, and to decide whether or not the person in question should be prosecuted.

Indictments.—After presentation of the case by the prosecutor the jury deliberates in private and determines whether or not to bring in true bills, or indictments, against the persons accused by the prosecutor. An indictment sets forth in formal terms the offense which the accused is supposed to have committed. On the basis of these indictments warrants are issued for the arrest of those who have been accused and the prosecutor continues with the case.

Influence of Prosecutor Over Grand Jury.—The grand jury is not restricted to a consideration only of those cases laid before it by the prosecutor. The jury may consider cases on its own initiative and bring in indictments even against the wishes of the prosecutor. He is nevertheless expected to proceed with such cases. But in actual practice grand juries are very much under the influence of prosecutors. Citizens are ordinarily impatient of jury service and are anxious to get through with their work as soon as possible. They have little inclination and practically no opportunities to investigate cases on their own initiative, or to consider the other side of a case that has been presented by the prosecutor. The members of the jury feel that the prosecutor knows a great deal more about the cases in hand than they do, that he is responsible for the successful prosecution of those whom he has accused, and that should the accused prove to be innocent all odium attaches to the prosecutor rather than to the jury. For these reasons grand juries are quite prone to bring in indictments which the prosecutor wants them to bring in and to drop those cases which he believes cannot be successfully prosecuted.

The grand jury is a very old institution and in nearly all the states an indictment by grand jury is required by law before the prosecutor may bring action. But contemporary writers are of the opinion that the grand jury serves no very useful purpose and that prosecutors should be allowed to proceed against lawbreakers entirely upon their own initiative, and without the formality of indictment by grand jury. It is pointed out that such reform could not possibly prejudice the interests of those who are subjected to prosecution and would eliminate a cumbersome, expensive and useless piece of judicial machinery.

Due Process of Law.—The first attempt to do away with the grand jury in one of the states was met by the contention that indictment by grand jury was an essential step in "due process of law," within the meaning of the federal constitution. The supreme court, however, held that indictment by grand jury is not essential to due process of law and hence so far as the federal constitution is concerned the states are free to eliminate the grand jury altogether. The result has been that a few states have eliminated the grand jury, and several others permit the prosecutor to bring suit "on information" without grand jury indictment even though the institution itself is still retained.

Cases Brought to Trial.—After indictments have been returned and the accused has been brought into the custody of the court the prosecutor prepares his case, and the defendant employs counsel and prepares his defense. A day is set for trial and the case wends its way through the machinery of the courts. A prosecutor is at liberty to drop a case at any time with the consent of the court, and this is done very frequently. Sometimes the defendant goes free, other times the prosecution is merely suspended, or abandoned temporarily, the prosecutor being free to take the case up again at a later date. Cases are frequently dropped for very good reason, as, for instance, when the prosecutor discovers evidence that convinces him the defendant is innocent, or when important witnesses have escaped the jurisdiction of the court. Other times flimsy cases are begun ostentatiously and with great publicity, the deliberate intention being to abandon them later, after public interest has abated.

Reform in Prosecutor's Office.—The principal weaknesses in the office of public prosecutor lie in conditions that will be extremely difficult to remedy. In the first place it is believed great improvement would result if prosecutors were under some authoritative supervision. Such supervision ought to be exercised by state authorities, certainly not the county board. The prosecutor should remain quite independent of all county officers; and as pointed out before he might very well be relieved of his duty of giving legal advice to county officers, and of representing the county in litigation.

Need of State Department of Justice.—But if he were to be brought under the control of state officers certain reforms should be effected in state administrative organization. A complete reform would involve the creation of a state department of justice headed by an attorney-general appointed by the governor. The local prosecutors could then be under the control of this department of justice which also could maintain a state police force. However, public opinion is hardly prepared for such a change as this and the local prosecutor is likely to continue in his present position of independence.

Another factor that works to the disadvantage of the office is that it is deeply involved in politics. It is always the goal of the corruptionist, it is eagerly sought by young and untrained lawyers who want the experience and publicity the office brings, together with the fixed salary; and it is often the last refuge of unsuccessful lawyers with a penchant for politics.

On the other hand, many of the foremost statesmen the nation has produced began their careers as brilliant prosecutors in the counties of their residence. Energetic young men find their way to the office and, fired with a desire to build a reputation, work tirelessly, and render services to the state of far greater value than is measured by the salaries they receive. But probably the best type of local prosecutor is the one who gives such satisfactory service to his constituency that he is elected term after term for a considerable number of years, is not too deeply fired with an ambition to become governor or to go to congress, and is content to remain a respected and influential member of his community.

THE PUBLIC DEFENDER

Is Machinery of Justice One-Sided?—In recent years there has been more or less comment to the effect that the machinery of justice is one-sided, that too much attention is given to the maintenance of the machinery of prosecution and not enough to the machinery of defense. Real justice cannot be attained unless the accused enjoys a fair defense at the same time that he is being subjected to vigorous prosecution. No matter if the theory of the common law be that the accused is innocent until he is proved guilty, the theory of the prosecutor's office invariably is that the accused is guilty. Under such circumstances the accused has small hope of justice unless he is supported by able counsel who will undertake to bring out all evidence that can possibly help his case. The prosecutor is not judicial minded. Once started on a case he is seeking a conviction, prejudging the accused as it were, before he has an opportunity of defending himself; and, assuming the guilt of the accused, the prosecutor launches an attack with all the skill at his command.

It is entirely proper that vigorous prosecutions should be conducted, and prosecutors cannot be expected to be judges as well as prosecutors. But in order that justice shall be done every defendant should have his side of the case fairly presented, and there should be no discrimination against penniless defendants. Comment is persistent that rich offenders escape punishment with the aid of high-priced lawyers and that poor offenders are at the mercy of the prosecutor. To remedy this situation it is suggested that a public defender, as well as a public prosecutor, should be maintained at public expense.*

As soon as a person has been indicted for a crime he at once employs counsel for defense, if he is able to do so. Right at this point, it is said, gross injustice occurs; the rich man is able to employ the best legal talent ob-

---

* See R. H. Smith, *Justice and the Poor*, M. C. Goldman, *The Public Defender*, and W. J. Wood, *The Place of the Public Defender*.

tainable while the poor man may be unable to employ any counsel at all. Both may be accused of the same crime, both must face the same prosecutor, but the rich man's chances of escape are infinitely better than the poor man's. The former can take advantage of every opportunity the law affords to present his case in the most effective way, for his skilled lawyers know how to do it.

Resources of Penniless Defendant.—The law, however, does afford some relief for the man who is unable to employ counsel. In the first place he is permitted to plead his own case if he desires to attempt it. This is an empty concession. Very few individuals would attempt to take advantage of this opportunity and it would be quite impossible for anyone not trained in the law to handle his own case even if he did attempt it. The other alternative provided in the law is that which requires the court to appoint counsel to serve for a defendant who is unable to employ legal aid for himself. The court has large powers in this connection and presumably can force any attorney practicing before the court to handle such cases. Counsel thus assigned may even be obliged to serve without pay. Further than this the court cannot go, and no sort of pressure can possibly compel assigned counsel to do good work in the interests of an unwelcome client.

Assigned Counsel not Satisfactory.—Assigned counsel are notoriously bad. Judges are not inclined to compel lawyers to serve when they are not willing to be assigned, particularly in view of the fact that there are always some attorneys about the court who are quite ready to take assigned cases. But attorneys who are seeking such assignments are likely to be young men with nothing to do, hoping for some experience and a little publicity; or else they are lawyers actuated by some ulterior motive. If the case in hand bids fair to be sensational and is calculated to bring much publicity to the attorneys for defense, able and ambitious criminal lawyers will seek assignment and do brilliant work for their clients, simply for the advertising which it brings to themselves. More than one famous criminal lawyer has had his start by serving as assigned counsel in some sensational murder case.

But the petty burglar, the hold-up man or sneak thief, and the ordinary disturbers of the peace, can promise no fame to the lawyer who defends them; and since able lawyers do not want assignments to such cases they are regularly turned over to incompetent lawyers, or intrusted to someone who hopes to victimize his client. Judges attempt to avoid letting cases fall into the hands of this latter type of lawyer, but the practices of such men are so subtle and insidious that it is difficult to discover them. They seek to prey at once upon their client's friends and relatives, often mulcting them out of larger sums than would be required to employ trustworthy counsel.

Need of Public Defender.—It is unnecessary to elaborate further on the situation in order to convince the most casual observer that defendants who are unable to employ counsel find themselves at a distinct disadvantage in the criminal courts. As might be expected conditions are worst in the urban centers; but even though cases are less numerous in the rural communities and smaller cities, the circumstances work just as much to the disadvantage of penniless defendants. Hence comes the suggestion for a public defender.

He would be a county officer paid by the county and would enjoy the same status as the prosecutor. It would be his function to defend all criminals who might be unable to employ counsel, or might choose not to do so. He would never be overburdened with work for he could not possibly have more cases to handle than the prosecutor, and probably never as many, for those persons who could afford it would usually employ private counsel.

Arguments in Favor.—It is argued in favor of creating such an office that the poor criminal would then be sure to have just as good counsel to defend him as would be found in the prosecutor's office to prosecute him. Thus he would not be obliged to suffer disadvantage because some assigned counsel did not know the law, or failed to take an interest in his case, or through blundering and indifference left him to be subjected to unduly severe punishment. A public defender, it is said, would at least afford him all the relief which the law permitted in his case. A public defender would also put to rout the unscrupulous lawyers who attempt to exploit the poorer class of criminals, their relatives and friends.

The presence of a public defender, it is also maintained, would do away with certain of the fraudulent defenses that prosecutors have to deal with. Bribed witnesses, false affidavits, corrupted experts, garbled testimony, purchased jurors, and other such factors would not appear in cases handled by a public official. The public defender would endeavor to afford his client every legal safeguard, but no corruption would be practiced.

Furthermore, it is insisted that if a public officer were handling the defense much of the vicious antagonism that develops between prosecutors and counsel for defense would be eliminated. Both prosecutor and defender would seek real justice. They might indeed consult together on a case before going into court, and later when the case comes to trial they could very quickly present both sides without prejudice to either. There would be no spectacular attacks designed to obscure the real facts in the case. The prosecutor would not be forced into unfair practices and the defense would not resort to corruption.

Arguments Against.—These arguments in favor of establishing an office of public defender in the county are met with vigorously hostile objections from those who do not approve of the idea. It is said that it is quite absurd for the county to employ one man to prosecute and punish criminals and another one to set them free. This argument loses some of its force, however, when it is reflected that it is not the primary business of the prosecutor to punish the accused persons but rather to seek justice, in the name of the state. It is possible that justice would be done more effectively in many cases with the aid of a public defender.

Another objection is that the maintenance of such an office would increase the cost of government. This is answered by the statement that a great many criminal cases would be settled out of court by the two public attorneys in conference; that trials would be very much shorter; that many of the obviously guilty offenders would be persuaded to plead guilty; and that in this way the expense of the defender's office would far more than be offset by a saving of time and court costs.

It is further maintained that a public defender would not be fired with the same keen sense of responsibility to his client that a private attorney feels towards the person who has employed him, and that hence the public defender would not strive to leave no stone unturned in order to save his client.

This may be true, but there is no denying that a public defender would take as much interest in his client as would assigned counsel. Of more weight is the suggestion that prosecutor and defender might form the easy habit of settling cases between themselves outside the court room. This could hardly be approved as a general practice but might very often occur in the cases of those obviously guilty. And the interests of the general public would not be adversely affected by such a practice, anyway.

Another point is urged that might be looked upon by some as an argument in favor of a public defender, and by others as an argument against. It is, that even though such an officer did exist, those defendants who could afford it would still employ private counsel, and thus the wealthy man would still have a very great advantage. Of course this is true, and yet it is urged that if the county affords to every criminal counsel for defense who presumably is possessed of as great ability as the public prosecutor, no more can be expected.

Method of Selection.—The method of selecting a public defender presents some difficult problems. If he be popularly elected, as is the public prosecutor, very keen rivalry might easily develop between the two officers in such a way as to prevent the coöperation and good understanding on which the success of the plan is based. If both officers were appointed by state authority better results might be expected; but such a step as that must remain far in the future. The defender might possibly be an appointed subordinate in the prosecutor's office, but obviously such a method of selection would give the prosecutor too great a measure of control. Still another method of selection would be to have him appointed by the county board.

It may be said, however, that the success of the public defender in those few places where the office has been established, is not due so much to the method of selection as to the character and real enthusiasm of the individuals who have held the office.

Summary.—In briefly summarizing the suggestions that have been made concerning reorganization of the county law offices let it be recalled that it is almost universally the practice to elect a public prosecutor who exercises the threefold function of acting as legal adviser for county officers, of representing the county as a corporate body in all litigation, and officers in their official capacities, and lastly of prosecuting all lawbreakers in the name of the people of his state. He is usually the only law officer of the county, and is permitted to employ assistants when they are needed. But it has been suggested that he might be relieved of his first two functions, and that a county counsel might be appointed by the county board to perform them. A further reform would provide for bringing the public prosecutor under the direct control of a state department of justice. And lastly there is the suggestion that a public defender be appointed by the county board to defend those who are unable to employ counsel. There would then be three distinct law officers: the public prosecutor, the county counsel, and the public defender.

CHAPTER XI

THE FINANCE OFFICERS

The County Treasurer.—The county treasurer is by far the most important of the local finance officers. The county is the area through which practically all taxes are collected and the money all goes through the hands of the county treasurer. He is all but invariably an elected official and the usual term of office is two or four years. Sometimes he is not permitted to serve two terms in succession, but this unnecessary prohibition has been eliminated in most of the states. The principal effect of such a restriction has been to make it reasonably certain that the treasurer shall always be more or less inexperienced.

Office Combined with Others.—The person who exercises the functions of treasurer may hold other offices, too. Thus it frequently happens that the treasurer is also county collector; and such illogical combinations as treasurer and recorder have been permitted. In those states where a single individual is allowed to occupy two such offices the law may leave the matter to chance in a certain sense. That is, if one person chooses to run as a candidate for both offices and is elected to both he may occupy them both. Otherwise the two offices will go to two persons. Party leaders are inclined to disapprove of the practice of combining offices, however, and this has served to prevent the practice to a large extent, except where the law very definitely combines two such offices as the treasurer's and the collector's.

The treasurer is a full-time officer, but since his work

is heaviest at certain seasons of the year, when taxes are coming in, it is customary to provide him with a temporary staff of assistants at such times. As treasurer he is likely to be paid a fixed salary, and that is the way he should be paid, although the baneful fee system has been applied to his office as well as to other county offices. On the other hand, if he also serves as collector he is likely to be paid for his services in that capacity entirely with fees.

Treasurer's Bond.—Inasmuch as the treasurer handles such large sums of money he is required to provide heavy bond. In the more populous counties wherein he receives the taxes for large cities, the amounts handled through his office reach many millions of dollars; and even in the distinctly rural counties the amounts handled by the treasurer are relatively large. Hence the heavy bond is required. This bond, a mere legal guaranty on the part of others to make good to the county any funds misappropriated by the treasurer, must be approved by the county board. In past years, and to-day to a large extent, particularly in the rural districts, it is the practice of county treasurers to secure the signatures of relatives and friends to their bonds. And there has been a sorry record of defaulting treasurers whose thefts have been made good by farmers and rural bankers at the cost of nearly all they possessed.

There is, however, no excuse for the continuance of this practice. Great bonding companies are always ready to assume the bonds of public officers upon payment of a premium, the business being carried on in much the same way that insurance is handled. The county should pay the premium, for if the treasurer is obliged to pay it himself it means that his salary is, in effect, reduced by the amount of the premium.

Functions of Treasurer:

1. *To Receive Funds.*—The primary functions of a county

treasurer are very simple indeed. He is expected to receive county funds and keep proper records of them, to pay them out on proper authority, and to have the actual care of the funds in the meantime. The principal source of revenue is the taxes, though always there are certain fees, some income from property, and fines imposed by the courts, that bring money to the treasury. The taxes that are turned in to the treasurer are state, city, county, township, and various district taxes. Sometimes city treasurers or collectors receive city taxes but this is not usual; and certain of the minor districts are sometimes permitted to collect their own taxes independently of county officers. But by far the most usual practice is for county treasurers to receive all taxes into their offices, and then to turn the proper amounts over to state, city, township, and minor district authorities. In this connection, therefore, county officers appear in the character of direct agents of the state and minor districts.

This aspect of the treasurer's function requires the keeping of very extensive book accounts, and his office must be equipped with a formidable array of ledgers and cashbooks. A detailed account must be kept with each individual taxpayer, receipts must be prepared in considerable detail, and proper entries made in all the tax books. In these operations the treasurer comes in very close contact with the county clerk, or the auditor, as the case may be, who is primarily responsible for preparing the tax books. Indeed the two officers are compelled to use the very same records to a large extent, for it would be a needless duplication of effort if each were to have separate books. The clerk's work comes first, as described in a previous chapter; the books are then ordinarily sent to the treasurer and he uses them in the discharge of his functions. It may well be imagined that harmonious co-operation is sometimes not attained, due largely to the fact that the two officers are popularly elected, and quite independent of any common authority.

The treasurer's accounts, particularly that portion of them which he keeps in conjunction with the clerk, must always be sufficiently clear and up to date in order that taxpayers may discover at once just how they stand with the county. Of course all of his records ought always to be in presentable condition and up to date. Unfortunately they are many times not so. The fact must be appreciated that the treasurer is usually not in any sense responsible to any other officer. The county board is supposed to have general supervision over his office, as it does over other county offices, but this supervision amounts to nothing because the board has no authoritative control over him whatever. No other county officers even have a right to inspect his books in any other way than as private citizens. In a few states county auditors are found who examine the treasurer's books, and recent years have witnessed a growing measure of state supervision and control. Such a step is always followed by very good results.

Add to the fact that the treasurer is independent and more or less irresponsible, the no less significant fact that he is popularly elected, and it will be understood how his records may gradually fall into a deplorable condition. Popular election means that any individual enjoying the general qualifications of citizenship, age, and residence, may succeed in reaching the treasurer's office, for special qualifications calculated to insure fitness for the office are not generally imposed. The result is that a great many county treasurers are utterly incompetent to keep their records in a proper way. They do not provide themselves with adequate equipment, they are not familiar with standard methods of bookkeeping, and they are not inclined to apply themselves industriously to the task of learning how to do their work.

It thus happens that accounts may be kept in absurdly unsuitable books, not properly designed for the purpose. Entries are made in pencil, almost obscured by passing years; and even when made in ink they may be almost undecipherable. Erasures occur, lines and scratches are drawn through entries that were incorrectly made, pages are torn out, corrections and alterations appear on every page—pages that are soiled and damaged beyond description by incompetent and blundering hands. Books are sometimes lost, their covers are torn off, and ultimately they are stuffed into boxes and barrels and consigned to the benevolent obscurity of the courthouse basement. Most of these irregularities could be very quickly remedied by some system of authoritative supervision, which could be accompanied with an abundance of advice, instruction and assistance.

As the years go by it often happens that a deputy or first assistant to the treasurer is appointed and remains in the position for many years, being reappointed term after term by succeeding treasurers. This is a wise practice and saves many a treasurer from falling into difficulties. The deputy is appointed because of his fitness for the position, quickly acquires a knowledge of his duties and performs them well, taking the responsibility off the shoulders of his principal. These deputies not infrequently are women, entirely competent, untroubled with political aspirations and actuated by a real desire to keep their books in excellent condition. The present trend of the times would seem to indicate that the day may not be far distant when these servants of the public may occupy the office of treasurer themselves. But in any event the situation merely illustrates the fact that the proper way to secure a competent treasurer is by appointment, not by election.

Effective supervision by county authorities would be much better than none at all, but state supervision is much to be preferred. The state law should require that all accounts be kept on standard forms and that certain prescribed methods be pursued in all the operations. The law should require standard equipment in every detail for the treasurer's office. An adequate inspection service could then be maintained by the state auditor's office. All of these steps would go far toward accomplishing the reforms that are needed. This has been done in a number of states, and when this is the case the county treasurers, even though they are still independent elected officers, have no alternative but to keep their accounts in the manner prescribed by law. And they are stimulated by state inspectors to keep their records in proper condition at all times.

2. *To Disburse Funds.*—Another duty of the county treasurer than that of receiving county funds and keeping records of them is that of paying out the funds on proper authority. This is purely a ministerial task and involves the exercise of no discretion on the part of the treasurer. Warrants are signed by the county clerk or auditor and when they are presented to the treasurer he pays the amount named. As mentioned before, in connection with the duties of the clerk in this regard, the warrant properly signed is full protection to the treasurer. Any sum paid out by him, not covered by an official warrant, he may be required to make good himself. This machinery is very simple and effective. It provides an easy way to check up on this phase of the treasurer's work, and puts responsibility upon the one who signs the warrants.

Even in this process, however, irregularities may creep

in. The law is sometimes lax in failing to require specifically that warrants must be paid immediately upon presentation. If they are not paid immediately it becomes possible for the treasurer to indorse the warrant, which then draws interest for the holder, while the treasurer retains the money for an indefinite period and enjoys the interest or other perquisities that grow out of his care of public funds.

3. To Have Custody of Funds.—A third function of the treasurer is to have charge of public money. This would seem to be a very simple duty and not calculated to give rise to many difficulties. Nevertheless this simple duty has been shown to involve many vexed problems and legal questions that are not yet solved. For the most part they could be removed by appropriate legislation which state assemblies appear more or less reluctant to enact. Other of the difficulties might not be entirely removed by legislation.

Legal Questions.—The law usually states that the treasurer "shall have custody of the funds," and goes no further to any essential purpose. This is true particularly of statutes written many years ago and which remain unchanged. Obviously the question arises,—Just what shall he do with them?

Methods of Caring for Funds.—The treasurer may have very large sums of money in his possession for extended periods of time, and in the absence of any control exercised through legislation or a superior authority he is largely free to exercise his own discretion in the matter of caring for the funds. There are various alternatives. Conceivably he might invest them in stocks and bonds or even real estate, and a few examples of such a practice are not lacking. Naturally this is not countenanced by the courts even in the absence of statutory provisions to the contrary. A first requisite is that public funds should be cared for with a minimum of risk and in such a way that they will be quickly available when wanted, without a loss.

A somewhat more suitable way to care for the funds would be to keep them in a safe or vault. In the absence of instructions in the law it would seem that a treasurer fulfills his legal duty when he keeps the funds in this way. In early days it was practiced, and no doubt it is yet practiced in some remote counties where the sums in hand are not large. But it is obvious that the simplest dictates of political economy forbid such a custom.

The method now generally practiced is for the treasurer to deposit the funds promptly in some bank which will pay interest on the amounts held and which will stand obligated to turn them over on demand, or after stipulated notice. County treasurers were, and still are in a majority of cases, free to select the bank in which to deposit all the funds. This freedom at once opens the door to more or less corrupt bargaining with the treasurer and bankers.

Interest on Funds.—If the law does not forbid, the treasurer may retain for himself the interest that is paid on the funds deposited. In case the law does forbid him to retain the interest thus earned it is still possible for him to make arrangements with bankers whereby a low rate of interest will be paid over to the county treasury, but substantial gifts may be made to the treasurer on the side. These so-called gifts may take a variety of forms and are exceedingly difficult to discover.

This abuse has been going on for a great many years. In Cook County, Illinois, hundreds of thousands of dollars have been retained by county treasurers in past years.* Flurries of indignation are periodically stirred up by newspapers and civic associations in those communities where the abuse becomes particularly obvious. But popular indignation soon subsides, the old treasurer goes out with his spoils of office, a new one comes in, and the evil is forgotten. Occasionally a candidate for the office will proclaim during the progress of his campaign that he will guarantee to turn in to the treasury all interest earned, and he may indeed live up to his promise. But such action as that, virtuous as it may be, is no solution of the problem. The law ought to be unmistakable on this point and specifically to require that all interest earned on county funds be turned into the treasury. This is the case in a few states, and in some others the courts have taken it upon themselves to interpret the common law in such a way as to require treasurers to turn in all interest despite the absence of any statute covering the matter.

Selecting Depositories.—Furthermore it is altogether wrong that a county treasurer should be at liberty to select the bank in which he will deposit the county funds. It is not that he may exercise bad judgment and place the funds where they will be unsafe; the evil lies in the fact that his discretion in the matter gives him a tremendously powerful lever with which he can drive good bargains with banking institutions,—bargains through which he may profit enormously despite any law that could be written. Were he not to have this discretion the bankers would not bargain with him.

---

* *Documents on County Government*, published by National Short Ballot Organization.

J—"The Office of County Treasurer in Cook County, Illinois."

N—"A Second Plea for Publicity in the Office of County Treasurer."

The obvious solution seems to be to vest in the county board full power to bargain with the bankers. The contract for handling county funds could be arranged in the same manner and with the same publicity as contracts for building materials or anything else. The various banks could make their legitimate bids and the board could award the contract. These contracts would stipulate the amount of interest, and cover all other important points. The treasurer would then have no choice but to place the funds in the bank selected. There would still be the opportunity for collusion between board members and bankers, but that can hardly be obviated. In those states where this practice has been followed the periodical scandals involving county treasurers have been largely done away with.

Delayed Entries.—There are other devices, suggested by the ingenuity of unscrupulous spoilsmen, through which considerable sums of money may be directed to improper uses without depleting the actual amount possessed by the county. Treasurers may be dilatory about entering in their books sums of money received from taxpayers. Ultimately, when actually needed, the amounts are entered, but in the meantime large sums of interest may have been earned which the treasurer's accounts do not show. Again, the treasurer may be dilatory about turning sums of money over to the other areas of government to which they are due, and it occasionally happens that a city sues a county treasurer for amounts due the city. In the meantime interest has been earned. Another phase of this practice has been mentioned before,—it is that of delaying payments on warrants presented by private claimants.

Spoils of the Office.—It is seldom that a county treasurer, corrupt though he may be, is permitted alone to enjoy the spoils of his office. If such an officer falls into such practices he is at once surrounded by henchmen who do their utmost to keep him in power so long as he divides the spoils and helps to keep the party machinery in operation. This is true of course of any public officer who practices corruption.

Essence of Reform.—Those irregularities which cannot be effectively checked by legislation, can only be eradicated by thoroughgoing supervision and a system of audit. To a certain extent this can be accomplished even though the treasurer remain elective. Vesting the discretion which he now possesses in the county board always helps greatly, and the maintenance of state inspectors working under the state auditor helps a great deal more. These reforms are usually accomplished along with more or less comprehensive legislation that aims to leave no doubt as to the treasurer's duty in connection with interest on public funds and his obligation to make payments, and all the entries, promptly. With these changes the county treasurer might well remain an elective officer, especially in the light of public prejudice which strongly favors popular election.

But most students of government and administration are convinced that treasurers ought to be appointed rather than elected, and there would seem to be no valid objection to appointing them, except popular prejudice. If the treasurer were to become an appointive official it probably would be best if he were selected by the county board instead of by some state authority, for much of his work relates closely to county affairs and not at all to the state. But if he were appointed by the board this fact should not in any way be allowed to inhibit the application of state audit.

Statistics concerning the matter are not available and

probably never will be, but it can safely be asserted that irregularities and defalcations have occurred as frequently, relatively speaking, in the county treasurer's office as in any other office in the gift of the people. Men elected to the office of county treasurer are no better and no worse than men elected to other offices. But circumstances seem to have conspired in such a way as to break down moral resistance with greater frequency here than elsewhere.

Reasons for Defaulting Treasurers.—Numerous factors play a part in the composition of forces which exerts the pressure. Moralists are inclined to say that the remedy for public ills lies in selecting better men for public office. But there is much more to the problem than that. The method of selecting an officer, the official relationship that exists between him and fellow officials, the measure of supervision to which he is subjected, the legal provisions concerning his function, the equipment with which he is provided, and the temptations that are thrust in his path, are the factors which determine the kind of service he will render. If these factors operate in a negative direction they can undermine good character and break down moral resistance. If they operate in a positive direction they can actually serve to build up moral character by inculcating a sense of responsibility and pride in accomplishment.

The county treasurer's office is peculiarly adapted to illustrate this proposition, and those factors which so powerfully affect the treasurer may be summarized in such a way as to emphasize their importance.

1. Many Temptations.—In the first place the treasurer is beset with many temptations. They come from different sources. (1) He is subjected to very strong political pressure. Next to the prosecutor's office the office of the county treasurer is the object of the spoilsmen's attack. Corrupt party leaders and those who are influential in maintaining a vicious political ring do their utmost to get control of the treasurer's office. Any person occupying the position is subjected to insidious influence and great temptation. (2) He has relatively very large sums to handle. This in itself is a temptation, which is greatly heightened by the fact that (3) He is not subject to any real authoritative supervision. (4) County funds do not turn over rapidly, large amounts remaining idle in his hands for a considerable period. (5) His office is in some obscurity as are most of the county offices in fact. (6) He is obliged to keep a very large number of small accounts with the individual taxpayers, and thus opportunities for tampering with and falsifying accounts are greatly multiplied. These are the most obvious sources of temptation.

2. Law Obscure.—In the second place the law is likely to be very inadequate and obscure concerning the treasurer's office in the following respects: (1) As to just what disposition should be made of the funds in his care, and the measure of discretion vested in him in the matter of selecting depositories. (2) As to whether or not he is entitled to any of the interest earned on public funds, and whether it is legal for him to accept gratuities of any sort from bankers. (3) As to his obligation to enter receipts promptly, and (4) To pay warrants and turn funds over to other areas of government promptly when they are due, so long as there is money to meet these obligations.

3. Popular Election.—In the third place the method of selecting the treasurer results in: (1) Many unfitted men reaching the office. (2) Making it virtually impossible for any incumbent to enjoy anything like long tenure in office, such as would result in greatly increased ability. (3) Making him too independent. (4) Leaving him more or less vulnerable to the attacks of political spoilsmen.

Summary of Reforms.—The suggested reforms may also be summarized briefly. The principal steps in reform require that: (1) He be appointed by the county board instead of popularly elected. (2) State authorities be permitted to prescribe standard forms and methods. (3) He be subjected to a thorough and authoritative system of state audit. (4) The law be made more comprehensive and clear concerning his duties; and (5) He be deprived of any right to exercise discretion in caring for public funds.

COUNTY COLLECTORS

In some states there is to be found a county collector exercising his functions more or less independently of the county treasurer. His duties do not occupy his full time the year around, and therefore he is ordinarily a part-time officer enjoying comparatively small remuneration. He is popularly elected and holds office for the usual two- or four-year term.

Function of Collector.—His function is that of collecting taxes. His office is usually open only a few weeks, during the period when taxes are due and should be paid. This may be annually or semi-annually. A definite date is fixed when his office will be open and another date when it will be closed, after which taxpayers must go to the treasurer to pay their taxes with accrued penalties. The collector's office may simply be a spot temporarily arranged for the purpose, in his own place of business, such as a store or a real estate office. After the period has closed all the funds, books, records, and papers pertaining to the office are delivered to the treasurer.

More frequently the office of collector is a township or minor district office and a collector is then elected for each township, all of them turning in their funds and records to the county treasurer at the close of the stated period.

Method of Payment.—The method of paying the collector even when, as in a majority of cases, the office of collector and that of treasurer are combined, has always been the object of some disapproval on the part of students of public administration. He is ordinarily paid a percentage of the amount collected. A small fee is added to each taxpayer's bill and these fees constitute the collector's compensation.

In private business the usual purpose of paying a collector a percentage of the amount collected is simply to stimulate him to greater efforts in order to collect all that he possibly can. Obviously this motive is wholly lacking in the case of a tax collector. He is not expected to put forth any effort in order to induce taxpayers to pay their taxes. The law requires them to pay, and very definite penalties are prescribed for failure to do so. No collector could possibly be expected to exert any personal effort himself to bring further pressure to bear upon the dilatory property owner. Indeed in view of the fact that accrued penalties may even slightly increase the size of his own fee when ultimately the tax is paid, the collector is inclined to view delinquencies with some complacency.

The reason for paying this officer a portion of what he collects is then, that the accumulated fees are a fair measure of the labor involved in collection. That this has been substantially the case is evidenced by the fact that the method is pursued almost universally, even when a salaried officer such as the treasurer does the collecting. Only in the final balance, however, do the accumulated fees constitute a fair measure of the work involved, for taking each collection separately it can easily be seen that the work involved in collecting a dozen small sums aggregating a few hundred dollars far exceeds the labor and expense of collecting one sum of several thousand dollars; yet for collecting the latter sum the fee is several times as great.

The fee system has been the bane of all local offices. Clerks, treasurers, sheriffs, coroners, supervisors, commissioners, recorders and collectors—all have been paid in whole or in part with fees at one time or another. Always it is supposed the fees bear a fair relation to the work involved, or else are calculated to stimulate the officer to do his work the better. Yet seldom has this been the case. The present tendency is to abandon the fee system so far as compensating public officers is concerned, and as for the collector no difficulty would be involved in determining a reasonable and fixed compensation based upon the amount of time he is occupied with his duties.

Treasurer Should be Collector.—That no good reason exists for separating the office of collector from that of treasurer is clearly shown by the fact that most of the states bestow the function of collecting taxes upon the treasurer. Any person who collects taxes must necessarily use the treasurer's books. The work only covers a short period of time, and in case it becomes necessary it is a simple matter to employ additional help in the treasurer's office when the load is heaviest. Sheriffs, constables, clerks, official and unofficial collectors, have all had their turns at collecting taxes; but it may be anticipated that the future will witness universal centralization of the function in the treasurer's office, and abandonment of the fee system.

COUNTY AUDITORS

Function of County Auditor.—It will be recalled that in the discussion of the county clerk's office it was pointed out that in some states there is to be found no county clerk but only a clerk of court, and a county auditor who exercises all the functions elsewhere exercised by a county clerk. In a few states a county auditor's office has been established in addition to the county clerk's, and where this is the case the county clerk relinquishes his function of signing warrants and examining finance accounts of other officers to the county auditor. Even though this office has been created only in recent years it has generally been made an elective office in spite of the fact that experience had already indicated that little advantage would grow out of an office of such a nature. The creation of such an office merely lengthens the ballot, sets up an additional independent officer, and takes from the clerk a function which under the circumstances cannot be exercised to any better advantage by the new officer upon whom it is bestowed.

A county auditor cannot possibly exercise that authoritative supervision which is essential to effective auditing. Were he appointed by the board the situation would be very slightly improved, but really substantial improvement could not be expected unless both the auditor and treasurer, and certain other officers as well, were appointed by the board. Then a county auditor could indeed act as an agent of the board and exercise authoritative supervision over the finance activities of all the county offices and institutions.

Auditing a State Function.—But the function of auditing is best performed by state authorities. An auditor should be entirely free of political pressure and local influences, he should be appointive and responsible to a superior far removed from local politics. These facts are quite generally appreciated and no doubt will lead to the practice of state supervised auditing rather than to the inauspicious creation of additional independent county auditors.

COUNTY ASSESSORS

Assessing Often a Township Function.—In most of the states where townships are to be found in the enjoyment of any of the prerogatives of local self-government, the function of assessing property for purposes of taxation is vested in a township assessor. In other states, where townships do not exist or where they are not characterized by the same vitality that they possess in certain North-Central states, the function of assessing property is vested in a county assessor.

Popular Opposition to Change.—Public opinion has always been exceedingly jealous of the function of assessment in view of the fact that assessments determine the relative amount of taxes that each property owner shall pay; the amount of county tax that each township shall pay; and the amount of state tax that each county shall pay. Vigorous and effective opposition is invariably raised against any attempt to alter the essential features of the general property tax, or to centralize authority over assessors, or to do away with the popular election of assessors. And any official who appears in a garb that suggests the character of a tax-gatherer from "the outside" is always an object of disapproval and suspicion. So if there be one official upon whom, more than another, a community likes to have its own hands resting heavily, it is the assessor.

Status of Assessors.—Hence it may be said in general that assessors are almost universally elected; their terms are ordinarily short; they are not subject to superior officers but are largely independent; and they are likely to be elected in the smallest possible governmental units, which happen to be the townships in many states. Elsewhere the assessor is a county officer with deputies to assist him. However, the general and steady decline of the township as an important area of government cannot but indicate that township assessors are destined to disappear, in spite of the fact that the assessor's office is likely to be one of the last strongholds of the township.

The General Property Tax.—The functions of the assessor are exercised in connection with the application of the general property tax. This tax is the principal source of revenue in every one of the states. It is not used by the federal government because of certain constitutional requirements which it would be exceedingly difficult to satisfy. It is a very old tax and has always been used in America, and when reduced to its lowest terms the process of applying the general property tax is very simple.

Fixing Tax Rates.—Each governing area determines the sum of money which it will be necessary for it to raise. Then it is necessary to fix a money value on all the taxable property owned within the taxing jurisdiction. The sum of money which it is desired to raise, when divided by the total value of all the property within the area, will produce a fraction which can be expressed in terms of percent. This may be looked upon as a tax rate, which if applied to every piece of property within the jurisdiction will produce the sum of money required. It has already been explained that there may be many different jurisdictions competent to impose a tax rate, subject to the limitations of the law. And it should be added that it is permissible to impose special rates for many special purposes. Thus county authorities may impose special rates for school, road, bridge, park, or other purposes. Local authorities are always eager to be permitted to impose these special rates, for it is then possible to spend more money for general purposes without raising the rate. The practice of imposing special rates becomes more general every year. Many of them are very small, but in the aggregate they make the tax burden ever higher.

Importance of Assessment.—The sum of all the rates, state, county, city, township, district and special, is the rate which is applied to the property of each taxpayer; and it will be seen that it is a matter of vital importance to fix a money value upon every piece of taxable property within the jurisdiction. This is called assessment.

It cannot be too firmly emphasized that in connection with no other governmental process has the spirit of democracy, local jealousy, and a desire for self-government been more evident, more determined, uncompromising and insistent. Public opinion has demanded for three hundred years that local officials, locally elected, locally controlled, and independent of outside authority shall do the assessing.

But even though local assessors do remain for the most part popularly elected and absolutely independent, there are boards of review competent to alter the assessments once made. Thus boards of township trustees review the assessments made by township assessors and correct injustices as between individual property owners. City councils may have this function within city limits. County boards review total assessed values as between smaller districts, and a state board equalizes values as between counties. But this does not affect the local assessor whose function it is to fix a money value upon every piece of taxable property within his jurisdiction.

Theory of General Property Tax.—The theory lying back of the general property tax is that the value of everything a person owns can be expressed in money, and the total will represent his wealth, against which the tax rate can be applied. Thus a person's land, buildings, household goods, stocks and bonds, farm machinery, animals, grain, jewelry, wearing apparel, etc., must all be listed and assessed at their true value in money. This was formerly a very much easier task than it is to-day. Every year the assessor's problem becomes harder. A bewildering combination of factors combine to determine real estate values, and the problem of discovering the value of securities, franchises, and intangible wealth generally, has revolutionized the assessor's task in the last few decades.

Classification of Property.—For the purpose of discussing the subject of assessment it will be found convenient to classify property. There are two great classes of property, real and personal. Real property consists of (1) Land, and (2) Buildings and improvements in and on the land. Personal property consists of (1) Tangible personalty, such as household goods, machinery, jewelry and movables generally, and (2) Intangible personalty such as stocks, bonds and securities in general. Real property is assessed and taxed within the jurisdiction where it is found, no matter where the owner may reside. Personal property is ordinarily taxed in the jurisdiction where the owner has his residence.

Difficulties of Assessing.—Each sort of property presents its own problems to the assessor, and even if no obstacles were put in his way the difficulties of his task would be sufficiently forbidding. If no political pressure were brought to bear upon him, if the records of all land sales were easily available, if all people were honest, if the doors of private homes were wide open to him, if he were helped on every hand, and himself possessed rare wisdom, even then his task would be hard enough. Suffice it that such conditions do not exist but are supplanted by other factors that serve to enhance the inherent difficulties of assessment.

Two Principal Abuses.—The result is that two grave abuses have appeared: (1) Real property is generally under-assessed, resulting in great inequities as between individuals and as between minor areas of government. (2) Large amounts of personalty, particularly intangibles, are never assessed at all, resulting in throwing undue burdens upon owners of realty, and those who declare their personalty. These evils are universal and appear to be inevitable concomitants of the general property tax. In some counties the boast is made that assessed values of real estate reach ninety percent of real values, and it may be true. It is known on the other hand that in many counties assessed values fall as low as twenty percent of real values. Somewhere between these two extremes is the average of a typical county. As to personalty, it is quite impossible to hazard a guess. It is known, however, that in some cities the total assessed value of all personalty is not as great as the wealth possessed by one individual. A brief examination of an assessor's function may indicate how this situation has come to exist.

The Assessor at Work.—In the county offices the assessor will find maps and records of every piece of land within his jurisdiction. He has at hand the old valuations and is much inclined to let them stand as they are, making a few changes here and there as seem proper to him. But there is every temptation to let these valuations remain as they are until such time as the board of review chooses to make a uniform horizontal raise on all property within their jurisdiction. The assessor, however, cannot escape responsibility for making changes in values that grow out of special conditions. The extension of public utilities such as water, gas and electric light, all have their bearing on property values. Paving is an important factor. The movement of population and the shifting of business centers affect property values very materially. The establishment of parks, street car lines, railroads, improved highways, and drainage systems, affect the value of adjacent property. The assessor must be continually on the alert to estimate the effect of these and other changing factors on real property values, and must note them in his assessment books.

In order to determine the value of buildings and improvements in and on the land the assessor must personally make thorough investigations. The elements of this problem are manifest and need not be discussed at any length. Building goes on continually. The value of buildings is dependent upon a thousand and one factors and an assessor must needs be very skillful if he keeps abreast of changes that are made.

Reasons for Under-Assessment.—The chief reasons why real property is under-assessed may be enumerated: (1) The inherent difficulties are great under the best conditions, and assessors naturally prefer to err by way of under-assessing rather than by over-assessing. (2) Political pressure brought to bear upon assessors all tends to make them place assessments low. Those who elected the assessor to office will surely desert him at the polls if he is too aggressive in making his assessments. Local authorities also desire that total assessed values shall be low in order that the local area will not be obliged to pay more than its share of state taxes. (3) There is a moral pressure brought to bear upon assessors,—an intangible sort of psychological pressure. In his contacts with property owners, with men whom he meets upon the street, and with people everywhere, he is conscious of their suspicion, their tendency to mislead him, their affected friendliness, their obvious jealousy of neighboring property owners, and their readiness to quarrel over any hint about raising their own assessments. Such an atmosphere cannot but have its influence upon assessors. (4) The assessor has no superior. He is not accountable to anyone. Hence it is very easy to let old values stand, and to ignore changes that demand new and higher assessments. Boards of review may alter his assessments, but he is not subject to their authority. (5) Popular election results in a great many incompetent, easy-going men getting into office; and the electorate is usually willing to keep such men there.

Thus assessed values of real property are likely to be far below real values. State legislatures from time to time recognize the situation and by law authorize the assessor to assess property at a fraction of its real value, as one-half or two-thirds. This is supposed to equalize conditions and to put all property owners on the same level. But such a move never solves the problem. The same tendency continues until it is necessary once more to change the law.

Assessing Personalty.—As regards personal property the evil lies not only in the tendency to under-assess tangible personalty, but in failure to assess intangible personalty at all. Assessors must rely upon the declarations of property owners. Every property owner is supposed to make a sworn statement of all the personalty of which he is possessed, together with his own estimate of its value. The assessor may change this after consultation with the owner. But due to the failure of property owners to make honest returns, and the inability of assessors to discover concealed personalty, the personal property tax has come to be a jest among officers of local government and property owners generally from one end of the country to the other. Nowhere is any pretense made that all personalty is declared.

The result is that assessors are virtually obliged deliberately to under-assess tangible personalty that is declared, for if this were not done the tax rate applied to that small portion of personalty which is declared would result in confiscation. The assessor has no alternative, he is in the midst of a conspiracy of silence and he cannot be expected to do much better than he now does so long as conditions remain unchanged.

Possibilities of Reform.—The situation ought to challenge the attention of legislators in every state; and indeed some reforms are being effected every year. But it is not the purpose to discuss tax reform in this volume and the remedies that seem to promise most good will merely be enumerated.

1. More Rigid Law Enforcement.—Exceedingly severe laws have been passed designed to make the general property tax work in practice as in theory. Such laws uncompromisingly require the assessor to assess all property at its true value in money, and impose heavy penalties upon property owners who fail to make honest returns. Tax ferrets, or persons who make secret investigations, are employed to discover evasions. They are paid a proportion of the value of untaxed property which they discover. These laws are very unpopular and for the most part unsuccessful.

2. Classification.—Property has been classified in many states in order that different rates may be applied to different kinds of property. Stocks and bonds, for instance, are then not subjected to the same rate of taxation as real estate. This involves a modification of the old theory of the general property tax. Classification is approved by tax experts everywhere, but public opinion is slow to sanction it, chiefly because it is not understood.

3. Separation of Sources.—Separation of sources is a device sometimes tried. The idea is to let the state government tax certain sources such as income and corporations; and to leave the local areas alone to rely upon the general property tax. This would eliminate the rivalry that develops between counties to escape their portions of the state tax. But the objection to separation of sources usually is that the state is not left with an adequate source of revenue.

4. Abolition of General Property Tax.—Complete abolition of the general property tax has been proposed, and in its stead it is believed an income tax might be applied, together with such other taxes as would seem proper and desirable.

5. Perfection of the Machinery.—But it is possible to improve the machinery of taxation without radical reforms, and without abandoning the principle of the general property tax. Efforts are being made in this direction every year, and for our purposes it is desirable to inquire as to what changes might be made in the office of assessor.

In the first place there is no doubt that men of greater skill could be chosen if assessors were appointed rather than elected. And appointed assessors would be relieved of much political pressure. It is furthermore desirable that responsibility for assessments should be centralized in an area not smaller than the county. This would eliminate a large number of independent, popularly elected assessors functioning in very small districts, and would insure that assessments would be uniform within a given county at least.

An Appointed County Assessor.—If these suggestions

were acted upon there could be a county assessor, appointed by the county board, with a staff of assistants such as he might need. The county board itself could serve as a board of review, though it would still be necessary to retain a state board of review to equalize assessments as between counties.

CHAPTER XII

LOCAL CHARITIES AND PUBLIC HEALTH

Poor Relief a Function of Local Government.—It has been a generally accepted proposition, at least since the sixteenth century, that each governmental area should take care of its own poor. This proposition is recognized in the law, in the common law and in statutes. Of course any minor area of government can be compelled to care for its own poor, and to care for them in any way that may be prescribed by the law. But even in the absence of any statutes imposing such an obligation, or defining the way in which it shall be discharged, minor areas of government cannot shift responsibility. Thus villages, towns, boroughs, cities, townships, counties, parishes, and any other areas of government or political units enjoying a measure of self-government are expected to provide for their own poor. Many times there are overlapping jurisdictions, and it is a nice legal problem to discover just where responsibility does rest; but the general proposition has been clear for at least five hundred years; poor relief is a function of local government.

The Common-Law Rule.—But the common-law rule does not pretend to say how the poor shall be cared for. It can go into no details. Destitute persons could all be thrust in jail and kept on bread and water if local authorities chose to fulfill their duty in that way, and if there were no statutes dealing with the matter. And exactly that disgraceful practice has been quite general in years past, in this country as well as in England. The basic principle of the common-law rule brings out an elementary function of government in its brutal simplicity—the government cannot allow people within its jurisdiction to die of starvation and exposure. The proposition is clear and logical, and certainly humanitarian considerations could not admit of less.

These principles were carried over to American soil, and no sooner were minor areas of government established here than local authorities began to assume the responsibility of caring for the poor. The little New England towns, the villages and boroughs, the parishes in the South, and where none of these minor areas existed, then the counties, set up machinery and institutions for the care of the poor. This practice has continued until the present day, and in the absence of special legislation to the contrary, the smallest area of government is expected to extend some kind of poor relief. The entire situation can of course be altered by legislation at any time. Thus special obligations can be imposed upon counties, and the townships be entirely relieved; or the state itself may take over the function of poor relief. The common-law rule has not been sufficient, and in recent years more and more legislation has been written in the statute books in order to remedy the unfortunate conditions that have been uncovered, and to provide more effective means of extending poor relief.

Until some years after the Civil War very little had been done through legislation. The minor areas handled their own problems as they saw fit, and conditions frequently were most deplorable. All manner of dependents were kept in abominable surroundings, many times in the local jail, for of other public buildings there were none. Indeed an extended account of poor relief in the United States during the first half of the nineteenth century would conjure up an ugly picture that may be passed over here and left to the historian.

The Move away from Extreme Decentralization.—But in the years following the Civil War the desirability of doing something to improve existing conditions was gradually impressed upon the public mind, progressive steps were slowly taken and led to much improvement in the years that followed. The first step toward improvement was to break away from extreme decentralization. It was observed that from most every point of view it was highly undesirable that the smallest areas of government should exercise the function of poor relief independently.

Considerations Leading to Centralization.—There were several considerations pointing to this conclusion: (1) In the first place it was not economical. Even the niggardly relief that was extended by the small areas, would in the aggregate cost ever so much more than would a much better sort of relief if extended by a larger area, or by the small areas coöperating. Thus one large institution can be maintained at a lower cost than half a dozen small ones, and yet accommodate just as many persons. (2) Again, the fact could not escape attention that different types of dependents needed different sort of care, and this could only be given through coöperation. The small units could not afford to render specialized care to different types of dependents. (3) And if better care were given to dependents the problem of poor relief would at least tend to be eliminated. Intelligent poor relief tends to lessen the need for subsequent relief. (4) Furthermore, if responsibility for poor relief were vested in some authority having jurisdiction over several smaller areas, then the disgraceful scramble to shift responsibility from one small jurisdiction to another would tend to be eliminated.

Who is Entitled to Relief?—This last evil had been

recognized in earliest days, and there has always been some law upon the subject. The question arises—To what persons must local authorities extend relief? And the answer is—To destitute persons who are residents within the jurisdiction. A resident is ordinarily one who has established a domicile or who has lived within the jurisdiction a long enough time to justify the conclusion that he intends to become a resident. The law is vague and cannot well be otherwise. A person may come into a jurisdiction and establish himself with the deliberate intention of remaining indefinitely. In the eyes of the law he has established a domicile and has become a resident at once. He is entitled to relief if he needs it. On the other hand, a wandering derelict may have no domicile anywhere, he resides, as it were, in the fields and the gutters, in freight cars and back alleys. And it is difficult to say just when the obligation to relieve him rests upon local authorities.

Legislatures have attempted to solve the problem but have not altogether succeeded. The rule usually is that residence within the jurisdiction one year entitles an individual to relief, unless he has been ordered to leave before that time. The case of wandering derelicts is not so clear. They wander about from place to place, leaving their accustomed haunts for a few months, and then returning again, never really establishing what could be considered a domicile. They are residents of the state most certainly, but of what county? what city? what township? It is frequently impossible to say.

Rivalry to Escape Responsibility.—Out of this confusion there has arisen an unseemly rivalry among minor areas of government, each endeavoring to shift responsibility upon the neighboring jurisdiction. The early New England towns met this very same problem by refusing to admit persons who bid fair to become public charges. To-day no area of government can refuse admittance to law-abiding citizens; but it is possible to send them on their way, however. Hence the very general practice has developed among towns, villages, small cities and counties, of passing on their undesirables. Such persons are given formal notice to depart, and the serving of such notice prevents a person from establishing a legal residence. Sometimes they are literally assisted to depart. Tramps, derelicts, loafers, drunks, drug addicts, prostitutes, and even the feeble-minded, are hurried on from town to town; and ever and anon they reappear and are again dispatched upon their way. When they are utterly destitute and unable to move, local authorities may pay their car fare to the next town. This item of expenditure is always found in local budgets. Thus a vicious circle is maintained, the practice is contagious, no locality dares stop, for if it does the undesirables immediately begin to accumulate to a most alarming degree.

Common sense and humanitarian considerations forbid the practice of such a silly custom, for it accomplishes no good for anyone. The victim has no chance to get upon his feet, and falls lower and lower until finally he reaches the very bottom of the scale and must be cared for by some locality. And yet it is important that no town or county should be obliged to care for dependents that properly belong to another jurisdiction. A dependent once acknowledged and accepted as a public charge upon the locality where he happens to be found, may remain a public charge for fifty years; and it is no light matter to assume such an obligation. Naturally there are many dependents, women, children, the sick or insane, who cannot be passed along indefinitely, and each locality has some of these, for whom it must provide.

Coöperation of Local Areas.—It will be seen that much of this rivalry can be eliminated and the situation greatly improved if responsibility for extending poor relief be centered upon county authorities rather than left for smaller local areas. Even so rivalry would still exist among counties, and this can hardly be eliminated unless the state assumes responsibility. But it has come to be the case that to-day in nearly every state the county is required by law to assume certain responsibilities in connection with poor relief. Not infrequently it happens that counties and smaller areas, the villages and townships, coöperate in the care of the poor, either voluntarily or as a result of legal requirements. The county frequently maintains control over the necessary institutions while the smaller areas pay for the support of their own poor, in the institutions. This leads to more or less bickering and dissatisfaction, however, and it is much better for the counties to assume full responsibility and control. Sometimes a number of counties voluntarily unite in order to maintain a better type of institution such as no one of them could possibly afford to maintain. This is a step but very little short of state control.

Dependents not a Homogeneous Group.—Accepting the fact that poor relief to-day is very generally a county function it is necessary to examine into the various aspects of it. In the first place it must be clearly understood that the poor do not constitute a homogeneous group by any means. There are many different types of destitute persons each requiring a different sort of care. They possess but one characteristic in common which is that of being poor or destitute. Indeed this is the essential factor in making an individual dependent in the eyes of the law and thus entitled to relief. It is sometimes necessary to conduct an inquiry through court proceedings in order to determine whether or not a certain individual is poor enough, is near enough to destitution, in order to be considered a dependent; but it seldom comes to this. But once a person is so poor and so nearly destitute as to qualify unmistakably as a dependent, he is entitled to be protected against starvation and exposure. This means, in its lowest terms, that he must be provided with food, clothing, and shelter.

Classification of Dependents.—But the poor can immediately be classified into several distinct groups. Various bases of classification at once occur. They are: (1) Men and Women, (2) Able-bodied Adults, (3) Aged and Infirm, (4) Sane and Insane, (5) Healthy or Diseased, (6) Children of Indigent Parents, (7) Orphans and Foundlings. These bases of classification are the most obvious and it is clear that each group is likely to need distinctive sort of care.

Methods of Extending Poor Relief.—In general there have been three different methods that have been pursued by local authorities in extending poor relief. They are: (1) Outdoor relief, (2) Farming out, and (3) Institutional care. Sometimes one method alone is followed, sometimes all three, other times townships will extend one sort of relief, counties another. At any rate the three methods are well defined. The first two present very simple governmental problems and may be discussed very briefly.

1. Outdoor Relief.—Outdoor relief is extended through individual officers of the government. In the case of the county this officer may be the county poor-master, the overseer of the poor, the individual members of the county board, or some special agent employed by the board. It formerly was the custom to elect a county poor officer called the poor-master or overseer of the poor. He was independent like all the other county officers, had charge of the county almshouse if there was one, and had charge of outdoor relief.

He was expected to investigate all cases of destitution upon his own responsibility, and to look into all cases that were brought to his attention. If in his opinion the destitute person or family could be relieved in their own home he laid the case before the county board, and if the board was willing to make the appropriation he provided the destitute person with clothing, food and fuel. Sometimes aid in other forms can be extended to very good purpose. Very frequently poor-masters render the necessary aid on their own responsibility, expecting the board to reimburse them. This is called outdoor relief for it does not require that the persons involved be cared for in an institution.

County poor-masters and overseers of the poor as independent officers have largely disappeared, and it is well they have. Outdoor relief is still extended, however, through persons employed by the county board, or through the activity of members of the board themselves. County supervisors or commissioners assume responsibility for discovering destitute cases, and outdoor relief is extended upon their authority directly. They are assisted in this matter by special investigators and private charitable organizations.

This method is quite generally practiced and is altogether appropriate in certain kinds of cases. It obviates the necessity of breaking up homes, it saves the victim from the stigma imposed through institutional care, and it frequently affords the destitute person that small measure of temporary aid which is sufficient to give him a new start and to get him on his feet again. However, the abuses that grow out of the system are manifold. If it is to be carried on intelligently it is necessary to have the services of some person of experience and quick appreciation. The practice must be safeguarded by frequent and thorough investigations. The sort of aid extended must be intelligently adapted to the needs of the victim. These requirements are seldom met, and outdoor relief becomes a source of great extravagance and petty graft, to say nothing of its demoralizing effect upon the recipients when it is extended in unworthy cases. Large sums may be expended in this way even though no investigation whatever has been made into the circumstances of the people who receive the charity.

If outdoor relief is to be practiced by the county, and it ought to be if done intelligently, it should unquestionably be carried on through some trained person employed by the county board and in every sense of the word responsible to it. Except in those counties that are so sparsely populated as to have very few cases it is quite inadvisable that county board members carry on this work themselves. It is done too clumsily and unintelligently, and results in great extravagance. In some counties each of thirty or forty members of the county board, township trustees, justices of the peace, and various other persons may carry on outdoor relief. In one Pennsylvania county one hundred and thirty-nine such officers were counted. Under such a disorganized system ablebodied loafers, and even families of some means, may be provided with food and fuel indefinitely. The evils of this nature that may arise need not further be discussed.

2. Farming Out.—Farming out is another method of extending poor relief. It involves the making of a contract between the local authorities and some private citizen who undertakes to assume charge of, and care for a dependent, on specified terms. This method in the past has been quite generally practiced in the case of children, the aged and infirm, and to a lesser extent in the case of feeble-minded persons. The danger of this practice is readily appreciated. The person who contracts to care for a dependent person does so in the hope of making a profit. Thus no matter what the understanding with the local authorities may be, the destitute person is in danger of being victimized, inadequately clothed and fed, subjected to brutal treatment, and obliged to work beyond his strength.

Sometimes the practice is attended with good results. Aged or infirm people who are not afflicted with disease or vicious habits, may in this way find excellent homes where they can make themselves useful to the advantage of all concerned. In the case of children it is not likely to result well. If a person is not willing to adopt a child outright it is hardly safe to put the child in his care for compensation.

On the whole the practice of farming out is not to be approved. The many evils which grow out of it vastly outweigh the few advantages; and when practiced wholesale for mercenary reasons the evils are greatly multiplied.

3. Institutional Care.—Institutional care has generally displaced the other methods of extending poor relief; and for the most part institutions are maintained by the counties, either independently or in coöperation with other areas of government. It has always been necessary to make use of public institutions in some cases, even though it be the jail or the basement of the townhall; but county poorhouses have gradually superseded all other institutions, and now in turn they are being displaced very slowly by state institutions, and local institutions of specialized type such as hospitals, orphan asylums, schools for the blind, and for the care of other special types of dependents.

The Poorhouse.—The county poorhouse is erected and maintained at the expense of the county. The county may be reimbursed by the contributions of townships, towns and cities, which it is intended shall cover the cost of supporting individuals whom they have sent to the county poorhouse. But the management and control of the poorhouse is vested in county authorities. In theory at least the county board has general supervision, and always makes the appropriations for maintenance. When a popularly elected poor-master has charge, then the county board is in a difficult position in the matter of exercising any real supervision. But this is very rarely the case. Poorhouses to-day are quite generally managed by stewards or superintendents who are employed by the board and are directly responsible to it. This is of course the best way. Boards of specially elected trustees for the management of such institutions, independent of the county board, are not entirely unknown but ought to be. Until the state takes over full control of institutions for extending poor relief the present method of selecting resident superintendents can hardly be improved upon.

Admission.—Any person found destitute within the boundaries of the county and not a legal resident of some other county in the state is eligible for admission to the poorhouse. Factors of age, sex, and condition, seldom play any part in the matter of eligibility. The poorhouse is the last refuge for all kinds of dependents who cannot be cared for elsewhere. Persons ordinarily gain admission to the poorhouse either through orders of a court or on a commitment order signed by any one of a number of local officials. Thus members of the county board, township trustees, and justices of the peace frequently are authorized to sign commitment orders for the admission of persons who require care.

Commitments and Fees.—This is not altogether a satisfactory practice. An official who signs a commitment order is entitled to a small fee for his trouble, and even these small sums stimulate officials to commit persons who are not deserving of relief, and to neglect to make the investigations that ought to be made before commitments are signed. Persons who are needlessly committed often leave the institution shortly after having been sent there, and presently they appear again seeking admission once more. This means another fee for the county supervisor or township trustee and he readily signs another commitment order. This petty graft can be carried on indefinitely although the whole procedure is perfectly legal. One obvious way to lessen this abuse is to abolish the fee system and to have fewer officers competent to sign commitment orders.

Opportunities for abuse are multiplied due to the fact that public authorities do not have the power to detain persons committed to the poorhouse. The superintendent must admit, and care for as well as he can, any person who appears at his institution with a commitment order. And when a person desires to leave, the superintendent has no alternative but to open the door, for a commitment order names no time limit. It therefore happens that irresponsible derelicts come and go very frequently. They stay long enough to get rested and well fed, then go upon their wanderings again and after a time appear once more in need of rest, food, and possibly medical care. They always appear in considerable numbers as cold weather approaches, and leave again in the spring. The superintendent can do nothing to prevent this, and it would be a difficult problem to deal with even if he did have authority.

Superintendent's Authority.—The superintendent is further embarrassed in that he cannot exercise disciplinary authority over his charges. They are of all kinds and conditions, often very disagreeable, troublesome, stupid, and lazy. They are inclined to be unamenable to rules, and the superintendent must be a man of strong character, tact, firmness, and infinite patience. He cannot exercise the coercive measures that are the resource of a jailer or the superintendent of an insane asylum, and hence he must fall back upon other, less effective resources. These are quite apt to fail him utterly and the poorhouse is then in serious danger of degenerating into an ill-managed, dirty, disorderly loafing place.

The superintendent may usually expel a person who persistently makes himself obnoxious, will not obey the rules, or who is apparently no longer deserving of support. But a superintendent is rarely inclined to expel any of the inmates. Especially if his compensation is measured by the number of inmates in his institution, he is anxious to keep all of them that he can. And, furthermore, an expulsion is quite apt to incur the displeasure of that official who signed the commitment order, and superintendents fear to make political enemies. They have but little to gain through being severe taskmasters and may lose their positions. There is every temptation, therefore, for a superintendent to follow the line of least resistance and to promote as little trouble with the inmates as is possible.

Fortunately conditions in the poorhouses of the country bid fair to be rapidly improved in the next few decades. Much progress has been made in recent years, and there is no sign that it has stopped. In the past, conditions have been exceedingly bad, partly because county authorities have been unwilling to make the necessary expenditures, partly because it has been impossible to segregate different types of dependents, and partly because resident superintendents and board members have been indifferent, incompetent, and in general thoroughly unfitted to deal with the problems of institutional care in a scientific way.

The result has been that men, women, and children, in all stages of mental and physical deterioration have been herded together in dilapidated, inadequate, unhealthful, and unsanitary buildings, in violation of the simplest dictates of common sense and decency. Conditions have been worse than in the county jails, for prison bars can at least keep some of the inmates from personal contact. But in the poorhouses the feeble-minded mingle with children, the diseased go uncared for and communicate their ills to other inmates, the vicious characters may corrupt the morals of fellow lodgers, and conditions reach a point that is intolerable. Superintendents have sometimes been unable to remedy conditions because of lack of funds, sometimes they have been tempted to let things go unnoticed from ulterior motives, seeking to profit by serving bad food and misappropriating funds which they were expected to devote to the improvement of conditions; and sometimes they have simply not known how to meet their problems.

But there is no reason why the county poorhouse cannot be a thoroughly admirable institution, and it requires no radical reform in county government to accomplish it. This is evidenced by the ever-growing number of splendid poorhouses scattered about here and there, with buildings well kept, adequate and sanitary, grounds and outbuildings in creditable condition, fences in good repair—all bespeaking an atmosphere of respectability and good order.

A competent superintendent, well paid, and supplied with funds that are necessary, can bring these things about in a remarkably short time. Many of the inmates, tactfully managed and supervised, can do a great deal toward keeping the institution in good condition.

The Poorfarm.—The poor*farm* idea has led to much improvement and in many counties has supplanted the poor*house*—a great bleak building without extensive grounds. County boards have acquired farms, erected proper buildings thereon, and have employed superintendents who undertake to run the farm with the aid of some of the inmates and some hired help. This has led in many cases to excellent results. The farm produces much of the food that is used and enough more of agricultural products to go far toward maintaining the institution. The farm also has great advantages over the urban locations for the care of county charges.

We are warned, however, by those who have practised it that the farm idea may be somewhat overdone. It has been said that, "The poorfarm, however, was destined to assume an important place in its demands upon the time of the steward of the poorhouse. He has really become primarily the steward of the poorfarm and secondarily of the poorhouse. Most of the latter functions have been turned over to his wife as matron. He has become the farmer, rejoicing more in making the farm pay than in making the poorhouse a home for the aged and infirm; taking more pride in his fine cattle, hogs or chickens, and in the spacious barns, than in the comfort, usefulness, and happiness of the inmates of the poorhouse, or in the buildings in which they are housed. We must not forget, however, that these men only reflect the attitude of their employers, the members of the boards of supervisors, and that the latter simply carry out the policy which they

know the taxpayers consciously or unconsciously hold." *
The last words of this statement hint at a factor which
too often lies at the basis of evil conditions in the poorhouse.
The poorhouse is not conspicuously in the public view,
and being out of sight is out of mind; and taxpayers are
more or less reluctant to spend much money on such an
unprofitable institution.

Specialized Institutions.—But the most promising sign
of improvement in methods of poor relief lies in the tendency to create specialized institutions in the counties
themselves, and particularly the tendency on the part of
state governments to create specialized state institutions
which immediately relieve the county poorhouses. It
has been pointed out that one great source of trouble has
been the apparent necessity of housing all types of dependents in one institution. If certain types could be
removed to other institutions where they could receive the
specialized care which their condition demands, the poorhouses would profit greatly. Very few counties indeed
could afford to maintain several different kinds of institutions, there not being enough dependents of one particular
type to warrant this. However, a specialized state institution designed to accommodate all the dependents
of a particular type in the whole state would serve the
purpose.

State Insane Asylums.—The first step in the direction
of establishing specialized state institutions was taken
some years ago when state insane asylums were created.
They are now found universally. These state insane
asylums take care of patients who are not dependents as
well as those who are, but for the present purpose it is to
be noted that when a state insane asylum exists there
no longer is any excuse for keeping insane dependents in

* Gillin, *Poor Relief Legislation in Iowa*, p. 143.

the county poorhouse. With them gone, one source of difficulty is removed.

Violently insane persons are always sent to the insane asylum. On the other hand, there are still to be found a great many harmless insane people in the poorhouses. It must be realized that a person is not insane in the eyes of the law until declared so by a court of competent jurisdiction. This means that many mildly insane persons find their way to the poorhouses as ordinary paupers, living out their lives there, with but little attention being paid to them. No one makes complaint, and the county board lets well enough alone, for if the insane person is removed to the state asylum his maintenance there must be paid for by the county. It is much cheaper to maintain such people quietly in the poorhouse. But at least the state insane asylums do afford an opportunity to eliminate one type of dependent from the county institutions.

Epileptics; Feeble-Minded.—Epileptics and the feeble-minded are in the same position as the insane, but there are fewer state institutions for their care. In the meantime they wander about the county poorhouses, objects of commiseration to everyone who sees them.

The Physically Defective.—Another type of dependent needing specialized care which only the state can afford is the physically defective. Those who are deaf, dumb or blind, may often be restored to a condition of usefulness if given proper care. Such care cannot be given in the county poorhouses; but dependents thus afflicted accumulate in those institutions as ordinary paupers and there they stay. But as soon as a state government establishes a school in which to train them there is no excuse for their remaining in the poorhouses. Some states have made great progress in this direction, others very little. And again the same difficulty arises as with insane people. That is, county boards are reluctant to go to the expense of sending their afflicted dependents to these relatively expensive institutions. It is much cheaper to maintain them in the poorhouse.

Orphans.—A similar situation exists with regard to children. It is very unwise to keep children in a poorhouse. They are subjected to demoralizing influences, and the general atmosphere of the place is not at all conducive to their betterment. Privately endowed orphan asylums afford opportunities to get the children out of poorhouses, and for the most part they find their way to these institutions or into the homes of people who adopt them. But there are still too many of them cared for in the poorhouses, and but very few state governments maintain institutions to which they can be sent unless they are defective. Dependent children can be maintained at very little cost in a poorhouse, and it is not likely that county orphanages will become very numerous.

The Diseased.—Another type of poorhouse inmate is the one badly in need of medical attention. In the poorhouse such victims are not likely to get the attention they need. If there be a county physician he makes occasional visits and renders some aid, but all too frequently people who are afflicted with loathsome or contagious diseases, afflictions that slowly grow worse and worse, persons suffering with tuberculosis or other illnesses less serious perhaps, are to be found in nearly every poorhouse. They remain there until their condition becomes so bad that they virtually die of neglect or are sent to public hospitals and supported there at the expense of the county. If there were county hospitals to which they could be sent, not only would the poorhouses be relieved of their presence but the victims themselves would be vastly benefited. A few counties have established hospitals, and some states maintain tuberculosis sanitariums. But up to the present time little progress has been made in this direction.

An Ideal Poorhouse.—It is obvious that if specialized institutions are maintained either by the county itself or the state government, the condition of poorhouses could very quickly be improved, if county boards were willing to take advantage of the opportunities. The poorhouse could thus become merely a refuge for the aged and infirm—an old people's home in fact, and the problems of management would be greatly simplified.

There is very little state supervision of county poor relief, and reform is not likely to take this direction. The erection of state institutions, not only for the insane but for the feeble-minded and epileptic, and the defective, is much more likely to be the means of solving present problems.

THE COUNTY PHYSICIAN AND COUNTY HOSPITALS

The County Physician.—In a good many counties there is to be found a county physician. Fortunately he is not a popularly elected officer but is appointed by the county board. His chief duty has been to give medical attention to destitute people of the county when they require it. This does not occupy all of his time by any means and he is merely subject to call, being paid accordingly. He treats some people in their homes, orders them removed to public hospitals at county expense if necessary, and gives them attention there. He makes his rounds of the jail and poorhouse and renders to the inmates such medical aid as they need.

Relation to Coroner.—Often his services are required by the coroner who desires him to make analyses and examinations in the hope of uncovering or clearing up mysterious poison cases; and the coroner's jury has the benefit of his expert testimony. In populous counties the coroner may have a physician as a permanent member of his staff; or the physician may be connected with the public prosecutor's office.

But in any event, it is necessary that the county board should have, subject to its control, a physician who can undertake the medical care of dependents who are ill.

County Hospitals.—With the development of county hospitals, the position of the county physician takes on new dignity and importance. He is still charged with giving aid to all county dependents, but may become the superintendent of the hospital on a regular salary.

County hospitals are of very recent origin. The idea was first originated in such a way as to find expression in the law, by Doctor E. E. Munger of Spencer, Iowa.[*] It was first necessary for him to get such legislation passed by the state assembly as would permit counties in his state to erect and maintain hospitals. It was accomplished in 1909. It would be necessary to take this preliminary step in any state, inasmuch as counties enjoy only enumerated and delegated powers. After the legislation was passed it was only necessary to hold a referendum in any county in order to determine whether or not a hospital should be erected. Similar bills were passed in other states and now there are a number of states wherein counties are permitted to build and maintain hospitals.

Need for County Hospitals.—It must be said that the purpose of erecting such hospitals is not by any means solely to accommodate public charity patients and to relieve congestion in the poorhouses. The principal idea is, on the other hand, to afford the rural population hospital facilities such as townspeople possess. There are many

[*] *Documents on County Government*, "O" pp. 1-8—"A New Kind of County Hospital."

counties in which no city is to be found, at least no city populous enough or wealthy enough to maintain a hospital. This means that people in these large areas must travel many miles to the nearest city in order to find hospital facilities. Many such rural counties are quite able to maintain hospitals even though there be no one city or town within the county limits that could afford to do so. The possibilities of the county hospital are gradually dawning upon the people of the rural districts and it may be expected that such institutions will become more numerous. The Cook County Hospital in Chicago is one of the finest of its kind in the country, though this institution is not primarily intended to accommodate a rural population.

PUBLIC HEALTH AND SANITATION

Public Health and Counties.—In recent years a great deal has been done in the interests of public health and sanitation. But not much activity has been carried on through county government. Cities have had their boards of health and health officers for a great many years, but not so the counties. And later the state governments created state boards of health and health offices which have done a great deal; but the counties for the most part have not had a prominent place in the governmental machinery for maintaining public health. The reason for this is obvious. The problems arising in this connection usually reach an acute stage only in the urban centers. Governmental machinery has therefore been established only in the urban centers to deal with the situations that develop there.

Need for Rural Health Agencies.—However, even though the problems of public health do not reach the acute stages in the rural areas such as they do in cities, it is a very great mistake to assume that public health in the rural districts is all that can be desired. Relative to the density of the population, disease is as prevalent there as in the cities. Sanitary precautions and preventive measures are not practiced there to anywhere near the same extent that they are in the cities, and there is just as much to be done there through governmental agencies, relatively speaking, as there is in the cities.

Food inspection is every bit as necessary in the rural districts as it is in the cities, for there is the very source of food supply. Sources of water supply should be under the eyes of health officers, and it is particularly necessary that milk be handled under strict supervision. Preventive measures designed to reduce the inroads of tuberculosis and other diseases are just as necessary in the rural areas as elsewhere. And a visit to a country school would ordinarily convince anyone that if medical examination of school children is necessary in the cities, in order to detect cases of under-nourishment, bad teeth, poor eyesight, and other afflictions, it certainly is needed no less in the rural areas. Unhealthful swamp lands go undrained for years. More or less polluted wells are regularly used, producing each year an array of typhoid cases that are quite unnecessary. Milk and butter are prepared for the market under most unsanitary conditions. Diseased animals are allowed to live with no intelligent effort being made to cure them. Under-nourished children grow to maturity, permanently handicapped by afflictions of the eyes, teeth, and respiratory organs.

There is no intention here to create a false impression of rural life in the United States, which is on the whole as healthful and altogether as wholesome as anywhere in the world, no doubt. But the fact should be emphasized that, per unit of population, there is just as much to be done through governmental agencies in the rural districts as in the cities. Country people are just as much entitled to the benefits to be derived through such agencies as anybody else, and the county is the unit through which health authorities could function most conveniently.

State authorities are doing something in the various states. In many of them a very thorough milk and butter inspection is carried on. Serious epidemics that afflict not only human beings but farm stock as well, are handled by state health authorities. But there is need of some local authority to deal with the somewhat less serious matters. County boards are ordinarily competent to pass ordinances requiring the suppression of unhealthful nuisances, and the pollution of streams; and county or township officials are very generally engaged in drainage projects. But other activities, hinted at above, can only be carried on by men of special training or aptitude for the work. A county board of health, composed of three physicians, or of two physicians and a layman, assisted by a health officer who could do the actual work of inspection, might be the solution of the problem. Such a board certainly ought not to be elective, but rather appointive by the county board.

Few counties have such boards of health, although county health officers working independently of a board are to be found in about one-third of the states. If a state department of public health were developed sufficiently to exercise close supervision over county health officers it would be unnecessary to maintain county boards of health. This will probably be the ultimate outcome, for county authorities are not inclined to increase county expenditures in this direction but rather prefer to wait, expecting the state to act sooner or later.

CHAPTER XIII

SCHOOLS AND COUNTY SCHOOL OFFICIALS

Public Opinion and Education.—Education is by no means necessarily a function of government. At least it is not so in the same sense that certain other governmental activities are. Peace must be maintained, at least some relief must be given to the poor, and there must be some machinery of justice; but a school system is not essential. This fact is the more significant, and reflects the greater credit upon the early settlers, for schools were established and have been maintained at public expense from earliest colonial times. They were established simply because public opinion demanded it, and have been maintained ever since for the same reason. Ways and means of extending education have changed and developed throughout the years, and progress has been very rapid in the last few decades. For while in some parts of the country very little or nothing has been done, in others a great deal has been accomplished. Nearly everywhere in the meantime, private initiative, working particularly through church organizations, has accomplished something. But the impulse given to public education in the early New England towns determined the sort of governmental machinery through which schools were to be managed for the next three hundred years.

Schools in New England Towns.—Originally the school organization was part and parcel of the town government. This simply means that the same officers who had charge of the town government managed the schools.

In town meeting it would be determined that a school should be erected and a schoolmaster employed. The selectmen would then proceed to erect the school building, to hire a schoolmaster and to give him his instructions in the minutest detail. Not only would the selectmen determine the length of the school year, which was likely to be no less than fifty-two weeks, and prescribe a course of study; but they outlined minutely the régime which the schoolmaster should follow. Certain days were set aside for religious instruction, certain hours were set for the administration of correction to scholars, visitors' hours were fixed; and the schoolmaster was required from time to time to make reports to the selectmen.

Thus was the school brought directly into the democratic machinery of the New England town. Town officers had charge of the school in exactly the same way that they had charge of almshouses and poor relief, jails, road building, and bridges. And taxes were levied and appropriations were made for the support of schools just as for other purposes.

However, this precise situation did not obtain in general outside of New England, for the very obvious reason that towns of the New England type did not appear outside New England. Yet even so it can hardly be doubted that New England practice in the matter of school management did, to a very large measure, determine the character of school organization that emerged elsewhere. It had been satisfactorily demonstrated in New England that management of a school was very properly the direct, personal concern of those people who sent their children to the school and contributed to its support. The school had proved to be a point of contact between all the people in a community who sent their children to it. In the New England town of course, there were a great many other points of contact, and factors that made for a sense of unity and solidarity; but the school also was one of the factors entering into the composition of forces which held the townsmen together.

Schools Outside New England.—Outside New England, on the other hand, the town as a unit of government failed to appear, as has been shown. The loosely organized township took its place, and further south and west even the township decayed and disappeared, giving place to vigorous county government. But even where this happened the school retained its essential character, it still remained a vital point of contact between the people of a comparatively small group and did not necessarily have to be bound up closely with the machinery of government. No matter how large the basic area of government might be, be it a town, township, or county, the school community in the very nature of things could not grow, for there were very distinct limits to the area which one school could serve.

Thus it may be said the institutions of local government grew away from the school community. Poor relief could be administered over a much larger area as a unit, the maintenance of peace, the collection of taxes and all the other functions of local government, could be carried on over larger areas as units; but the school community remained essentially as it was, a unit that could not grow. The school remained a central point of social and, to a certain extent, political unity. And it is so to-day. Even in the heart of great cities a single school is frequently the center of a very distinct social group, and social workers are striving constantly to make all schools real effective social centers. In rural areas the school continued to be the center of a political group as well as a social group.

The School District.—The people of a given school

community in early days were intensely interested in the management of their school; and it is one of the most striking manifestations of the spirit of democracy that as other activities of local government outgrew the school community, the people of the school community organized, set up machinery of government, and undertook to manage their own schools directly, through governmental machinery of their own. Thus appeared the familiar school district found in nearly every state of the union in one form or another—an area through which local self-government is practiced in its purest form.

Organization.—The typical school district has been ordinarily nothing more nor less than an area accommodated by a single schoolhouse. The governmental machinery for handling the business of the school district has been quite independent of other governmental machinery. Thus in some states the people of a school district assemble at stated intervals and determine the important matters that arise, leaving the actual management of school affairs to school officials who are elected by the people of the district. These meetings are primary assemblies in the same sense that town meetings and party caucuses are primary assemblies. They are a relic of pure democracy. The meetings determine major policies, make appropriations and fix a tax rate. But the general meeting has been for the most part discontinued, and even in those states where it still is held the attendance is likely to be very small. The result is that actual management of school district business invariably falls to a board of some kind. This board may be controlled in the determination of major policies by the referendum. Thus a favorable popular vote is often necessary before a new schoolhouse can be erected. The referendum process becomes in this way a substitute for the primary assembly.

Trustees.—Ordinarily a small school board of trustees is elected, the members serving a short term. This board of trustees perfects its simple organization by choosing from its number one to serve as clerk and another to serve as chairman. The trustees thereupon proceed to the business of their district. They have full charge of the schoolhouse. If authorized by the voters of the district, through general meeting or referendum, they let contracts and superintend the building of a new schoolhouse. They make full provision for the maintenance of the building and grounds. They employ a teacher at as low a wage as possible, and in the absence of legislation imposing limitations upon them the trustees map out the school régime in complete detail. The length of the school year is fixed, the hours of the school day, the subjects that shall be taught, and the books that shall be used. The trustees are expected to give school affairs their personal and constant attention. And most important of all, the trustees at one of their regular meetings are expected to determine the tax rate which it will be necessary to impose in order to yield the amount of money needed for school purposes.

Limitations of State Law.—As years have passed by the people of school districts and the boards of trustees have not been as free to exercise their own discretion in managing school affairs as the above account might intimate. Restrictions have come through state legislation; but they have come very slowly. In early days the local school authorities had almost unlimited power, to-day in some states their functions have been reduced to a point where they do but little more than administer state regulations. The demand for reform and centralized control has resulted in a breakdown of the characteristic school district system and has also resulted in a serious curtailment of the power of local authorities over school affairs.

One invariable limitation imposed by state law forbids local school authorities to fix their tax rate above a certain maximum. For the most part school trustees have been very willing to remain within the limits set.

But for many years no other significant limitations were imposed. Hence the school year varied in length from place to place. Salaries paid to teachers varied widely. The character and quality of instruction was not by any means uniform. Some districts had excellent school buildings, others got along with disgracefully inadequate structures.

Tendency Toward Standardization.—But public opinion has gradually reached a point where it will not tolerate so many and such wide variations. Workers in the field of education are striving constantly to secure ever so much more uniformity than has been accomplished anywhere as yet. Progress so far has been along certain pretty well-defined lines. In addition to limiting the tax rate, state laws may fix the length of the school year, and by means of a compulsory attendance law people may be required to send their children to school during this period. This immediately establishes a certain measure of uniformity. Then may come a law determining in general outlines the course of study and the type of books that must be used. Minimum salaries are established for teachers; and candidates for positions are required to possess certain qualifications that are determined by examination or diploma from a normal school. Then come building standards fixing certain requirements with regard to the character of the school building. These are aimed to do away with the buildings that are overcrowded, inadequately lighted, improperly heated, ill-ventilated and unsanitary.

It will be observed that the moment any or all of these limitations or requirements are fixed in state law, the local authorities find their measure of discretion cut down just to that extent. An independent school board is then no longer able to cut a school year down to six months, to employ an untrained girl at starvation wages as a teacher, or to send the children to a dilapidated schoolhouse—cold, dark, and unsanitary—all for the purpose of saving money. Their right to do these things is, to be sure, bound up with the right to local self-government. But the right to local self-government, splendid and worthy of admiration as it is in theory, has been abused so grossly in so many connections that it is no wonder public opinion is reaching a point that will permit the abandonment of local self-government in the interests of better education.

Even so, the desire for local self-government as regards school affairs has been plenty strong enough to resist extensive reform, and complete state control. Many states have accomplished virtually nothing of importance, and in these states the rural districts are as independent as ever they were. Nearly every state that has made any progress at all has done so with hesitating and compromising steps.

"**State Aid.**"—Instead of making the desired regulations compulsory, and instead of obliging local authorities to live up to them, state legislatures have set up certain standards as an ideal to be attained. Then in order to induce the local authorities to meet the ideal standards a certain sum of money is set aside which is distributed in the form of gifts to those districts which attain the standards. This practice is known as "state aid," but the various methods of administering it need not be discussed. Suffice it that "state aid" has done a very great deal to improve rural school conditions. In addition to the desire to receive some state aid, another factor enters the equation. Something of disgrace attaches to those districts which have not reached the standards which entitle them to state aid, and a sense of pride stimulates them to improve such conditions. Thus "state aid" has done much to improve conditions without doing very great violence to the desire for local self-government.

But even though such a practice is to be approved, and even though it is much better than doing nothing at all, it is a temporizing, compromising, halfway policy. Certain desirable standards as regards school year, curriculum, teachers' salaries and training, and the character of school buildings, ought to be firmly established in law beyond the power of local authorities to circumvent them. Some steps in this direction are being taken every year and great progress may be expected.

Along with the tendency to impose certain requirements upon local school authorities is to be observed another tendency. As standards are fixed, and as the factor of discretion is cut down, local interest in school affairs takes on a different complexion. People are confident that their schools will be maintained at certain standards because the law requires it, and they immediately cease to have any desire to take a personal part in managing school affairs. They do not come to district meetings, they will not even go to vote for school officers; and this attitude of indifference is reflected in the conduct of local officials themselves. In a word, the bonds that made for unity in the school district tend to be completely loosed, and it thereupon becomes a mere artificial area as soon as any considerable measure of state control is imposed.

Centralizing Control.—This fact, together with other considerations, leads to a still more rapid centralization of control over schools, and the creation of administrative systems embracing a number of school districts. The variations from state to state in this connection are manifold. In some states all the district schools are brought under the control of township officers. The district trustees are then not to be found and a township board assumes control over all the schools within the township. Sometimes a township that is not particularly populous constitutes a single district itself. Another device is to permit a number of small districts to combine their resources, abandon their tiny district schools, coöperate in building one fine structure at a convenient spot, employ good teachers, and then provide transportation for the children.

Consolidated Districts.—Thus appears the so-called consolidated school district. The consolidated school district has a school board and possibly a superintendent of its own. The consolidated district has much to recommend it. The buildings in such districts can be as good as city buildings, for they may be adequately lighted and heated. Playrooms and other facilities may be provided which afford the country children all the benefits enjoyed by city children, and sometimes even more. And much better teachers can ordinarily be employed to work in these schools. It is possible to classify the children into grades, and to give them much better instruction. But no reform measure can be without its strong opponents, and objections are raised because consolidated schools are so much more expensive than the old-time district schools. Indeed the factor of expense has been the chief impediment to progress along these lines. Other problems arise in connection with the transportation of the children. This can never be solved until good roads are made, and kept in good condition.

County Unit Administration.—The most promising tendency in the direction of centralizing control over the school system lies, however, in vesting full local authority in county officials, and in making them responsible to state officers. There is no longer any reason why autonomy should be permitted in an area smaller than the county. Public education is of concern to the entire state, and if one small section of a county is backward the entire state suffers. Standards of education ought to be as nearly uniform as possible and they never will be uniform if petty local officers are to have control. The county is a small enough unit ordinarily for satisfactory school administration and each county should have governmental machinery for managing its schools, until such time as state control shall supplant all local authority.

There have been county school boards and school superintendents in a majority of the states for many years, but the trouble has been that they possessed little or no real authority over the district school officials. County school boards have existed that had actually nothing whatever to do; and county superintendents have held office and occupied their time with making perfunctory inspections that led to nothing, and with giving advice to district authorities and teachers that was deliberately ignored. The law has required superintendents to make investigations, to give advice and assistance, and to file reports—sometimes with the county court, sometimes with state officers. But under such circumstances district authorities do not find their own prerogatives invaded to the slightest degree, for the superintendent is nothing but a figurehead who can be ignored completely.

The county superintendent's hand has been greatly strengthened in those states that have adopted the practice of giving state aid, and aid is given based largely upon his recommendations. Under such circumstances it can be seen that his influence in the various districts would be quite considerable. It has also been the function of the superintendent to conduct examinations for teachers when the state law requires all teachers to have met certain requirements. And where the state law makes requirements concerning the school year, compulsory attendance, curriculum, text-books and building standards, it is the business of the superintendent to make investigations and report violations. On the other hand, district trustees do still for the most part employ their own teachers, have direct charge of their school buildings, and determine the tax rate for their districts.

County School Board.—Complete centralization of control in county authorities would involve the abolition of school districts as independent entities, and hence the abolition of district trustees. A county school board would then be necessary. There are various ways of selecting such a board. Popular election is possible, but is strongly to be condemned. In some states the school board is composed of all the presidents of all the district boards ex-officio, but this could not be under the reorganization here contemplated. Probably the best method of selecting a county school board would be to have it appointed by the county board. And it ought to be relatively small in number of members.

Such a school board would have the function of determining all school policies for the county in so far as state law left it free to determine policies. State law should at least: (1) Fix the maximum tax rate, relative to the value of property, or number of children in the county. (2) Fix the length of the school year. (3) Provide for compulsory attendance. (4) Determine minimum salaries for teachers. (5) Fix requirements for qualifications for teachers. (6) In general terms outline a curriculum, and (7) Determine building standards.

Within these limits the county school board could

exercise its discretion by: (1) Determining the number and location of school buildings. (2) Furnishing them and keeping them in condition. (3) Letting contracts for supplies. (4) Employing teachers. (5) Preparing the school budget, and (6) Determining the tax rate.

The County Superintendent.—The county school board might also select a county superintendent who would be directly responsible to the school board in every sense of the word. It has been the custom to elect the county superintendent of schools by popular vote, and this is still the practice in somewhat more than one-half of the states. However, inasmuch as the superintendent should not be vested with any large measure of discretion in determining important school policies there is no reason why he should be popularly elected, and, furthermore, the superintendent should possess a certain fitness for his office which cannot by any means be assured if he is popularly elected.

The duties of a county superintendent would be primarily to serve as an agent for the school board. He would exercise general supervision over the schools of the county, examine candidates for teachers' positions, give advice and aid to teachers and principals, conduct rigid and frequent inspections, superintend the distribution of supplies, make recommendations to the board in the matter of employing teachers, prepare school statistics, keep various records that are needed, and make complete reports to the county board. These functions are already performed by county superintendents for the most part, but not with the same thoroughness and effectiveness that could be expected if district authorities were abolished, if the state laws were made more complete, and if the superintendent were appointed by and responsible to a county school board.

State and Federal School Authorities.—State boards of education are found in some states and there are state superintendents of education in a large number of the states, but their functions do not come within the scope of this volume. Furthermore, there is considerable agitation for the creation of a federal department of education, with a secretary at its head who would have a place in the President's cabinet. The activities of such a department would certainly be greatly hampered by the limitations of the federal constitution unless very broad interpretations were countenanced by the courts. Yet even in spite of constitutional limitations, the possibilities are very great.

City Schools.—City school systems have not been touched upon in this discussion. They are quite independent of the rural school system, each city being a school district and possessing its own organization with a school board and a superintendent of its own. This is as it should be. The county school organization should embrace only the area outside of city limits, and the city school system should not come under the control of county school authorities. All of them should, of course, be included in the machinery of state control.

CHAPTER XIV

ROADS AND HIGHWAYS

Highways in Ancient Times.—The establishment and maintenance of roads and highways has been a function of local government since ancient times. Central governments have seldom been interested in the matter except to the extent of maintaining a few great arteries that would connect principal points and facilitate the movements of military forces. The Roman roads still remain as monuments to their builders, and a few great arteries running throughout England are of particular interest. But the law concerning highways in early England was chiefly negative. By this statement it is meant that laws were not frequently passed looking toward the maintenance of these highways, no special duties or obligations were ordinarily imposed upon local communities with respect to maintaining them; but there was plenty of very strict law concerning the maintenance of peace upon the king's highway, and severe penalties were inflicted upon anyone who obstructed free passage upon it. The reason for this is obvious, the Norman kings and their successors were determined that channels of communication between them and their people should be free, unobstructed and safe, as far as possible. To be sure the ideal was not attained for some hundreds of years but that has nothing to do with the theory.

Highways in Colonial America.—Except for these few great national highways the people of each community were left free to maintain roads or not as they saw fit.

The same situation prevailed in colonial America. **If any road building was done it was done by local authorities,** for the colonial governments took scant notice of the matter. Clearly enough in early times there was very little that needed to be done. Trails from one community to another were blazed by hunters and explorers. But as time went on it became necessary not only to maintain streets in a relatively passable condition inside the limits of urban districts, but to build roads from one community to another that could be used for trading purposes, for the delivery of mails, and for general intercommunication. Yet even after the period of statehood the whole matter was left largely to local authorities, the counties and townships assuming full responsibility. They were given power to impose meager taxes for the purpose and then were left to their own devices.

Highways and the Federal Government.—The newly established federal constitution gave Congress power to establish post roads, but this power has never been exercised to any important degree. Back in colonial days Benjamin Franklin expressed some interesting and constructive ideas concerning national highways, particularly for purposes of facilitating the mail service; and statesmen of national prominence have been sporadically interested in the matter ever since. The Cumberland Road was the most significant national highway ever attempted, and although during the thirties and forties the Whig Party voiced great plans for national highways, but little came of them, attention being directed rather to waterways. From that time until the present little has been done by the national government.

Highways and State Governments.—State governments also were neglectful of the highways all during the nineteenth century. This is a little difficult to explain. It was natural enough that the federal government should have neglected them, in view of the political controversies concerning the powers and purposes of a central government. But that the states, in the very moment when they were claiming sovereign powers and expressing resentment against interference in local affairs on the part of federal authorities, should have neglected their highways, is not so easy to explain.

Reasons for Neglect of Highways.—Yet there are certain considerations that do shed a little light on the matter. They may be enumerated. (1) Distances were rather overpowering in their magnitude. Settlements were scattered over very broad areas, and the prospect of building roads between them was quite forbidding. These overpowering distances never faced the people of Europe, and it is not to be wondered at that in the press of other matters the statesmen of this country were content to let alone the problem of building endless highways. (2) The population was relatively scanty, being spread over a vast area, and hence the demand for roads was not so insistent as it might have been. (3) There was no occasion to move great military forces on foot. The necessity for doing this was one of the principal factors in the development of good roads in the old country. (4) The railroads developed with the population and made good highways somewhat less necessary. Had the steam engine continued to remain a thing unknown, there is no doubt that as population developed the demand for good roads would have become more insistent. (5) The state governments preferred to leave the matter with the local areas in response to the demands for democracy and local self-government. These considerations explain in part at least why such little progress was made until the present century.

Since the respective state governments through all this period have been so neglectful, the whole problem of road building and maintenance has rested upon the counties and the townships. This fact has necessitated the establishment of local government machinery for the purpose of exercising this function. Policies had to be determined, money necessarily had to be raised for the purpose, and the work actually done through instrumentalities of local government.

What is Involved in Highway Control?—The local governmental machinery for road building and maintenance was simple. Power to determine policies was vested in town boards of selectmen, township trustees, and county boards; and in so far as state governments have not taken over control of certain highways, these boards determine policies to-day. Determination of policies and the general management of roads and highways involves: (1) The selection of routes and the locating of bridges. (2) The purchase or condemnation of property where necessary. (3) The determination of the amount of road work to be done in a given period. (4) The determination of the character of the work and improvements to be undertaken. (5) The letting of contracts for the purchase of all the equipment, material and supplies that may be needed. (6) The employment of workmen. (7) The general supervision of the work, and. (8) The fixing of a tax rate necessary to raise the money needed.

Special Road Officials.—Actual supervision of the work of road construction and maintenance has always been vested in special officials. There have been township road supervisors, county highway commissioners, and district highway officials. In some cases they have been independently elected officers, but that situation has been largely done away with now, the person who takes direct charge of road work usually being appointed by, and under the control of, the board which determines policies.

The actual work in early days, and to-day in distinctly rural sections, was done to a large extent by citizens themselves. A road tax was often imposed upon every adult man in the community for purposes of road maintenance, and men were given the alternative of paying the tax or of doing an equivalent amount of work upon the roads themselves. In spite of the fact that this is still done in certain communities it is obviously a very undesirable practice. The work done by such men is not of the best, it is irregularly done, and is in many ways unsatisfactory, especially in present times when good roads are needed more than used to be the case. But it is not yet a rare sight to see farmers out along the roadside with their teams and wagons, plows and scrapers, working out their road taxes.

City vs. Country.—Governmental machinery for road building and maintenance to-day ought to be highly organized. All roads do not require the same sort of attention. Certain of them may properly be left to the care of local authorities while others ought to be controlled by the state. The condition of rural crossroads is primarily the concern of dwellers in rural districts, but the condition of a main highway leading from one city to another is of concern even to the whole state. It should not be that the people of a sparsely settled township can leave that portion of a main highway running through their jurisdiction in such condition that it is impassable, while large populations on each side of them are demanding a means of quick and easy communication.

On the other hand, it is not proper that the people of a sparsely settled township should be obliged to go to the expense of building a fine highway chiefly to accommodate the city populations.

Just as certain aspects of the school problem outgrew the machinery of local government, so have the modern problems of road building and maintenance outgrown it. Minor areas are utterly incapable of meeting the demands of present times. Even counties are not large enough and wealthy enough to be intrusted with the more important highway problems. They, as well as smaller units, must be deprived of some of their prerogatives in connection with the highways, for the needs of the state cannot be denied on account of the provincial backwardness of local authorities and the poverty of rural districts.

Classification of Highways.—These considerations suggest the possibility of roughly classifying all the roads and highways. It can be done, although it is not consciously done in very many of the states.

1. Country Roads.—In the first place there are the least important roads,—country crossroads leading from farm to farm, and to the little villages, the country schools, and railroad stations. These are country roads in the best sense of the term. In common parlance no distinction is made between the words "road" and "highway," and indeed there is no very important distinction to be made. But it may be said in general that "highways" are always public "roads." The highway is owned by the government, the government has complete control over it, and it is maintained at public expense. With "roads" this is not always the case. "Roads" may be privately owned and maintained, "highways" never. In rural districts there may be a good many miles of much frequented, well-kept road that is not highway. Nevertheless we are not dealing in these pages with such private roads, but only with roads which are indeed highways.

Yet in deference to common usage it is quite permissible to speak of the least important country "highways" as country "roads."

These roads are not subjected to heavy traffic or to constant use. It is not necessary that they be permanently improved but merely kept in reasonably good and passable condition. These are the roads that are of primary interest to the people of the rural districts themselves. It is entirely proper that they should have control over them through the machinery of local government.

2. Highways Connecting Cities.—Another class of roads is composed of those that connect all the cities of a state. The condition of these highways is a matter of great concern to the urban population of a state as well as to the rural groups. These highways are necessary to the development of trade and social intercourse, which, in turn, is essential to national progress. Such important highways ought not to be left to the control of authorities in areas smaller than the counties.

3. Cross-State Highways.—Still more important highways are those running clear across the state, connecting the largest cities and facilitating interstate communication. These are few in number, but they are of primary concern to the people of the whole state and should be controlled largely by state authorities.

4. National Arteries.—Yet another class of highways includes those great national arteries which exist in contemplation rather than in actual fact. The federal government might well assume a certain measure of control over them.

As said above, this more or less artificial classification of roads and highways is not always consciously recognized in highway legislation. But in actual practice it is at least tacitly recognized in a majority of cases. Country crossroads are invariably left to the care of township or county-district authorities. More and more those highways which connect the cities are taken over by the counties in the states where townships have had control in the past. In so far as state governments assume any responsibility whatever they are devoting attention to just a few cross-state highways connecting the great cities. And the federal government is concerned with only a few great national arteries. This division of function tacitly recognizes the fourfold classification here suggested. The problems in connection with each class will be touched upon and particular attention given to the position of the counties.

Maintenance of Country Roads.—The elementary tasks that arise in connection with road building, such as the blazing of trails through the woods and wilderness, no longer present themselves in very many cases; yet there are plenty of rough, unfrequented, and partially overgrown roads that suggest the difficulties of early days. These, and the country crossroads connecting farm, school, and country store, are maintained by township or county district authorities. These roads can be cared for without expensive machinery and materials, without skilled engineers and armies of laborers. The local supervisor or other road official, working with his neighbors or with the help of a few laborers, can do all that needs to be done. This means frequent scraping and dragging with rude farm machinery, the erection of rough bridges across small streams, the clearing away of obstructions, fallen trees and underbrush, and the digging of drainage ditches to prevent washouts. The expense of this work is met in the local budget, the township or district officers determining a tax rate for the purpose.

The time has been when all roads were virtually in this

class and were cared for in just this manner. Even to-day they are likely to constitute from fifty to one hundred percent of road mileage in any given state. These roads are the residuum, those that are left after the more important ones have been selected for better treatment, and brought under the control of authorities superior to the local officers.

Care of the Highways Connecting Cities.—Public opinion is demanding that the highways directly connecting the cities and most important urban settlements be taken out of this residuum of country roads. It is demanded that the highways connecting urban populations be permanently improved in such a way that they will remain passable during ordinarily bad weather and constant usage. This demand becomes the more insistent in the light of certain considerations. (1) Expanding population makes it more necessary to have good means of intercourse in order to maintain business and social relations. Old facilities are no longer adequate. (2) The discovery and invention of new materials in recent years makes it a much easier matter to build good roads than it used to be. (3) The engineering problems involved in bridging streams, cutting through steep hills, and blasting rock, are more easily solved than they used to be. (4) The impetus given to the good roads movement by the rapid development of the automobile need only be mentioned to be fully appreciated.

The character of the permanent improvement demanded, as distinguished from the rough care given to the country roads, may involve anything from merely covering them with gravel, crushed stone, or other like materials, to paving them with brick, cement, or even something more expensive. Making of these improvements involves the determination of policy, the purchase of expensive machinery and vast quantities of material, the letting of great contracts to specialists in road construction and engineering firms, and the employment of a great many men.

This work is done through counties ordinarily. County boards select those roads which they choose to subject to permanent improvement and then undertake full control of them. These roads are then looked upon as a system of county highways as distinguished from the residuum of unimproved country roads. They may constitute anywhere from one to fifty percent of the road mileage in a given state.

Road building is rapidly coming to be one of the most important activities carried on through county government. It involves the expenditure of greater sums of money and the letting of larger contracts than any other undertakings ordinarily assumed by counties. County board members often spend a large proportion of their time personally inspecting and supervising road work. Old-time county road officers, popularly elected, have virtually disappeared and county boards now employ surveyors and engineers to do the work which they cannot do themselves.

Methods of Doing Road Work.—In general there are two principal methods of procedure by which a county may undertake to improve its system of highways. The first method is to purchase all the necessary machinery, equipment, and material, employ a county engineer, and permit the work to be done under his supervision directly. This means the investment of a considerable amount of money in machinery and equipment, and the employment of many laborers. The other method is to enter contracts with construction companies for the improvement of certain sections of the highway. The county engineer then functions as an adviser to the board, and as an inspector. He also is responsible for the maintenance of the highways after construction work has been completed. Both methods are used quite generally, the second apparently being the favorite.

It must be said that the ambitions of county officials and the desires of the public are likely far to outstrip their ability and willingness to pay. Legal limitations upon the tax rates, and clamors of the taxpayers, prevent the development of good roads in keeping with the demand of the times. Populations of great cities demand improved highways stretching across many intervening counties. The cities are impatient of delay, and yet some of the intervening counties may be quite unable to finance the building of the sort of highway that is wanted.

"State-Aid" Roads.—This situation has led to the practice of "state-aid" in road building. Many states have created state highway commissions and the commissioners do much toward aiding local authorities. Actual financial aid is given in many cases. State highway officials will indicate a certain few of the most important cross-state highways which ought in their opinion to be paved. The counties are then informed that if they will proceed with the improvement along the lines dictated by the state officials the state itself will contribute substantially toward the expense.

These highways often become known as "state-aid" roads. The practice has given considerable impetus to road building, for counties are usually eager to take advantage of these contributions. Thus "state-aid" roads are becoming more numerous every year. In some cases they are taken entirely out from under the control of local officers and thus become in every sense of the word state highways.

The National Highways.—Still another type of highway has been mentioned—great national arteries that exist in contemplation rather than in actual fact. The Lincoln Highway, the Yellowstone Trail, and the Dixie Highway, are some that have already been marked across the continent, at least upon a map. Statesmen have in mind a great system of national highways which may materialize sometime in the future. It is to be supposed that they would be under the control of federal authorities, or that substantial federal aid would be given to those states which would improve that portion of the national highway lying within their boundaries. Indeed Congress already has appropriated very large sums of money as "aid" to road building, and federal agents conduct inspections and exert a considerable measure of control over the work that is done with federal aid.

But for the present there are no true national highways. Those that have been blazed across the continent have been improved by state and local authorities to a certain extent, in some cases with federal aid and sometimes without. In those states which maintain state highways or practice state aid, the projected national highway is likely to become part of the state system. In other states the counties alone are responsible for the maintenance of that portion of the proposed national highway which lies within their boundaries. And in certain backward communities the national highway must necessarily degenerate into nothing more than an ordinary country road—scraped, dragged, drained, or neglected by officials of the smallest areas.

CHAPTER XV

REFORM OF COUNTY GOVERNMENT

There has been presented here a picture of typical county government in the United States. The exact situation in no one state has been described. And it has been observed that variations are numerous, particularly as regards the less important aspects. However, it has been possible to discuss in some detail those governmental activities usually carried on through areas of local government, the character of the political machinery and organization through which the functions are exercised, and to a certain extent the methods that ordinarily are pursued. It was noted too that many factors contributed to a determination in each state as to what the functions of local government should be, the character of the governmental machinery, and even the methods that should be followed. Now it is desirable to turn to the problem of reform of county government as a whole and see what factors must be dealt with in this connection.

Changes in Function.—In the first place it must be emphasized that the present situation has developed gradually and without conscious direction. New functions have been bestowed upon areas of local government from time to time as it became necessary for the government to do new things, and certain functions have been taken away. But more particularly the functions themselves have taken on a new complexion as years passed by. The function of maintaining peace is not what it used to be, nor is the function of poor relief. Road building and education are no longer the simple problems that they used to be. These functions have altered very slowly either as a result of deliberate legislative action or as a result of social forces. At any rate, functions have changed, and the machinery of local government has not been changed to keep pace with the changes in function. Here lies one of the problems of reform.

Changes in Organization.—On the other hand, the machinery of local government has been altered from time to time, but not consistently or in harmony with changing functions. New offices have been created on the spur of the moment without any effort being made to maintain the county organism as a unit. Lines of responsibility and authoritative control have not been made clear, and hence the machinery of county government is disorganized, and the various parts are calculated to work at cross purposes. Here, too, lies a problem of reform.

Changes in Method.—And lastly, changing conditions demand that new methods be pursued in the performance of old functions. The county clerk must have office equipment which fifty years ago was unknown. The treasurer's books and the recorder's records must be kept in better ways than they used to be. County purchasing and budget making, and the assessing of property, are the same old functions that they used to be, but new methods ought to be pursued in exercising them. So here again lies a problem of reform.

Outline of Reform Programme.—A programme of reform in county government can be outlined. It would involve a consideration of:

I. Changes in function.
    (a) The assumption of new functions.
        (1) Either taken over from smaller districts such as the townships (thus, the

county might take full charge of assessments, poor relief, and road building), or
(2) Taken on as new projects altogether (thus, counties are building hospitals and maintaining parks and libraries).
(b) The abandonment of old functions.
(1) To the state (the possibilities have been suggested in connection with the care of defectives, rural education, highways, and maintenance of peace), or
(2) To smaller districts (this rarely occurs and is not to be approved).
II. The reorganization of government machinery.
(a) The abolition of certain officers (coroner, collector, overseer of the poor, highway commissioner).
(b) The creation of new offices (civil service commissions, county manager, hospital superintendent, public defender).
(c) New methods of selecting officers (appointment instead of election).
(d) Establishment of clear lines of responsibility and control (thus making the county clerical officers accountable to the board, making the public prosecutor or school superintendent responsible to state authorities).
III. The adoption of new methods in all phases of county activity.

Public Interest in Reform.—In the light of this outline one is tempted to inquire: (1) What specific suggestions have come from reliable sources as regards reform? (2) Which of these can be harmonized in such a way as to effect a practical reform with a minimum of legal action and without too much uprooting of old institutions and violence to popular prejudice? (3) Just how much has already been accomplished? Suggestions, and answers to these questions are coming from many sources. Such organizations as the National Short Ballot Organization, the National Municipal League, the various political science associations and clubs, and civic bodies everywhere, are turning their attention to the problem.

The Chief Problem: Structure.—The chief problem in this outline, the one that commands immediate attention and presents the most baffling complications, is that of reorganizing the structure of county government. Changes in function are taking place steadily by slow degrees. Functions are slowly passing from the control of townships and minor districts to the control of county authorities, as has been indicated in the body of the text. And the same tendency leads to the relinquishment of certain functions by the county in favor of the state. Improvement in methods also goes on apace. But the great stumbling-block is the reorganization of machinery, particularly the unification of the county organism and the clear delineation of lines of responsibility and control.

Changes in this direction are considered radical by the public generally and often are condemned as undemocratic. They are generally opposed by those who are in office and those who hope to be. Changes in this direction often involve constitutional amendments and the uprooting of old institutions that are deeply imbedded in the political experience of the people. Hence this problem stands out as the most difficult of all. So, while the other points in the outline should not be forgotten, the problem of reforming organization may well be the center of any discussion of reform in county government.

Typical County Structure.—On page 291 will be found

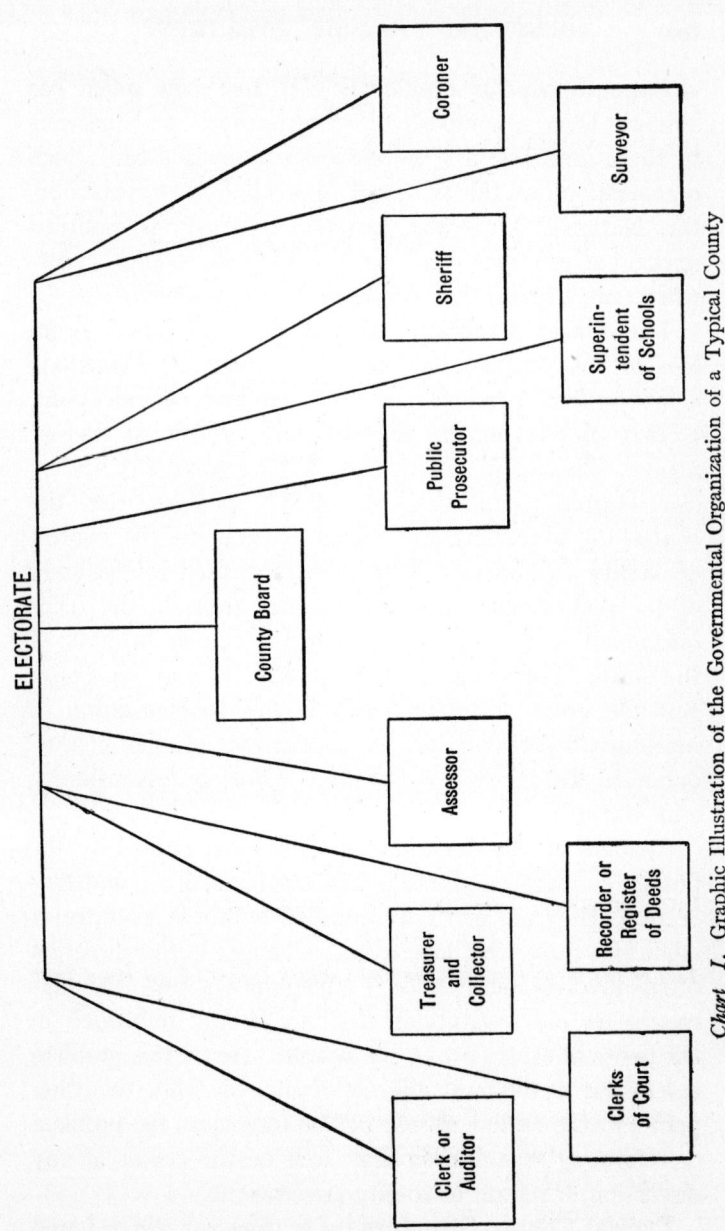

Chart I. Graphic Illustration of the Governmental Organization of a Typical County

Chart I which illustrates graphically the governmental organization of a typical county wherein all of the important officers are popularly elected. It will be observed that lines of responsibility and control run directly to the electorate, leaving the county machinery disunited and not focused around any responsible central authority. The evils of this situation were sufficiently discussed when the various offices were under consideration.

Suggestions for reform of the situation depicted in Chart I vary from those which contemplate the establishment of a county commission with a county manager, to those which merely involve picking out an officer here and there and causing him to be appointed by the board instead of popularly elected.

Enumeration of County Officers.—It will be observed that on Chart I there are not to be found certain of the officers and boards that were discussed at considerable length in the body of the text. They are left out of the graphic illustration simply because they are not to be found in typical counties, or else they exist as distinctly subordinate appointees of other officers. Chart I is intended to picture a thoroughly typical county. But in order that all of the officers which have been discussed in the text may be kept in mind as the discussion of reform proceeds, a compact list is given below:

List of the Principal Boards and County Officers That Have Been Discussed in the Text

County Board
Board of Review
Board of Election Commissioners
Board of Road Commissioners
Board of Health
School Board

Civil Service Commission
Sheriff
Coroner
Public Prosecutor
County Counsel
Public Defender
County Clerk, or Auditor
Recorder
Clerks of Court
Auditor
Treasurer
Collector
Assessor
Superintendent of Schools
Overseer of the Poor
County Physician
Health Officer
Superintendents of Institutions
Highway Commissioner
Surveyor
Engineer

Suggested Reforms Summarized.—A mere glance at this list will bring to mind most of the suggestions for reform that have been made in the text. They are such as could be effected gradually, one at a time indeed; they do not involve any serious invasion of the prerogatives of local government, nor do they involve any novel or strikingly new ideas of government. They merely involve a simplification of the machinery of county government. These suggestions for reform may be summarized and then presented in a graphic illustration.

The County Board.—The county board should consist of from three to seven members, depending upon the population of the county. The members should be popularly elected either at large or from districts, and for a term not less than four years; and they should be paid a fixed salary. This board might be known as the Board of County Commissioners.

The functions of the board should be virtually what they are at present, namely: (1) to determine policies, (2) to exercise supervision over all county activities, (3) to make appointments, (4) to fix the tax rate, (5) to make appropriations or pass a budget, (6) to let contracts, and (7) to pass on claims. These should be the chief functions of the board.

It is to be remembered that certain of the functions ordinarily exercised by a county board are in some cases exercised by special independent boards or commissions, particularly in the more populous counties. But on the whole it is highly desirable to avoid the multiplication of such boards and commissions.

Board of Review.—In this connection it will be recalled that county boards ordinarily serve as boards of review, to equalize assessments. This is a proper function of a county board and thus a special board of review is not needed.

Election Commissioners.—County boards usually have full supervision of elections, though in some states the county judge has certain administrative duties in this connection, and in other states boards of election commissioners have been created which supervise the machinery of elections. But in the ordinary county there is no reason why the entire machinery of elections cannot be put under the direct control of the county board itself.

Highway Commissioners.—With the rapid development of good roads there has been a tendency to create highway departments in the county organization, or to create special boards of road commissioners. However, the regular county board ought to be entirely competent to undertake full supervision of the county highway system.

Boards of Health.—County boards of health are appearing in some states. They are needed, for the regular county boards, composed of laymen, are not altogether competent to determine policies with regard to public health. A board of health need not be large, nor need the members give very much time to their duties. Their salaries could be very low. A county board of health might well consist of three members, two physicians and one layman, appointed by the board of county commissioners, for a period of four years.

The School Board.—It is desirable that the governmental machinery for the management of schools be made more or less independent of the rest of the county organization. Hence, a county school board of from six to a dozen members, serving without pay or for very small compensation, could be selected by the board of county commissioners and have full charge of the county school system.

Civil Service Commission.—If civil service examinations are desirable in connection with appointment to federal, state, and city offices, they are desirable in connection with appointments to county offices. Certain county appointees ought to be exempt, but the clerical officers, the finance officers, the superintendents of institutions, and most of the other county appointees ought to be subjected to civil service examinations. The civil service commission which would administer the examinations could consist of three members. They should be independent of the regular board of county commissioners because the purpose of the civil service merit system would be to restrict the county board itself in the matter of appointments. The civil service commissioners could be popularly elected, either at large or from districts. Their compensation could properly be very small.

The Sheriff.—The sheriff ought to remain an elective officer until such time as he is embraced in a reorganization of state government. And no changes in his functions can profitably be made until such time. His term should be at least four years and he should be paid a fixed salary and no fees.

Coroner.—The coroner's office may be abolished.

Public Prosecutor.—The public prosecutor should remain a popularly elected officer until such time as he is included in the organization of a state department of justice. He should be simply a prosecutor, however, and be relieved of certain functions that would fall to a county counsel.

County Counsel.—A county counsel should be appointed by the board of county commissioners. He should serve as legal adviser to county officers, represent the county and county officers in litigation, and take over any other legal duties now discharged by the public prosecutor but not related strictly to prosecution.

Public Defender.—A public defender, if such an officer is considered necessary, should be selected in the same manner as the public prosecutor, if that officer be under the control of a state department of justice. Otherwise it were better for the defender to be appointed by the board of county commissioners. If such were the case, it is not impossible that the functions of county counsel and defender be combined in one individual. The two functions are not necessarily incompatible in their nature.

Clerical Officers.—As to the clerical officers, the county clerk—in some states known as the county auditor—ought to be appointed by the board of county commissioners. He would then be directly responsible to the board in every sense of the word. His functions would be very largely what they are at present. He would be a secretary and an executive agent for the board, and he could render the board much more valuable assistance than is now possible, particularly in connection with: (1) the exercise of general supervision over all county activities, (2) purchasing supplies, (3) examining claims (4) preparing a budget, and (5) negotiating contracts.

The recorder should be an appointive subordinate in the clerk's office.

All clerks of court should be appointed by the judges of the courts.

Finance Officers.—The finance officers too might very well be appointed. The board of county commissioners should appoint a treasurer whose functions might be the same as they are at present. His office should be surrounded with legal safeguards, however, that would serve to eliminate as far as possible the abuses that might otherwise develop. The treasurer ought to function also as collector.

An assessor should be appointed by the same authority as the treasurer until such time as it is thought proper to bring the function of assessment under state control. The county assessor ought of course to displace the township assessors.

A county auditor is not needed. The function of auditing accounts is much better performed through instrumentalities of the state.

Superintendent of Schools.—The superintendent of schools should be selected by the school board and be directly responsible to it.

Charity and Public Health Officers.—In connection with public health and charities certain special officers are necessary. An overseer of the poor should be appointed by the county board to superintend outdoor relief and to conduct all the investigations concerning charity cases.

Superintendents of various institutions ought also to be appointed by the board. The board of health would have need of an executive officer whom it should appoint. He would be the county physician and health officer, and serve full time or part time as need be.

Highway Officials.—The county board itself should have full charge of highways and should employ an engineer and surveyors as might be necessary.

Essence of Reform: Centralization.—All of these suggestions are brought together and illustrated graphically in Chart II, page 299. This chart thus graphically illustrates a reformed county organization. It will be observed at once that the principal features of the suggested reforms lie in doing away with the popular election of many county officials, in greatly strengthening the position of the county board, and in making it the center of a unified county governmental structure.

This scheme for reorganizing county government is by no means satisfactory to those who have little faith in the administrative ability of county boards. These people are of the opinion that all administrative responsibility should be concentrated in one individual, and they turn to the city manager for inspiration. There are also those who refuse to compromise with the offices of sheriff and public prosecutor and believe that these two should at once be put under the direct control of state authorities. And there are still others who believe that all the present-day functions of local government should be carried on by the state.

It would be impossible to reconcile all of the radical proposals that have been made concerning the reform of county government; but the essential features of the county manager plan may briefly be described.

County Manager Plan.—The plan involves first the

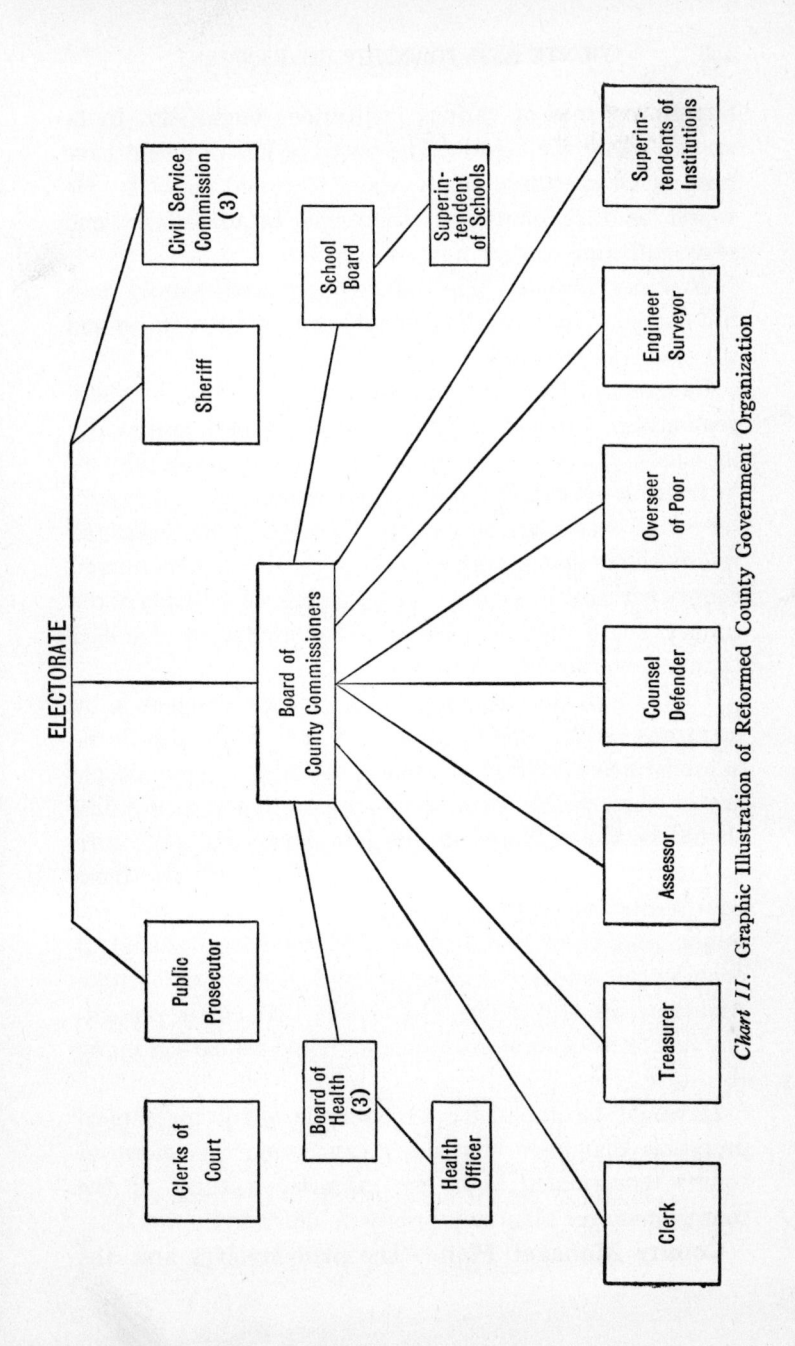

Chart II. Graphic Illustration of Reformed County Government Organization

popular election of a board of from five to nine. The members would be elected for a four-year term and serve for very low pay.

The chief function of the board would be to employ a manager from among those who could pass the civil service examinations for this office or show other evidences of fitness and ability. The remaining functions of the board would be few and simple although of primary importance. The board would: (1) pass ordinances under which county activities could be carried on, thus determining policies; (2) determine the tax rate; (3) make appropriations or pass a budget; (4) pass on claims; (5) authorize contracts as negotiated by the manager; and (6) ratify appointments made by the county manager.

The manager himself would necessarily be a highly paid official and devote full time to his work. He would have direct personal control over all the business and administrative work of the county, recognizing responsibility only to the board. He would appoint all the subordinates necessary to the administration of county affairs, such as the clerical officers, the finance officers, and those concerned with public charities and institutions. He would exercise constant supervision and authoritative control over all of them. In addition he would (1) have personal charge of all public works; (2) negotiate contracts on behalf of the county; (3) serve as purchasing agent for offices and institutions; (4) prepare a tentative budget to lay before the board; and (5) approve or disapprove all claims before they were submitted to the board.

The county manager idea it is believed is particularly adapted to urban counties, although enthusiasts are by no means convinced that it is not suited to universal application.*

* See *Documents on County Government*.

The Commission Plan.—Another radical reform scheme of county government which might or might not include the manager idea, involves an adaptation of the city commission plan to the county.* It involves the classification of county activities into several departments with a departmental head for each. Three departments have been suggested. They are: (1) Public Works, which would include highways and bridges, buildings and parks. (2) Finance, in which department the treasurer, collector and assessor would be found. County purchasing would be done through this department and the budget would be prepared there. (3) Charities, and Public Welfare, which would include public health activities and the control of charitable institutions and poor relief. The departmental heads would be chosen by a board which would exercise the usual policy determining functions. The county clerk, the county counsel, and the superintendent of schools would be outside the departments.

Obviously there are a great many variations and combininations which could be effected. The purpose here is merely to suggest possibilities and to point to the ideas that are being worked out by civic agencies. It should be stated that at present none of these plans is in operation anywhere. The nearest approach to them has been reached in certain of the California counties where city-county combinations have been effected.

Home Rule for Counties.—The movement for reform of county government is bound up with the demand for home rule. Home rule for cities has been practiced with some success for many years and it is urged that there is no reason why home rule for counties would not also be followed by good results.

In order for the counties of a state to enjoy opportunities

* See *National Municipal Review*, August, 1920, p. 504.

for home rule it would be necessary to provide by law for a referendum on the question in any given county whenever a certain number of petitioners might demand it. If a favorable vote resulted from a referendum it would indicate that the people of that county wished to abandon the regular county organization and establish a different form of county government for themselves. A commission could then be selected as provided by law, either appointed or elected. This commission would then devise a scheme of county government which in the opinion of the commission would meet the needs of the county, and submit the plan to a referendum. If the vote were favorable at this referendum, the new government could be established. The proposed scheme would necessarily have to be within whatever limitations may have been fixed by law, such as stipulations that certain officers must be popularly elected.

This is the essence of home rule. It has been suggested particularly for those counties in which are to be found cities of considerable size.

The City-County Problem.—The development of urban centers to such a point that they absorb a large proportion of the area and population of the county in which they happen to be situated gives rise to some special problems of reform in county government. In the case of the larger cities it is apt to occur that: (1) The city becomes larger than the county and even absorbs more than two counties. This is the situation in New York City. (2) The city is virtually coterminous in area with the county. This is the case with Philadelphia, St. Louis, Denver, and several other cities. (3) The city is not as large in area as the county but contains by far the largest proportion of the population and wealth of the county. The most conspicuous illustration of this condition is Chicago.

Whenever any of the situations enumerated above exists, conflicts of jurisdiction, duplication of function, wastefulness, and more or less inefficiency and confusion arise in the effort to exercise county and city functions harmoniously. Indeed the difficulties that arise in such situations begin to appear whenever a city reaches such a size that its population, its wealth, and its governmental activities begin to overshadow the county in which it is located. The difficulties appear in cities far smaller than any that have been named above; but when such cities reach the size of those that have been named the difficulties come to be almost intolerable and demand solution through a system of reorganized county government.

Two Assemblies not Needed.—In such situations the county board and the city council appear as quasi-legislative bodies determining governmental policies, making appropriations, and fixing tax-rates for practically the same area and the same population. There is real need for only one such quasi-legislative body, for even though the law may clearly define the sphere of activity for each body, the functions are essentially similar in their nature and might well be performed by one assembly. Thus the same assembly could very well determine municipal policies and also determine policies with regard to county activities as well—policies that deal with the construction of highways, the extension of poor relief, education, the administration of tax laws, and elections.

Other Duplications.—The exercise of police functions is quite likely to raise difficulties. The county sheriff and city police have the same powers, but their activities are frequently not coördinated. The law officers and the finance officers of each unit are discovered duplicating each other's work; or at least it soon becomes apparent that one staff of law officers or one staff of finance officers could very easily perform all the law and finance functions that must needs be exercised in behalf of both the city and the county. Also the distinctly clerical functions of both areas can very well be performed through a single staff of clerical officers. And obviously such institutions as poorhouses, hospitals, jails, orphan asylums, libraries, and schools do not require the existence of two entirely separate structures of government.

A certain degree of wastefulness is sure to grow out of such duplication. Confusion in the exercise of functions is almost sure to arise; particularly is this true in connection with the administration of tax laws. And it is indeed fortunate if unseemly conflicts do not arise between authorities of the two areas seeking to do the same thing, or to perform functions that bring them into close contact with each other. The citizen furthermore, when he thinks about the matter at all, is quite likely to be much confused as to the jurisdiction of various authorities and to resent the necessity of dealing with two sets of officials on matters that might well be handled by one. The organization of the county is adapted primarily to the needs of a semirural area, and those functions which county officers perform and which must also be performed within city limits, could very readily be transferred to city officers.

Thus it appears from practical considerations as well as theoretical that within large cities there ought to be just one structure of government, just one governmental organization, to perform all the functions ordinarily exercised through the county and the city. There should be just one board, council, or quasi-legislative assembly, one staff of clerical officers, one centralized police department, one staff of law officers and one staff of finance officers. There would then be no such thing as overlapping jurisdiction and conflicts of authority, certain economies could be effected, and the confusion that now exists could largely be done away with.

City-County Consolidation.—Such an arrangement would bring into being a consolidated city-county, for each city subjected to such reform would also be a county. A certain very few such combinations do now exist.* In a somewhat larger number of cases the city and county are coterminous in area.† But even when this is the case it is customary to retain the two separate governmental organizations functioning in the same jurisdiction. On the other hand, there is a very large number of cases where no attempt has been made to improve conditions although it is obvious that a combination of the two areas would be highly desirable.

Problems of territorial adjustment arise in connection with plans to make county and city jurisdictions coterminous when the boundaries of the two areas are not already nearly identical. Thus to take a city of considerable size out of a county as it were, and to make of it a county in itself, is apt to leave the surrounding rural area completely adrift. To leave this rural area organized alone as a county, without including the city, would usually be quite out of the question, for the remaining area is likely not to be sufficiently populous or wealthy to justify its remaining alone as a county, to say nothing of other considerations. And to attach such rural area to neighboring counties might involve the readjustment of county lines to an extent that is not desirable.

These distinctly practical considerations often stand in the way of accomplishing the reform of consolidation, except when the city and county are very nearly coterminous anyway. Of course it is always necessary to secure a special

* See *Documents on County Government*.
† This is the case with the cities in Virginia.

charter for a city in order that it may have a structure of government adequate to the exercise of county functions as well as city functions. Several such charters are in existence to-day and others are in contemplation.*

Whenever such a consolidation is effected the county activities are necessarily submerged in and subordinated to the municipal functions and activities. The problems involved in consolidation do therefore fall quite fittingly within the field of municipal government rather than county government.

* See *Documents on County Government*, particularly CC—"City and County Consolidation for Los Angeles."

CHAPTER XVI

TOWNSHIPS AND COUNTY DISTRICTS

TOWNSHIPS

Similarity in County and Township Functions.—Virtually all of the functions of local government which are exercised through the township have already been discussed in connection with the consideration of county activities in the same field. Such functions as assessment, road building, and poor relief, are cases in point. Whether they be exercised through the county or the township they are exercised in very much the same way in either case, and present similar problems. It is unnecessary, therefore, to consider these functions a second time. Township boards, clerks, treasurers, assessors, collectors, road supervisors, school officials, and poor-masters do exactly the same things that similar officers do for the county. It only remains, then, to consider the general features of township organization.

Townships in the United States.—In turning attention now to township government in the United States it must be remembered that in over half of the states no townships are to be found. Townships are to be found, at least in name, in the following twenty-two states:

Arkansas	Missouri	Ohio
* California	* Montana	Oklahoma
Illinois	Nebraska	Pennsylvania
Indiana	* Nevada	* South Carolina
Iowa	New Jersey	South Dakota
Kansas	New York	Wisconsin
Michigan	* North Carolina	
Minnesota	North Dakota	

In Washington and some of the other western states the law permits the organization of townships but they do not exist. It will be observed that most of the twenty-two states in this list lie in a great central belt extending from New York, New Jersey and Pennsylvania on the Atlantic coast, through to and including Kansas and Nebraska. And it is significant that in the states lying conspicuously outside of this belt the township is nothing but a county district, not possessing the characteristic township organization and functions. This is true of townships in California, Montana, Nevada, North Carolina, and South Carolina. With these five states eliminated there are left just seventeen. In these seventeen states the township is a definitely organized area of local government, with a structure of governmental machinery and more or less important functions to perform. The characteristic features of the township organization, its functions, and the variations in type to be found among these seventeen states must be examined.

Origin of Townships.—In New York, New Jersey and Pennsylvania the township emerged spontaneously in very much the same way that New England towns emerged; and it was expected that these townships would exhibit the same elements of vitality and local jealousy that characterized New England towns. Why this did not happen

* Townships are nothing more than county districts in this state.

has been explained in Chapter III. However the more or less spontaneous origin of townships in these states accounts for their irregular shape and widely varying areas. At the time of their origin they bid fair to become social, economic, and political units growing out of a natural composition of forces. Hence the irregular boundaries.

Elsewhere the township has been for the most part artificial, and the boundaries are usually square, averaging six miles each way. Efforts were made by the national government in 1785 and 1787 * to stimulate a sense of unity and a desire for self-government in these small areas, and the state governments followed up these efforts. For the most part the old congressional townships were accepted and the civil townships were made coterminous with them.† In some states county boards are competent to alter township lines, but sometimes only following a favorable referendum on the question among the people involved.

Machinery of government was created and the inhabitants literally invited and urged to govern themselves through political institutions. But the township was destined never to possess very much vitality. Artificial stimuli have kept the machinery in existence, but the township as a unit of self-government is still declining, and even in those seventeen states where it does exist it is unable to command the vigorous interest of the people.

Closely to be associated with this situation are two outstanding facts that have already been discussed. First— It is the custom for communities to organize as petty muncipalities, thus taking the heart out of what otherwise might be thriving townships, very similar to New Eng-

* See page 56.
† See page 56.

land towns. Second—The county organization is always adequate and ready to take over all the township functions whenever public opinion is ready to have this done. Thus the township is between two forces, both of which are sapping its vitality. Social and economic forces are also at work to the same end.

Municipalities and Townships.—Municipalities, large or small, cities, villages, or boroughs, may or may not be part of the township in which they are found. The practice in the several states is not uniform in this regard. But in either event the municipality is organized for certain municipal functions independently of the township; and in this regard the township is always to be differentiated from the New England town. The township government does not exercise municipal functions, though it does exercise its township functions within the boundaries of a municipality except in those states where municipalities are entirely separate from the townships.

Legal Status of the Township.—In some states townships are incorporated, in others they are not, but usually at least are quasi-corporations enjoying prerogatives, powers and liabilities that accompany such a status. In those states where there is no township meeting or township board but merely a few administrative officers, and where the township is nothing but a county district, it does not possess even the quasi-corporate character.

As regards internal organization even greater and more confusing variations are to be found among townships in different states than were found among counties.

Township Meetings.—A township meeting is provided for and is supposed to be held in New York and New Jersey, the birthplace of the township, and in certain of the North-Central states—Michigan, Illinois, Wisconsin, Minnesota, the two Dakotas, and Nebraska. In the remaining states where townships are found there is no township meeting. The township meeting was intended to be a counterpart of the New England town meeting. The fact that such meetings were provided for by legislation is clear evidence of an intention to do all that could be done to stimulate the development of institutions of local self-government. All citizens who are voters within the township are expected to attend the meetings which assemble annually or semi-annually.

Functions.—The meeting has the full power of the township as a corporate entity, it *is* the township as a corporation. The chief functions of a township meeting are: (1) To determine policies as regards township activities. (2) To make appropriations. (3) To determine the tax rate. (4) To select township officers. In some states the policies which a meeting may determine have become so few and unimportant as to be neglected altogether. But the policies ordinarily determined have to do with poor relief, road building, schools, and drainage projects.

Meetings have degenerated to such an extent, however, that with the exception of a few cases in New York and Wisconsin not more than a mere handful of citizens appear.[*] Many times only the officers attend. They do the business of the meeting and remain in office a great many years. So it has come to be that the township meeting is nothing but the ghost of a one-time democratic institution. It commands no interest, is purely artificial, serves no important purpose, and in the light of present-day social and economic conditions cannot hope to be revived. The meeting is usually an institution that exists in addition to the township machinery such as is found in those states where meetings are not held. In these states everything that might be done at a meeting is done at the polls, where

[*] J. A. Fairlie, *Local Government in Counties, Towns and Villages*, p. 170.

referenda are held on important policies, and officers are elected. Township boards do all the rest.

Township Boards.—In all those states where the township exists as anything more than a mere county district, a township board is to be found. This board is usually called the board of trustees, though sometimes the members are known as supervisors. There are two distinct types of township board. One is the ex-officio board which is composed of the township officers such as supervisor, clerk, treasurer, and justices of the peace sitting together. The other is a board composed of officers elected specifically for this position. This type of board is ordinarily composed of three members. It is found in Indiana, Iowa, Minnesota, Missouri, the Dakotas, Ohio, Pennsylvania, and Wisconsin. In the other states some type of ex-officio board is to be found.

Functions.—The township board exercises the characteristic functions of determining policies, making appropriations, and fixing a tax rate, subject to the limitations of the law. In some states the township board also sits as a board of review to equalize tax assessments. It may serve as a school board, when the township is a school district, and sometimes as a local board of health.

One Principal Officer.—In about half of the states where townships exist there is to be found one outstanding principal officer. If there be a township board he is a member of it, and if the county board is composed of representatives from the townships he is the person who represents his township on the county board. In Illinois, Michigan, and New York he is known as a supervisor, while in Indiana, Kansas, Missouri, and Oklahoma he is the township trustee. In Wisconsin he is the township chairman. He is a very important officer in those townships which do not have a board, for then he alone determines policies concerning roads, drainage projects, and other matters. But in any event, whether he is checked by a township board or not, his is the most important office in the township for usually there is combined in him the functions that elsewhere are performed by separate officers. Thus he may be clerk and treasurer of the township, and possibly the assessor. He is overseer of the poor and road commissioner. And quite frequently he has charge of school matters.

Other Township Officers.—In those townships where there is no such officer as this there are to be found several independently elected officers each having a specific function to perform. There is the township clerk who keeps the records of the board meetings if there is a board. He keeps records, statistics and maps concerning his township, records which show the highways and improvements, the location of schools and other institutions. Indeed he does for the township what the county clerk does for the county, on a very much smaller scale.

The finance officers of a township are a treasurer and an assessor. The details of their work it is unnecessary to examine into, as the subject has been discussed in connection with the county offices.

There is also likely to be found in the townships an overseer of the poor and a road commissioner, if there is not a township trustee or supervisor to perform the functions in this connection.

Purposes of the Township.—This survey of township officers gives a pretty clear hint of the purposes for which the township ordinarily exists. It will be recalled that townships and counties often exist for some identical purposes and that when this is the case the township is permitted to exercise one aspect of the function while counties have control of another. Thus counties have supervision over certain highways, while townships control the rest; townships administer one type of poor relief, counties another. But the township of course never exists for as many purposes as the county and must always share its prerogatives with the larger area.

There are four outstanding purposes for which townships ordinarily exist. They are: poor relief, road building and maintenance, maintenance of drainage systems, and maintenance of schools. Outdoor poor relief is extended through township officers, and township officers are ordinarily competent to commit destitute persons to the county poorhouse. As to the maintenance of roads and bridges township officials usually have charge of the residuum of highways, that is, all that are not taken over by county or state. Improvements are made on these country roads by the township to whatever extent is possible in view of the money that can be raised for the purpose. Usually this means only dragging and scraping, more extensive improvements being carried on by the county. The erection and maintenance of drainage systems is a very important activity of township officers in some sections, and is often done in connection with road work. Swamp lands are drained, the courses of streams are changed, culverts put in and ditches cut to protect the roadbeds. And as to school matters they are not always vested in the care of the regular township officers but rather in the hands of special school district officials.

Other purposes for which townships exist are: the assessment of property for the purposes of taxation, the administration of the election machinery—townships often being precincts—and the administration of state health and sanitation laws.

Justices of the Peace.—Finally there are always to be found in the township one or more justices of the peace and several constables. Thus the township is an area for the administration of justice. Justices of the peace have a long history running back into early England. They have always presided over courts of petty jurisdiction. To-day they are found universally in the United States even where the township does not exist. Usually a justice of the peace is elected for a short term and is not required to possess any special qualifications for his office. His court has jurisdiction over civil and criminal cases and he usually is permitted to try cases arising anywhere in the county, even though he be elected by the people of a single township.

Civil Jurisdiction.—Civil jurisdiction is usually limited by the sum of money involved, as two or three hundred dollars, and justice courts do not usually have jurisdiction in cases involving title to land. Hence they are largely concerned with petty damage cases, controversies arising out of wage disputes, collections, and controversies involving wage earners and small tradesmen.

Justice courts are not usually courts of record and proceedings are often more or less informal, not to say irregular. Justices are quite apt to be ignorant of the law and not infrequently they descend to absurd and undignified bickerings with attorneys and litigants. Indeed the average justice of the peace cuts a rather sorry figure before a competent lawyer, and justice of the peace courts have been objects of jest and ridicule since the days of Shakespeare.

Appeal.—Cases may be appealed to the state district or county court unless the sum involved is very low. But it is ordinarily unprofitable for litigants to pursue their petty cases further than the justice court and hence, unsatisfactory as they are, the justice courts do finally dispose of a great mass of minor cases. These petty courts are one of the sore spots in the American system of judicial administration. Bar associations and students of the problem are at work constantly, seeking to improve conditions either by abolishing the justice courts or in some way eradicating the grosser abuses.

Criminal Jurisdiction.—As regards criminal jurisdiction the justice of the peace is empowered to try cases in which the punishment that may be inflicted does not exceed a certain minimum fine or a short term in the local jail. Trials are conducted with or without a jury, depending upon the desires of the defendant.

Cases of too serious a nature to permit of their being heard by a justice of the peace are held over to the higher courts. The alleged criminal is brought before the justice of the peace and bound over to the grand jury, the justice court proceeding being conducted merely for the purpose of inquiring as to whether the accused is legally held or not. Justices of the peace issue warrants for the arrest of criminals and thus are important factor in the whole machinery of justice.

Other Functions.—There are certain other functions performed by justices of the peace. They perform the marriage ceremony, they administer oaths and take acknowledgments; and oftentimes these are the only duties they care to perform as justices. They receive fees for the various services they perform, and many of them have no desire to conduct trials. This is particularly true in urban centers that remain part of the township in which they are located.

It has already been noted that justices of the peace may sit on township boards, and in a few states they still are members of the county board.

Constables.—For each justice court there is a constable. Hence there may be one or several constables in a township. The constable is popularly elected and is paid chiefly with fees. He is a general peace officer, but although he is not literally a subordinate of the county sheriff the constable is usually very willing to relinquish his responsibilities as a peace officer to the sheriff of his county and devote his own time and attention to acting as an executive officer for a justice court. It may be said however that the advent of the automobile has served to bring many rural constables out of their obscurity and to afford them an opportunity to arrest speeders as general peace officers. But for the most part the constable is concerned with executing the orders of the justice court to which he is attached, serving papers, bringing in witnesses, and being present at the justice court proceedings. There was a time when constables were responsible for the care of prisoners, but to-day prisoners are held in county jails under the authority of the sheriff. Even so the constable is responsible for his prisoners until he has turned them over to the sheriff.

Even though justices of the peace and constables are very important officers in the structure of township government they are not to be identified with the township organism any more than are the sheriff and the public prosecutor to be identified with the county organism.* The justice and the constable are quite apart from the business affairs of the township,—poor relief, schools, and highways,—unless indeed the justices are members of the township board. And the fact should be appreciated that justices and constables exist whether townships do or not.

Township Unnecessary.—On the whole the township has ceased to be a necessary institution of government. It serves no important purpose that cannot be more con-

* See page 165.

veniently and effectively served through other agencies. The mere fact that no townships are to be found in more than half of the states is eloquent proof of this. The four purposes which were emphasized as the most important ones for which townships exist do not necessarily demand the existence of townships. Poor relief, highways, drainage, and education are all matters that could be handled to better advantage through county machinery. Assessment of property, administration of elections, and enforcement of health regulations also do not require any machinery besides that afforded by the county. It will therefore be profitable to turn for a moment to those states which have no townships and see how these functions are exercised there.

COUNTY DISTRICTS

Distinction between Township and County District. —It has been the practice in these states, which include most of those in the South and West, to divide the counties into special districts through which may be exercised the functions that elsewhere are performed through instrumentalities of the township. These districts differ very distinctly from townships, however, in that they ordinarily do not possess any of the governmental machinery and powers that go with real local self-government. That is, they do not have political machinery through which policies can be determined, tax rates imposed, appropriations made, and governmental activities carried on more or less independently of other areas of government. Power to do such things is the essence of local self-government and ordinarily is possessed, to a certain extent at least, by townships. County districts do not have these prerogatives, and in the few cases where townships do not have them then the township is in effect nothing but a county district masquerading as a township.

One clear exception should be made to this statement concerning county districts. The school districts may be considered one kind of county district, and the school district does possess some of the prerogatives of local self-government in that through machinery of its own, policies can be determined, tax rates imposed, appropriations made, and business carried on. Other county districts, except in rare cases, cannot do these things.

Another point of difference between the county district and the township is that a considerable number of activities are carried on through the township while a county district ordinarily exists for only one, or possibly two purposes. Thus, through the township such activities as have to do with poor relief, highway construction, and assessment of property are carried on; while through county districts, such as road districts, drainage districts, and election districts, merely the one function indicated by the name is exercised. These districts may overlap each other and thus be in no sense coterminous.

Types of District.—Thus, also, in those states where there are no townships several different kinds of county districts are likely to be found. Of chief importance are the school districts which already have been discussed. There are also supervisor and commissioner districts. These are districts from which members of the county board are elected. The supervisor or commissioner may have special functions within his district, serving as overseer of the poor or road commissioner. In some states there are magisterial districts in which members of the county board may be elected, as in Virginia; and they may be used for other purposes as well, serving as areas through which property may be assessed, the poor relieved, and highways maintained. In other cases magisterial districts are merely areas in which justices of the peace and constables are elected and exercise their functions. Sometimes such districts are called justice's precincts.

Other types of county districts are assessment districts, election districts, poor districts, road districts, drainage districts, irrigation districts, sanitary districts, park districts, and forest preserve districts. Of course not all of these districts are to be found in any one county, but in some of the more populous counties most of them can be found, and sometimes they exist even in addition to the townships. Sometimes a few of them are coterminous, more often they are not. For the most part these districts are created by the county boards, sometimes following upon a referendum among the people concerned.

District Officers.—The officers functioning within these districts may be appointed by the county board, or in rare instances by state authorities; or, as is more frequently the case, they are popularly elected. Thus a county may be divided into assessment districts and an assessor is elected or appointed to function in each district. Counties must always be divided into election districts, precincts, or wards, for the purpose of conducting elections. Sometimes townships are precincts, but more often it is necessary to make the precincts smaller, for a precinct is an area accommodated by one polling place and necessarily its size is limited, and determined to a certain extent by the density of population. Election officials are either ex-officio township officers or are specially appointed by county authorities such as the clerk, the judge, the election commissioners, or the county board.

Poor districts are merely areas in which a poor-relief officer functions, either independently, as when he himself is a member of the county board, or, more rarely, he is appointed by and responsible to the board. Road and drainage districts are but little different from poor districts except in that officials functioning within them must either exercise considerable discretion and determine policies themselves or merely act in accordance with the policies determined by the county board. The latter is more likely to be the case, though in some states road commissioners are popularly elected and are quite independent of higher authorities. Tax rates are fixed by state law ordinarily.

Special Problems.—Irrigation, sanitary, and park and forest preserve districts are exceedingly rare; but their presence calls attention to a governmental problem that is not always easy to solve. Oftentimes it is desirable to carry out a project covering an irregular area that overlaps several jurisdictions. Thus drainage or irrigating projects must often embrace several townships and even cross county lines to be successful. In such cases it is almost necessary to create a special district embracing exactly the area involved and to provide for appointed or elected officials to carry out the one project within their district. This practice of creating special districts has developed very rapidly indeed in recent years.

The necessity for having a great many special districts may well be doubted. The tendency to create them for each new purpose that appears indicates a desire on the part of legislatures to compromise with the still vigorous popular demand for a measure of local self-government. If it were not for this demand many of the districts could be combined or abolished and all of the officers functioning in the districts that did remain could be appointed by the county board. The board itself could determine all policies, fix tax rates, and make appropriations. These districts would then be pure administrative districts such as were described in the first chapter of this volume. But public opinion is very slow to countenance this, and hence appears a compromise in the shape of a special district. These special districts, created in the spirit of compromise, grow directly out of the popular desire for local self-government, and a firm belief in administrative decentralization.

This particular type of compromise cannot endure. The evils that grow out of it are too numerous. And when public opinion comes to a realization of the fact that this sort of a compromise does not preserve the real essence of democracy it will give way in favor of a better type of governmental organization. A much more suitable sort of compromise between, or combination of, self-government and centralized administration, would involve the concentration of administrative authority in the county board. Local self-government could then be exercised to a full enough extent through the county.

CHAPTER XVII

SMALL MUNICIPALITIES

Classification of Small Municipalities.—As already has been pointed out the phrase "local government" has no very exact meaning.* Relatively speaking the government of one of the states in the American Union could be considered "local" government; and the government of cities is "local" government just as truly as is the government of counties. But simply by common consent the practice has developed of including within the phrase "local government" all areas of government which are subordinate to the state, with the exception of the cities. The result has been that small governmental areas such as villages, boroughs, and towns, have generally been classed with counties and townships for purposes of discussion. Nearly all writings that have dealt with city government have ignored the villages, boroughs, and towns—tacitly assuming that such small areas fall within the field of "local government." And writers in this field, few as they have been, have accepted the classification and have dealt with these small areas along with counties and with townships.

The Census Bureau.—The Federal Bureau of the Census also has adopted this classification and in its grouping of governmental areas has placed all districts embracing less than two thousand five hundred people in a class entitled rural, thus differentiating them from cities, and lending color to the very general assumption that in most essen-

* See p.1.

tial characteristics they are more closely related to rural areas such as townships, than to cities.

Villages, Boroughs, and Towns Are Like Small Cities.— These considerations seem to require at least a brief treatment of villages, boroughs, and towns in this volume. It should be clearly understood at the outset, however, that in spite of precedents to the contrary, these small areas of government are more properly classed with cities, than with counties or with townships. In three vitally essential particulars is this true:

In the first place the village, borough, or town is like a city in the matter of legal status. This, it will be remembered, would mean that one of these small areas would be created at the behest of the people who are to reside within its proposed boundaries, rather than at the desire of state authorities. Counties and townships, on the other hand, are created at the desire of state authorities, although local referenda may be required in connection with changing boundaries, and some other matters. Furthermore, as regards legal status, the village, borough, or town, is created primarily for the exercise of what are known as municipal functions. These may be exercised on a very small scale to be sure, but they are exactly the same kind of functions that are exercised by cities. And finally, the village, borough, or town, like the city, is very seldom used as an instrumentality of the state government. This is so because as a general thing the state either exercises its functions directly through agents responsible to state authorities, or else it makes use of counties, townships and administrative districts for the purposes in hand. Hence, as regards legal status the village, borough, and town are to be looked upon merely as small municipalities.

In the second place the village, borough, or town is like a city in the matter of governmental structure and organization. The most significant facts about the organization of counties and townships are: the complete lack of a chief executive; the combination of executive, administrative, and legislative functions in the same organ of government; and the general lack of unity of the governmental structure. The city, on the other hand, is always possessed of a chief executive, in the person of the mayor; executive and administrative functions are separate from legislative functions and the latter are exercised by a clearly defined legislative body, usually known as a council; and the whole governmental structure exhibits a considerable measure of unity, with a chief executive at the head. In all these respects the village, borough, and town very closely resemble the city, and may be looked upon merely as small municipalities.

In the third place the village, borough, or town is like a city as regards the functions which it performs. These small areas are concerned with such matters as: policing, and the enforcement of local ordinances; the enactment of local ordinances that determine rights, obligations, and conduct in civil and social relationships; fire protection, the maintenance of such public services as water supply, light, waste disposal and sewerage; paving and care of streets; the preservation of public health and safety; and the maintenance of parks, libraries, and playgrounds. These are municipal functions and are obviously to be differentiated from those functions which are ordinarily exercised through counties and townships. They are functions which it becomes necessary to exercise chiefly when relatively large numbers of people live together in a relatively compact community. In a word, these functions grow out of the mere physical situation created by comparatively dense population. Other functions, those exercised through counties and townships, are but slightly affected by the factor of population. And since the village, borough, and town exercise these municipal functions, they may be looked upon merely as small municipalities.

How They Differ From Cities.—But while they are in truth but small municipalities they differ from cities in a few respects—though chiefly in degree. For instance, their population is smaller, for the law usually provides that when population reaches a certain point the community may become a city, and usually the residents are eager to take advantage of this opportunity. Again, the governmental structure of the village, borough, or town, while similar to, is not so extensive as that of the city. The city usually possesses a larger council, and has more officers. And thirdly, the city is intrusted with greater powers than the smaller area, it can do more things, it can raise larger sums of money, and has greater freedom in the exercise of its municipal functions.

Emergence of Small Municipalities.—The circumstances that lead usually to the creation of a village, borough, or town may readily be imagined. Population gradually precipitates at a certain spot. A variety of forces induce people to build their habitations close together, and presently a rather small area comes to be thickly populated. This simple physical fact requires new activities on the part of government. Of course it is impossible to say just exactly when the new activities must be undertaken. Sometimes a rather thickly populated community will get along for years without enjoying the benefits that come from the exercise of municipal functions by the local government; and again, very small groups of people are sometimes organized for municipal purposes even before it really becomes necessary. However, the laws of the respective states must determine just when municipal organization may be effected, and what the procedure shall be.

The Practice in New England.—The laws of the various states on this question are by no means uniform. Nor is it possible to group the states into geographical classes as regards their law upon this point. The New England states exhibit the greatest uniformity. In these states, as already has been pointed out, the town government undertakes municipal functions when it becomes necessary, and thus the town in New England is a combined township and small municipality. Township functions are exercised for the entire area, and municipal functions are exercised for the thickly populated center by exactly the same governmental organization. The town government continues to exercise these combined rural and municipal functions until such time as the population in the urban center becomes so dense that a city may be created. But such is the conservatism of New Englanders that population in a small area may reach as high as twenty thousand before town government is abandoned.

The practice in New England very clearly illustrates the problem of classifying areas of "local" government. The Census Bureau explains the situation as follows: "The Census Bureau classifies as urban population that residing in cities and other incorporated places having two thousand five hundred inhabitants or more, and in towns of that size in Massachusetts, New Hampshire, and Rhode Island. In most sections of the country all or practically all densely populated areas having two thousand five hundred inhabitants or more are incorporated separately as municipalities, variously known as cities, towns, villages, boroughs, etc. In the three New England states just named, however, this is not the case.

" In Massachusetts and Rhode Island it is not the practice—as it is in practically all the other states—to incorporate, as separate municipalities, the relatively densely populated portions of 'towns' (which are the primary divisions of the counties), and no town as a whole is incorporated as a municipality until it attains a population greatly in excess of two thousand five hundred. In New Hampshire a similar condition exists, although there are in the state two incorporated villages, each of which has fewer than two thousand five hundred inhabitants. For this reason those towns having two thousand five hundred or more inhabitants in the three states named are treated as urban, although portions of their area are rural in character. The urban areas in the three states in question, as classified by the census, thus contain a certain number of inhabitants who in other sections of the country would be segregated as rural. Nevertheless, in most of the Massachusetts, New Hampshire, and Rhode Island towns having two thousand five hundred inhabitants or more by far the greater part of the population resides within the more densely settled areas, so that the proportion classed as urban, considering each state as a whole, is not greatly exaggerated by the practice adopted. . . .

"Urban population being thus defined, the remainder of the county is classed as rural, consisting of all unincorporated territory, and all incorporated places having fewer than two thousand five hundred inhabitants, except in Massachusetts, New Hampshire, and Rhode Island, where it consists of all towns under two thousand five hundred." *

In the other three New England states, Maine, Vermont, and Connecticut, the practice of creating small municipalities has made greater inroads upon the town system. Thus in spite of the existence of the typical New England town, villages are to be found in Maine

* Fourteenth Census of the United States (1920), Vol. I, p. 43.

and Vermont; and boroughs are to be found in Connecticut.

Outside New England.—Outside of New England, on the other hand, very small groups of people are permitted to organize small municipalities known variously as villages, boroughs, and towns. These words have no distinctive significance and are used in various connections that lend some confusion to a consideration of the areas to which they are applied. The popular use of the word town has been discussed.* The word village is used to designate a group of habitations which may or may not actually constitute a small municipality. The word borough is borrowed directly from England where it has been applied to small municipalities and parliamentary constituencies. It is not widely used in the United States.

Legal Significance.—But in spite of the careless popular use of these terms, each of them, in one state or another, does have a very distinct legal meaning, and is applied to the smallest of municipal corporations. These small municipal corporations are essentially similar, and hence the various names applied to them do not indicate any important differences for purposes of this discussion.

Sometimes none of these three terms are used and the small municipality is known merely as a city of the lowest class. When this is the case the terms village or town have no legal significance. Thus municipalities of the lowest class in Pennsylvania are known as boroughs, in New York they are villages, in Iowa they are towns, and in Kansas they are cities.

Provisions of State Law.—These small municipal corporations are provided for in the statutes subject to whatever constitutional limitations may apply. The statutes

* See p. 25.

are likely to provide that a municipality shall be organized only when the people who are to be within it express their desire for such an organization. This desire is usually expressed through a petition signed by a certain number of inhabitants and submitted to the proper authority. The only other requirements that usually apply have to do with area and population. Thus it might be provided in the law that a village, borough, or town may be created in case a certain minimum population is to be found within a certain maximum area. These limits are usually very liberal. Thus it may be that if one or two hundred people live within one or two square miles, they may organize a small municipality. In some states indeed, no limits at all are set.

Procedure for Incorporation.—The procedure is simple. Persons who are interested secure a sufficient number of signatures to a petition requesting that a village, borough, or town be organized. This petition is then submitted either to the local court of general jurisdiction, or to the county board, or possibly to the township trustees. The authorities to whom the petition has been submitted then proceed to order an election to be held for the purpose of giving the residents an opportunity to vote on the question.* If the result of this referendum is favorable, another election is immediately held for the purpose of selecting officers to function for the new unit of government.

The officers which shall be chosen are provided for in a law of general application, in most of the states. It formerly was the custom to create these small municipalities by special acts of the legislature,—in which the organization, powers and functions of the village, borough, or town would be prescribed. This was also the practice

* In a very few states this referendum is not held.

with regard to cities. But such great abuses grew up in this connection that at the present time state constitutions very generally forbid the legislature to create such public corporations by special acts. The general act,—one which shall apply to all cases of a similar nature—determines the procedure for creating the small municipality; it determines the officers and institutions which the municipality may possess, and it also defines its powers, functions, and obligations. This means that all the small municipalities will be alike in these particulars.

Internal Organization of a Small Municipality.—The organization provided for is essentially the same in all the states. A chief executive is the principal officer and his title is likely to be "president" if the new area be a village, and "mayor" if it be a town. This officer is popularly elected. There is also provided a council of some sort. The council is composed of from three to seven, or even nine members popularly elected at large. This assembly may be called the council or the board of trustees. Other officers are: a clerk and a treasurer. It is the custom to elect these officers. Certain other officers may be appointed by the chief executive. There is likely to be some officer concerned with streets, such as a street commissioner, there may also be an attorney or solicitor, and there is also a chief police officer often called the town or village marshal.

In case the newly created small municipality is to exercise township or county district functions as well as the new municipal functions, then it is necessary to have more officers to exercise them. Thus an assessor, justices of the peace, and constables may be elected, and they carry on the usual township functions within the municipality, although they are officers of the latter area. In many of the states, however, the county, township or county district officers carry on their functions within the small municipalities as well as in the rural areas.

Its Corporate Character.—As soon as all the officers have been selected and have assumed their duties the village, borough, or town comes into existence as a municipal corporation of the lowest class. And as a public corporation of this character it possesses all the qualities and the legal status discussed elsewhere in this volume as appertaining to such corporations.* It can sue and be sued, it can buy and sell property, it can enter into contracts, and it can employ and discharge employees,— all in the furtherance of its governmental functions.

Reorganization as Cities.—Provision is made in the law whereby these small municipalities may finally become cities. In a few states, such as Kansas, as already has been pointed out, small municipalities are known simply as cities of the lowest class and the terms village, borough, and town are not used. But ordinarily the term city is not applied until the population has reached a higher point.

Municipal corporations may be classified on the basis of population. Thus, for instance, all municipal corporations wherein the population is less than two thousand may be called towns, or villages, and possess a certain type of organization. When the population exceeds two thousand and has not attained to fifteen thousand the town or village may become a city of the second class and be reorganized. When the population exceeds fifteen thousand the city of the second class may be reorganized again and become a city of the first class. At each step the structure becomes larger, more councilmen appear, they are chosen by wards instead of at large, more officers are provided for, and the city is given a larger measure

* See p.89.

of power and a broader scope for its activities. Municipalities do not pass automatically from one class to another as soon as population reaches the necessary point. A petition must be circulated and the inhabitants must seek reorganization on their own initiative. Frequently this is not done until long after population is great enough to justify it.

Functions of the Small Municipality.—But so long as a small municipality remains in the lowest class it must be content with very meager municipal functions. The council is empowered to pass some ordinances regulating the life of the community, and to take steps for the purpose of promoting safety and public health. Petty police regulations are enacted—traffic regulations, ordinances concerning the suppression of nuisances, and other such matters. These are all enforced by the police officer and his aides who are directly responsible to the president or mayor. Indeed that official himself has the full powers of a peace officer.

Duties of Council.—The council is furthermore charged with the responsibility of determining policies. In a few states town or village meetings are held, in imitation of the New England town meeting. But this is not usual, and so the council becomes the policy-determining organ of the government. The municipality is organized for the purpose of engaging in the activities demanded by the increased population, and it is for the council to determine just what shall be done. Thus the council may decide to pave a street and to lay some sidewalks. It may decide to build a pumping station and to provide some kind of water supply for the townspeople. And when the town becomes sufficiently populous the council may decide to construct a sewer system and waste disposal plant. A fire department may be organized on a small scale, a chief is appointed, equipment is purchased, and firemen are employed either on part time, full time, or merely subject to call.

As the town grows and public opinion demands better things, gas or electric light service may be provided for by the council. Sometimes the municipality engages in the undertaking directly, other times private companies are granted franchises subject to the terms of the law. Service of this sort always is afforded in cities of any consequence, and people in the rural districts are impatient for the same conveniences. Following close upon the heels of such services comes the telephone, if it has not gone before. Large companies in neighboring cities can usually extend this service, and the authorities in the small municipality are seldom burdened with much responsibility in the matter.

The council will decide upon the feasibility of providing libraries, parks and playgrounds. It can be done in a very modest, inexpensive way, and yet this is just the sort of thing for which people seek incorporation into small municipalities. A single room with a few score volumes presided over by a woman for a few hours each day is in striking contrast to our vast metropolitan libraries. Yet in its essence the service is the same. A vacant lot provided by the town council, where the local band can render weekly concerts, and where the local ball team can meet its rivals, is a far cry from New York's Grand Central Park; and yet great things must spring from small beginnings.

Embarking upon these undertakings, inconsequential though they may seem to be, marks the transition from distinctly rural government to municipal government. Township organization is not suited to the performance of such municipal functions, and hence appears the irresistible tendency to create the small municipalities, which everywhere are taking the very heart out of the townships.

Fixing Tax Rates.—Naturally these undertakings require a much larger expenditure of money than would be necessary without them. The town council makes all the appropriations for these various services and is intrusted with the important responsibility of fixing a tax rate. In this matter the council is usually confined by very strict limits imposed by the legislature. The council may not be permitted to go into debt beyond a certain sum. It may not be permitted to impose a tax rate that is larger than a certain fixed maximum ratio to assessed values. Very specific limits may be fixed to the rates which may be applied for specific purposes. Thus so much may be allowed for parks, so much for the maintenance of cemeteries; and other matters are dealt with in the same way. But subject to these limitations the town council determines the tax rates necessary to finance town undertakings.

Duties of Chief Executive.—The mayor or president, as chief executive, is charged with the enforcement of all ordinances, and assumes supervision of the administration. And in accordance with the custom that prevails in a large majority of American cities he presides at the meetings of the council and may cast a deciding vote in case of tie. He appoints various officers provided for in the statutes, or by ordinance passed in council meeting. Naturally he has a large measure of control over these persons and is in a position to supervise the work which they carry on.

It is customary also for the chief executive in the small municipalities of some states to preside in a police court. Other times, however, a police magistrate is appointed to perform this function. The jurisdiction of such a court is very similar to the jurisdiction of a township justice of the peace court. Petty offenders against the law, and those who have violated local ordinances, are brought before the magistrate or chief executive. He conducts a hearing and may impose penalties of a minor nature—small fines and short sentences in jail. Appeals may be carried to the courts of general jurisdiction; and offenders who are charged with offenses too serious to be heard in these petty courts are bound over to the grand jury. When petty municipal courts of this nature exist the justices of the peace who have jurisdiction in the same area are likely to concern themselves chiefly with civil cases and non-judicial work.

Duties of Other Officers.—The functions of the other officers who ordinarily are found in a small municipality can be considered very briefly. Their titles give a clear indication of their functions. The clerk keeps a record of the council proceedings and does all the clerical work for that body. In the absence of an auditor he has the important duty of drawing warrants upon the treasurer. He also keeps all records which the council may require of him or which may be required by statute. He issues licenses that are authorized by the council. These may be issued to those who operate billiard halls, hotels or eating places, to peddlers, itinerant merchants, and other such persons.

The principal function of the treasurer is to have custody of the funds, and to collect them. When the municipality serves as the area through which taxes are collected, the office of treasurer assumes greater importance. He disburses funds on authority of warrants signed by the clerk.

The duties of the police chief or marshal, and the police magistrate, if there be one, have already been touched upon. The street commissioner is in effect the agent of the town council and takes direct supervision of the streets and bridges. Policies in this connection are of course determined by the council. The solicitor is an attorney whose business it is to give advice to the town officers and to represent the town in its corporate capacity. A solicitor is not always to be found in these small municipalities of the lowest grade.

Schools.—School administration has already been discussed in this volume.* But the question may arise: How does the small municipality fit into the school system? This can be answered by saying that usually the small municipality is in itself a school district. This is very generally the practice in those states where the school district system has been worked out. In other states the small municipality has power to create and maintain schools if it desires to do so, largely independent of any external control. The chief point to bear in mind in this connection is that village or town schools are not ordinarily subject to township or county authorities.

In any event the machinery for the administration of the schools is separated more or less from the machinery for civil government. The town council does not function as a school board and does not exercise direct control over the schools—as selectmen did in early New England towns. On the other hand, a small board of directors or trustees is selected and this group functions as a school board. In some cases they are popularly elected, and in other cases they are appointed by the mayor or president.

The custom has not altogether disappeared of holding school district meetings at which school officers are selected and the important policies determined. But it should be clearly understood that such meetings are not town meetings but merely school district meetings. The area of the school district is made coterminous with that of the town itself, merely for convenience. The school district is a distinct entity with machinery of its own and officers

* See Chapter XIII.

of its own, for the purpose of carrying on its own business.

The town or village school board performs exactly the same functions as the school boards perform for other school districts, subject to the provisions of the state law. If the small municipality is permitted to have a superintendent of its own, then practically there is no relation at all between the town or village schools and the county authorities. Otherwise the county superintendent has the usual power of supervision over the village schools as well as those of the distinctly rural districts.

Metropolitan Suburbs.—In concluding this discussion of small municipalities at least a word ought to be said about the little suburbs that cluster on the outskirts of the great cities. In legal contemplation they are no different from the other small municipalities that have been under consideration. They are organized as villages, boroughs, or towns. And yet to the casual observer they are very different indeed from the little towns and villages which are isolated somewhere out upon the plains. These suburbs are so close to the city that one is not conscious of crossing the boundaries that divide them from it. A street may be the boundary, and a person driving about in a great city may pass through a dozen separate and distinct municipalities without being aware of the fact that he has been outside the boundaries of the metropolis itself.

The Census Bureau on Suburbs.—The Census Bureau presents the situation thus: "In presenting population statistics for cities the Bureau of the Census must necessarily deal with them as political units, showing for each city the population actually residing within its municipal boundaries. In many cases, however, the number of inhabitants enumerated within the municipal boundaries gives an inadequate idea of the population grouped about one urban center. In fact, in only a few of the large cities do the municipal boundaries closely define the urban area. Immediately beyond the political limits of many cities, and connected with them by rapid transportation systems, are densely populated suburban districts which industrially and socially are parts of the cities themselves, differing only in the matter of governmental organization." *

There are listed in the census report thirty-two cities which are surrounded with what is called a "metropolitan district," that is an area within ten miles of the city limits proper, which is composed of contiguous villages and towns. Thus in the metropolitan district of Chicago are to be found nearly one hundred separate and distinct villages, to say nothing of a number of cities.

Thus it is that these suburban towns and villages have a character all their own. They have their mayors or presidents, they have their councils, their marshals and police magistrates, they possess municipal status and enjoy the same powers and have the same responsibilities as rural towns and villages. And yet they seem like a part of a great city.

This situation does of course very materially affect the actual activities carried on through the town or village. Public services such as water, gas and electric light are afforded through the same source that supplies the city. And while the suburb has its own police force the metropolitan police in practice do extend their activities into the suburban area. The same is true of fire protection service. Other services, such as waste disposal, may be exercised independently or in coöperation with the city.

Absorption of Suburbs.—It will occur to anyone to ask why such suburbs are not absorbed and actually made part of the great city itself. This is possible, usually only

* Fourteenth Census of United States (1920), Vol. I, p. 62.

with the consent of the people in the suburb, however; and it is done from time to time. But public sentiment within the suburb is quite apt to be distinctly opposed to such absorption. The reason is obvious. If the suburb become a part of the city its governmental machinery is swallowed up in that of the city and there is no chance left to control policies locally. But more important than this is the fact that city tax rates are apt to be very much higher than the rates applied by the suburb, and residents are unwilling to assume a part of the burden of maintaining the great city. The chief argument in favor of absorption lies in the possibility of greater centralization of public service agencies. Hence it is likely to be the case that those who pay taxes and who take a personal interest in the management of local affairs will be found to oppose absorption, while others exhibit considerable indifference toward the question.

Broad Range in Character of Small Municipalities.— Strangely enough this brief treatment of local government in towns and villages has led from the most remote, isolated, tiny and insignificant political areas to the most highly developed, wealthy and exclusive communities to be found in the length and breadth of the land. Surely this is rather significant evidence that existing types of government in the small municipalities have proved to be fairly satisfactory instruments of democracy.

INDEX

Abstracts of title, making of, 160

Accident, verdict of death by, 184

Administrative decentralization, reasons for, 14; results of, 14, 15; belief in, 87

Administrative districts, description of, 8–15; duties of officers of, 9; status of, in America, 9, 10, 11, 16; townships and counties as, 18, 19, 20, 49, 109, 110, 111, 112; arbitrary creation of, 21; status of, as corporations, 89

Aged, farming out of, for poor relief, 248

Agricultural statistics, report on, 153

Alabama, type of local government in, 60; county board in, 71

Almshouses, reports of, 153; officers in charge of, 246, 263

Appropriations, vote of county board on, 116

Areas for local self-government (see Local self-government areas)

Arizona, type of local government in, 60, 71, 72; state police organized by, 177

Arkansas, type of local government in, 63; type of county board in, 71; townships in, 308.

Assessment districts, purpose of, 320; officers of, 320, 321

Assessment of taxes, better machinery for, 105; equalization of, 132, 133, 234, 235, 312; method of, 230, 231; importance of, 231; review of, 231, 238; theory of, 231, 232; difficulties of, 232, 233, 234, 235; abuses in, 233, 234, 235; area in charge of, 288, 289, 307, 319

Assessor, county, duties of, 104, 105, 109, 165, 230, 231, 232, 233, 297; military data kept by, 109; value of property taken from books of, 148; opposition to, 229; status of, 229, 230; tax rates fixed by, 230, 231, 232, 233; difficulties of, 232, 233, 234, 235, 236; methods of, 233, 234; possibility of reform in office of, 236, 237; advantages of appointment of, 237, 238, 297, 299; relation of, to other officers, 291, 299; mention of, 293

Assessor, district, appointment of, 320

Assessor, town, office of, 59, 331

Assessor, township, duties of, 104, 105, 132, 133, 307, 313

Assessors, board of, duties of, 50

Attachments, making of, on lands, 159

Attorney, city, position of, 331

Attorney, county (see Prosecutors, public)

Attorney-general, state, failure of sheriff to coöperate with, 173; state police to aid, 177; relation of, to other law enforcing agents, 196, 197, 198; appointment of public prosecutors by, 200; department of justice in charge of, 204

Attorney-general, United States, law enforcement duties of, 196

Attorneys, appointment of, as counsel for defence, 206, 207

Auditing, duty of state to do, 228, 229

Auditor, county, relation of, to county board, 115, 117; budget in charge of, 128, 129; duties of, 138, 139, 140, 165, 214, 227, 228, 296, 297; selection of, 161, 228, 296; tax books prepared by, 214; warrants signed by, 217; supervision over, 228; advantages of state authority over, 228, 229; relation of, to other officers, 291, 299; mention of, 293; no need of, 297

Auditor, deputy county, appointment of, 126

Australian ballots, use of, 106; preparation of, 149, 150

341

INDEX

Australian Trooper Police, 176
Automobiles, enforcement of laws concerning, 95; demand for better roads due to, 103, 283; use of, by criminals, 174, 175

Bailiffs, duty of, to maintain order, 169
"Bailiwick," sheriff's, 168
Ballot boxes, provision for, 133
Ballots, preparation of, 106, 107, 133, 134, 149, 150; variations in, 150, 151; distribution of, 151, 152; counting of, 152; preservation of, 152
Bids, advertising for, 122, 123, 124
Births, records of, 41, 47, 99, 157
Blind, census of, 153
Board of review, service of county board as, 132, 133; mention of, 292; no need of, 294; function of, 294, 312 (see also Assessment of taxes)
Bodies, corporate, powers of, 90
Bodies, politic, status of counties and townships as, 90
Bonds, approval of, by county boards, 133
Boroughs, status of, as minor areas of government, 6, 323; representatives of, 35; status of, as corporations, 88, 89; duty of, to provide for poor, 239, 240; relation of, to townships, 310; similarity of, to cities, 324, 325, 326, 329; organization of, 325, 326, 330; functions of, 325, 327, 328, 329; definition of, 329; incorporation of, 330, 331, 332, 333; government of, 331, 332; officers of, 331, 339; powers of, 332; powers of councils in, 333, 334, 335; status of, as city suburbs, 338, 339, 340; absorption of, into cities, 339, 340; variations in, 340
Bridges, control of state over, 9, 34, 37; building of, 102, 120, 301; records of, 119; contracts for, 120; maps showing, 152; tax rate for, 230; town officers in charge of, 263; location of, 278
Budget, lack of, in New England towns, 33, 34; selectmen in charge of, 40; need of, in counties, 128, 129; making of, 297, 301; adoption of, 300
Buildings, control of county boards over, 119; contracts for, 120, 121, 122; supervision of, 137
Burial certificates, issuing of, 157

California, status of, in federal state, 3; type of local government in, 60, 71, 72; importance of counties in, 91; county commission plan in, 301; townships in, 308
Canadian Northwest Mounted Police, 176
Candidate, papers filed by, 149, 150
Cemeteries, record of, 119; maps showing, 152; tax for, 335
Census Bureau, Federal, classification of local government areas by, 323, 324, 327, 338, 339
Central states, local governments in, 61, 62, 63, 70; county boards in, 66–72
Centralization of authority, attitude of Americans toward, 9, 10, 11; hindrances to, 11, 12; advantages of, in poor relief, 241
Charitable institutions, selectmen in charge of, 40; management of, 99, 301
Charities and public welfare, department for, 301
Chart, on county officers, 291, 299
Chicago, Cook County Hospital in, 259; predominance of, in Cook County, 302; metropolitan district of, 339
Chief executive (see Executive, chief)
Children, school attendance required of, 37; employment of, 195; classification of, as dependents, 245; farming out of, for poor relief, 248; influence of poorhouses on, 252; need of medical examination of, 260
Circuit clerk, duties of, 139, 140; appointment of, 161
Circuit courts, work of, 157
Cities, status of, as areas of local government, 1, 5, 323; purpose of creation of, 4; charters of, 5; similarity of small municipalities to, 6, 25, 26, 324, 326; wards of,

INDEX

8; demand of, for home rule, 12; special legislation concerning, 85; status of, as corporations, 88, 89; contracts made by, 121; budgets in use in, 128; mayors of, 136; elections in, 150; crime in, 174; opposition of, to state police, 180; suits by, to secure tax money, 221; duty of, to provide for poor, 239, 243; public health agencies of, 259; food inspection in, 260; school systems of, 274; interest of, in roads, 279, 280, 281, 285; relations of, with counties, 302–306; relation of, to townships, 310; organization of, 325; classification of, 327, 329, 332; incorporation of, 330, 331, 332, 333; officers of, 331; powers of councils in, 333, 334, 335; absorption of suburbs into, 339, 340

City councils, duplication of, with county boards, 303, 304; consolidation of, with county boards, 305, 306; legislative powers of, 325

City magistrate, hearing before, 200 (see also Mayor)

City officers, enforcement of state laws by, 13; mention of, 331

City police, jurisdiction of, 166; relations of, with sheriffs, 168, 169; inability of, to handle labor disorders, 175; work of, 181; inquests requested by, 183; attitude of, toward public prosecutor, 199; duplication of work of, 303

City wards, status of, as areas of government, 8

Civil cases, jurisdiction over, 97, 157, 315; procedure in, 200

Civil jurisdiction of justices of the peace, 315

Civil service commission, creation of office of, 289; mention of, 293; function of, 295; election of, 295, 296, 299; pay of, 296

Claim register, keeping of, by county board, 119

Claims, county boards to pass on, 129, 130; collection of, through courts, 130; filing of, with county clerk, 142–146, 152; examination of, 297, 300

Clerical offices, status of, in counties, 136–161; mention of, 293; duties of, 296, 297

Clerk, county, origin of office of, 52; methods of selection of, 54, 83, 140, 154, 155, 161, 296, 299; position of, 98; need of, 100; service of, to county board, 115, 141, 142; independence of, county board, 117; budget in charge of, 128, 129; duties of, 138–156, 158, 165, 296, 297; courthouse in charge of, 142; correspondence of, 142; claims filed with, 142–146; warrants signed by, 146, 217; records kept by, 146, 147, 152; tax machinery administered by, 147, 148, 149, 214; services of, in elections, 149-154; licenses issued by, 152, 153; reports made by, 153, 154; reforms needed in office of, 154–156; land surveys ordered by, 161; fees of, 227; auditor serving as, 228; equipment of, 288; relation of, to other officers, 291, 299, 301; mention of 293

Clerk, town, land titles recorded by, 108; position of, 331; duties of, 336

Clerk, township, service of, on township board, 312; duties of, 119, 139, 140, 153, 155, 156, 157, 307, 313

Clerk of court, records kept by, 119; marriage licenses issued by, 153; method of choosing, 158, 161, 297, 299; relation of sheriff to, 168; relation of, to other officers, 291, 299; mention of, 293

Clerks of elections, appointment of, 106

Collector, county, taxes collected by, 148, 149, 225; treasurer as, 213, 227, 297; payment of, 226, 227; proposal to abolish office of, 289; relation of, to other officers, 291; mention of, 293

Collector, deputy county, appointment of, 126

Collector, town, election of, 39

Collector, township, duties of, 225, 226, 307; payment of, 226, 227

Collectors of internal revenue, districts for, 4, 5

Collectors of taxes, dislike for, 104
Colonial assembly, election of representative to, 35, 36, 52
Colonial governments, relation of, to local government, 47, 48; counties created by, 48, 49, 50
Colonies, American, attributes of original thirteen, 3; origin of counties and townships in, 24, 25; attitude of, toward towns, 27, 28; position of sheriff in, 164; roads in, 276
Colorado, type of local government in, 60, 71, 72
Commission plan for counties, departments in, 301
Commissioner, township, duties of, 319
Commissioners, county (see County commissioners, board of)
Common law, principle of, concerning defendant, 205; rule of, concerning poor relief, 239–241
Compensation, claims for, 129
Compulsory military training lack of, 108
Compulsory school attendance, 267, 269, 272
Condemnation proceedings, 125, 193, 194
Congress, enforcement of laws passed by, 14; act of, concerning public lands, 56; authority of, over roads, 276, 286
Congressional districts, division of states into, 18
Congressional townships, creation of, 56; combination of civil townships with, 309
Connecticut, type of local government in, 58; type of county boards in, 71; status of municipalities in, 328
Conservators, appointment of, by county courts, 156
Consolidated schools, advantages of, 270; objections to, 270; transportation of children to, 270
Constables, abolition of office of, 11; town meeting announced by, 29; service of, as sergeants-at-arms of town meetings, 30; selection of, 38, 57, 317; duties of, 38, 39, 41, 93, 95, 317; loss of prestige of, 52; office of, 59, 331; number of, 316, 317; fees of, 317; relations of, to other peace officers, 317
Constitutions, state, provisions in, concerning county boundary lines, 78–81; amendments to, 80; popular election of county officers guaranteed by, 82, 83; provisions in, concerning local government, 86, 87
Contractors, deals with, 120, 121, 122, 123, 124; difficulties of, 124
Contracts, control of, by states, 9; powers of corporations to make, 90; awarding of, by county boards, 116, 120–124, 127, 128; limitations on, 122, 123, 124; approval of, 143, 144, 300; litigation over, 193, 194
Cook County, money retained by treasurers of, 220, predominance of Chicago in, 302
Cook County Hospital, status of, 259
Coroner, county, duties of, 52, 182, 183; selection of, 54, 182; origin of office of, 182; relation of, to sheriff, 182; inquests held by, 183, 184, 185; warrant issued by, 185; possibility of abolition of office of, 186, 187, 200, 288, 296; abuses in office of, 187, 188; relations of, with other officers, 199, 200, 291; fees of, 227; relation of county physician to, 257, 258; mention of, 293
Coroner's jury, selection of, 183, 184; procedure of, 184; verdicts of, 184, 185
Corporate and politic bodies, counties and townships as, 88
Corporate powers, extent of, 90
Corporations, counties not to hold stock in, 86; definition of, 88; counties and townships as, 89, 90; influence of, with coroner's juries, 187, 188; state tax on, 237 (see also Public corporations and Private corporations)
Council, municipal, 331
Council, town, functions of, 333, 334, 335; tax rates fixed by, 335; schools not in charge of, 337
Counsel, appointment of, for accused persons, 206, 207

INDEX

Counsel, county (see County counsel)

Counties, status of, as areas of local government, 1, 15, 16, 17, 47-56, 60, 61, 62, 63, 64, 65, 66; overlapping jurisdictions of, 5; courts in, 6, 156; service of, as judicial districts, 6, 7, 18, 48, 49, 98; use of, as representative districts, 7, 18, 36, 54, 79, 80; reason for maintenance of, 13; chief characteristics of, 16, 20; functions of, 17, 18, 19, 20, 92-113, 162-188, 288, 289, 310, 313, 314; service of, as administrative districts, 18, 19, 20, 49, 109, 110; law enforcement in, 19; definition of, 21; origin of, 24, 25, 45, 48, 49, 324; importance of, in Pennsylvania, 45, 52, 53; status of, in New England, 47-51, 58, 59, 91; service of, as military districts, 49, 108, 109; collection of taxes in, 49, 50, 104, 105, 130-132; officers of, 50, 59; 136-161, 189-211, 212-238; status of, in New York, 51, 52; status of, in South, 53, 54, 60, 61; development of, in West, 55, 56, 60, 61; number of, in United States, 57; status of, in central States, 61, 62, 63; relation of, to townships, 66, 72, 80, 81, 307, 310, 313, 314; absence of, in Louisiana, 71; state control over, 71, 87, 119; legal status of, 76-91; powers of, 77; boundaries of, not to be altered by state legislatures, 78-81; election of officers of, 82, 83; special legislation concerning, 84, 85, 86; limitation on debt of, 86; status of, as bodies corporate and politic, 87-91; status of, as corporations, 89, 90; control of, over highways, 102, 103; control of, over elections, 106, 107; governing board of, 114-135; legislative power belonging to, 116; opportunities for graft in, 121, 122, 123, 124; civil service not used in, 126; need of budget for, 128, 129, 288; claims against, 129, 130, 142-146; clerical offices in, 136-161; census of, 153; issuing of annual reports of, 153, 154; police functions of, 162-188; division of England into, 163; sheriffs as officers of, 164, 165, 166; proposed reforms in government of, 181, 182, 287-306; law officers of, 189-211; counsel for, 192-195; finance officers of, 212-238; duty of, to provide for poor and dependents, 239, 240, 243, 244, 246, 247, 249, 250; hospitals maintained by, 258, 259; public health work of, 259, 260, 261; schools in charge of, 264-274; roads maintained by, 278, 282, 284, 285, 286; purchases for, 288; government of, 290-299; manager for, 300; commission plan for, 301; home rule for, 301, 302; relations of, with large cities, 302-306; creation of, 324; organization of, 325

Country roads, importance of, 280, 281, 282; maintenance of, 282, 283

County attorney, name of, 189 (see also Prosecutors, public)

County board, service of county justices as, 53; number of men on, 68, 69, 70, 71, 72, 114, 115, 292, 293; selection of, 72, 83, 293, 294, 319; division of authority of, 99; creation of, by state legislatures, 114; meetings of, 114, 115, 141, 142; organization and work of, 114-135; secretary of, 115, 139; quorum of, 116; legislative functions of, 116, 117; supervisory powers of, 117, 118; administrative functions of, 117-135, 138; records of, 118, 119, 141, 142, 152; policies determined by, 119, 120; contracts awarded by, 120-124; purchase of land by, 124, 125; rules made by, 125; officers appointed by, 125, 126, 161, 296, 297, 298, 299; poor relief in charge of, 126, 245, 246, 249, 250, 253, 255, 256; supplies provided by, 126-129; control of, over claims, 129, 130; services of, as boards of review, 132, 133; bonds to be approved by, 133; duties of, in supervising elections, 133, 134; minor functions of, 134, 135; relation of county clerk to,

140, 141, 142; reports of county officers made to, 154; land surveys ordered by, 161; local duties of, 165; jails maintained by, 170, 171, 182; public prosecutor as legal adviser to, 190; county counsel to be appointed by, 193, 211; need of legal counsel for, 193, 194; authority of, over funds for criminal prosecutions, 198, 199; public defender to be appointed by, 210; supervision of, over treasurer's office, 215, 222, 225; banks selected by, for public funds, 221; assessor to be appointed by, 238; county physician employed by, 257; public health work of, 261; roads in charge of, 278, 284, 285; accountability of clerical officers to, 289; relation of, to other officers, 291, 298, 299; salary of, 294; functions of, 294, 298, 299; service of county clerk to, 296, 297 (see also County boards)

County board districts, status of, as areas of government, 8

County boards, types of, 66–72; number of, 134, 135; duplication of, with city councils, 303, 304; consolidation of, with city councils, 305, 306

County commissioners, board of, election of, 53; duties of, 53; organization of, in south-central states, 63; discussion of, 66–72; small number on, 72; service of, 114; fees of, 227; poor relief in charge of, 246

County counsel, need of, 192, 193, 211; mention of, 293; duties of, 296; appointment of, 296, 299; independence of, 301

County courts, status of, 18; organization of, 30, 50, 51, 53, 54, 156; function of, 50, 51; establishment of, 53, 54; appointment of judges of, 97; standards of, 98; probate functions of, 99; administrative functions of, 99, 100; jurisdiction of, 156, 157; sheriffs as officers of, 168–170; appeals to, 315, 316

County districts, status of, 318; types of, 319, 320; officers of, 320, 321; special problems of, 321, 322

County executive, lack of, 136

County farms, provisions for, 100

County funds, care of, 213, 214, 218, 219; sources of, 214; records of, 215–217; disbursements of, 217–218; custody of, 218, 219; interest on, 219, 220; depositories for, 220, 221, 224; delayed entries of, 221, 224

County government, complexity of, 18; variations in, 287; changes in, 287, 288; reform programme for, 288–306; reorganization of, 290, 298, 299; typical structure of, 290, 291, 292; new plan of, 298, 299; county manager plan for, 300

County institutions, reports of, 153

County judge, status of, 18; place of, on county board, 71

County manager, creation of office of, 289; principle of, 298, 300; term of, 300; employment of, 300; pay of, 300; subordinates appointed by, 300; duties of, 300

County manager board, election of, 300; duties of, 300

County officers, enforcement of state laws by, 13; indefinite status of, 19, 98; taxes collected by, 19, 104, 105; location of offices of, 81; selection of, 82, 83, 125, 126, 181, 289, 295; salaries of, 83, 84; supervision over, 117, 292; supplies for, 120, 121, 122, 126–129; bonds of, 133; information concerning 153; reports made by, 153, 154; list of, 161, 292, 293, 299; public prosecutor as legal adviser to, 190–195, 203

County officers, deputy, appointment of, 125, 126

County offices, legislature not to abolish, 83, 84; election of, 87; filling of vacancies in, 134; papers filed by candidates for, 149, 150

County police, lack of, 175

County school board (see School board, county)

County seats, distance of boundary lines from, 79; restrictions on moving of, 81, 82; location of offices at, 81, 82

INDEX

County superintendent of schools (see Superintendent of schools, county)
County supervisors (see Supervisors, county)
Courthouse, location of, at county seat, 81; maintenance of, 98; contracts for, 120; rules concerning, 125; merit system for employees in, 126; county clerk as superintendent of, 142
Courts, districts for holding of, 5, 6, 7; holding of, at county seats, 81, 82; kinds of, 156, 157; records of, 157; sheriffs as executive officers of, 168-170
Courts, county (see County courts)
Courts, district (see District courts)
Criminal cases, jurisdiction over, 97, 157, 316
Criminal jurisdiction of justices of the peace, 316
Criminals, function of public prosecutor in conviction of, 195-199; deficiencies in agencies to apprehend, 199, 200; arrest of, 200; hearing of, 200; indictment of, 200, 201, 202; trial of, 203
Cross-state highways, 281, 282
Cumberland Road, importance of, 276
Curriculum, regulation of, 269, 272, 273

Dance halls, licenses for, 134, 152
Deaf, census of, 153; care of, 255
Deaths, records of, 41, 47, 99, 157; investigation of, 182, 183
Decentralization, administrative, belief in, 13
Deeds, giving of, for lands, 159; recording of, 159, 160
Defectives, state care of, 289
Defendant, presumption of innocence of, 205; counsel provided for, 206, 207
Defender, public, need of, 204, 205, 206, 207, 208; position of, 207, 208; arguments in favor of, 208, 209, 210, 211; duties of, 208, 296; objections to, 209, 210; selection of, 210, 211, 296, 299; creation of office of, 289
Defense, need of provision for, 204, 205, 206, 207, 208

Delaware, type of local government in, 60; type of county board in, 71
Democracy, significance of term, 3; self-government as a factor in, 12, 14, 17; inefficiency as price of, 13; town meeting as illustration of, 28
Denver, county absorbed by, 302
Dependencies, self-governing, character of, 3
Dependents, care of, 13, 74, 99, 100, 101, 240, 241; county courts in charge of, 156, 157; responsibility for, 243; groups of, 244, 245; farming out of, 247, 248; segregation of, 252; medical aid to, 257, 258
Destitute persons, relief granted to, 242
Detective work, state police for, 176, 177
Diseased, care of, 100, 256
District attorneys, United States, law enforcement work of, 196
District courts, creation of, 99; work of, 157; sheriffs as officers of, 168-170; appeals to, 315, 316 (see also Courts)
District officers, duties of, 9, 10; appointment of, 320
Districts, purposes of, 4, 5
Districts, administrative (see Administrative districts)
Districts, judicial (see Judicial districts)
Districts, representative (see Representative districts)
Dixie Highway, making of, 286
Documents, recording of, 158, 160
Dogs, licenses for, 152
Domicile, establishment of, 242
Drainage, township control over, 311
Drainage districts, reasons for, 15, 320, 321; creation of, 110; maps of, 152; function of, 319, 321
Drainage projects, control of, by counties, 86
Drainage systems, supervision of, by states, 9; records of, 119; townships in charge of, 314, 318
"Due process of law," meaning of, 202

INDEX

Earl, shire ruled by, 162; political power of, 162, 163
Education, attitude of people toward, 262; status of, as a function of government, 262; importance of, to state, 271; federal department of, 274; change in, 287, 288; state supervision of, 289; control over, 303, 304 (see also Schools)
Eighteenth amendment, provisions for enforcement of, 14; mention of, 134
Election ballots, printing of, 121
Election cases, county courts in charge of, 156, 157
Election commissioners, board of, mention of, 292; function of, 294; no need of, 294
Election districts, towns in New England as, 59; function of, 319, 320; officials of, 320
Election officials, appointment of, 320
Election returns, canvass of, by county boards, 134
Elections, counties as units in, 52; administration of, by local authorities, 105-107, 111, 112; methods of conducting, 105-107; officials of, 106, 107, 151; supervision of, by county boards, 133, 134; conduct of, by county clerk, 149-154; returns of, 152; control over, 303
Engineer, county, appointment of, 125, 298, 299; duties of, 161; employment of, on roads, 284, 285; mention of, 293
Engineer, highway, 102, 118
England, representation in, 35; sheriff's office in, 162, 163, 164; coroner in, 182; roads in, 275; justices of the peace in, 315
Epidemics, control of, 261
Epileptics, state institutions for, 255; care of, in poorhouses, 255
Equalization of assessments, county boards to provide for, 132, 133 (see also Boards of review)
Europe, administrative districts in, 8
Ex parte proceedings, 99
Executive, chief, lack of, in counties, 136; duties of, 136, 137, 196

Executive department, possession of, by states, 4
Executive functions, enumeration of, 136 137

Farming out, plan of, in poor relief, 247, 248; abuses in, 248
Federal agents, laws enforced by, 166
Federal government, administrative centralization of, 13, 14; limitations on powers of, 77; maintenance of peace by, 93, 94; interest of, in education, 101; contracts made by, 121; marshals of, 166; authority of, over roads, 276, 281, 286
Federal legislation, enforcement of, 14
Federal prosecuting attorneys, duties of, 14
Federal state, status of units of, 3, 4
Feeble-minded, efforts to get rid of, 243; farming out of, for poor relief, 248; presence of, in poorhouses, 252, 255; state institutions for, 255
Fees, retention of, by sheriffs, 169, 170; payment of county officers by, 227
Fence viewers, mention of, 39
Fences, town rules concerning, 37; inspection of, 40
Feudalism, relation of sheriffs to system of, 162, 163
Finance department, 301
Finance officers, duties of, 41, 297; supplies for, 126; account of, 212-238; mention of, 293
Finances, control of, by states, 9; control of board of commissioners over, 53
Florida, type of local government, 60, 71, 72
Food, contracts for, 120, 121, 122; inspection of, in rural communities, 260, 261
Forest preserves, control of states over, 74; guarding of, 177; districts for, 320, 321
France, status of, as political unit, 2; gendarmes in, 176
Franklin, Benjamin, good roads advocated by, 276

INDEX 349

Functions of counties and townships, 92-113 (see also Counties and Townships)

Gambling, enforcement of laws concerning, 14, 195, 197, 198; state police to prevent, 177
Gendarmes, mention of, 176
Georgia, type of local government in, 60; type of county boards in, 71
Gerrymander, danger of, in changing county lines, 79, 80
Government, greater areas of, 1-4; local areas of, 1, 4-20, 54, 55, 56, 57; complexity of, 5; inefficiency of, 13; factors in determining form of, 42, 43
Governmental areas, classification of, 1-20
Governor, arrest of, in Illinois, 94; position of, at head of state, 136; sheriff's accountability to, 164; appeal of sheriff to, for militia, 168; authority of, over law enforcing agencies, 196, 197, 198; attorney-general to be appointed by, 204
Grand jury, indictment of prisoners by, 200, 201; personnel of, 201; meetings of, 201; influence of public prosecutor over, 201, 202; proposal to eliminate, 202, 203
Greater areas of government, definition of, 1-4
Guardians, appointment of, by county courts, 156

Health, board of, mention of, 292; need of, 295; members of, 295; appointment of, 299; township board as, 312
Health officer, appointment of, 125, 298, 299; mention of, 293
Health regulations, enforcement of, 13, 109
Highway commission, state, creation of, 179
Highway commissioner, town, office of, 59
Highway commissioners, duties of, 102, 278, 279, 294, 295; proposal to abolish office of, 289, 295, 298; mention of, 292, 293
Highway engineer, 102, 118

Highway officials, approval of contracts by, 143, 144; local duties of, 165; roads in charge of, 278, 279
Highway overseers, duties of, 102
Highways, authority of county court over, 51, 99; towns in charge of, 59; control of, by local government areas, 102, 103, 111, 112, 277, 301, 303, 317, 318, 319; record of improvements on, 119; removing obstructions from, 134; officers in charge of, 161, 278, 279; maintenance of, 275, 281, 282, 283; attitude of federal government to, 276, 285, 286; distances covered by, 277; neglect of, 276, 277, 278; routes of, 278; work on, 279; definition of, 280; classification of, 280-282; need of improvement of, 283, 284; state control of, 289
Home rule, success of, in cities, 12, 301; adoption of, in counties, 302
Hospital superintendent, creation of office of, 289
Hospitals, county, location of, 81; counties permitted to build, 84, 86; maintenance of, 110, 118; rules concerning, 125; supplies for, 143, 144; reports of, 153; care of dependents in, 248; establishment of, 256, 257, 289; duty of county physician in, 258; origin of, 258; need of, 258, 259; control over, 304
Houses of correction, county court in charge of, 50; need of, 96
Hunting, licenses for, 152

Idaho, type of local government in, 71, 72
Illinois, pioneer period in, 55; type of local government, 61; type of county board in, 71; arrest of Governor of, 94; duties of county officers in, 139, 140; bill for state police defeated in, 179, 180; townships in, 308, 310, 312
Income tax, collection of, 11, 14
Incomes, state tax on, 237
Indiana, pioneer period of, 55; type of local government in, 63, 71, 72; townships in, 308, 312
Indictments, service of, by sheriff, 168

350 INDEX

Innkeepers, licensing of, 53
Inquests, procedure in, 183, 184, 185; holding of, unnecessary, 185, 186; substitute for, 186, 187
Insane, control of state over, 9; care of, 12, 100; county courts in charge of, 156; keeping of, in poorhouses, 255
Insane asylums, state, advantages of, 254, 255
Insanity cases, hearing of, 99
Institutional care, plan of, for poor relief, 248, 249
Institutions, county, supplies for, 120, 121, 122, 126–129; land for, 125; rules for, 125
Institutions, provisions for, in local government areas, 96; care of dependents in, 248, 249; special types of, for poor relief, 254–257; mention of, 293; superintendents of, 298, 299
Iowa, type of local government, 63, 71, 72; duties of county officers in, 139, 140; county hospitals established in, 258; townships in, 308, 312; towns in, 329
Irish Constabulary, Royal, 176
Irrigation districts, purpose of, 320, 321

Jails, provision of town meetings for, 37; location of, at county seats, 81; need of, 96; rules concerning, 125; reports of, 153; supervision of, 165, 166; sentence of prisoners to, 169; maintenance of, 170, 171; sanitary conditions in, 171; control over, 182, 304; care of dependents in, 239, 240, 248; segregation in, 252; medical care for inmates of, 257; town officers in charge of, 263
Judge, county, election of, 100
Judges, districts for, 5; election of, 97, 98; appointment of clerks by, 161, 297; sheriffs accountable to, 164
Judges of elections, appointment of, 106, 133
Judgments, records of, 157; execution of, by sheriffs, 169
Judicial authority, development of, in New England, 48, 49
Judicial districts, status of, as areas of government, 6, 7, 16; boundaries of, 6, 7; counties as, 18; creation of, 98; public prosecutor elected for, 189
Jurors, summons for, 157
Jury, list of persons eligible to, 134, 151; summons for, 168; sheriff in charge of, 169; unwillingness of citizens to serve on, 202
Jury, coroner's (see Coroner's jury)
Justice, administration of, 6; control of state over, 9; administration of, by local areas, 59, 96–98, 110, 111, 112
Justice, state department of, suggestion of, 181, 203, 204
Justice courts, appeals from, 157
Justices, appointment of, 50; service of, as county court, 50
Justices, county, appointment of, 53; duties of, 53, 54
Justices of the peace, office of, 59, 314, 315, 331; townships as districts for, 60; position of, on county boards, 71, 114; jurisdiction of, 97, 315, 316; ridicule of, 98; appeals from, 157, 315, 316; hearing before, 200; persons committed to poorhouse by, 250; service of, on township boards, 312; criticisms of, 315, 316; other functions of, 316; pay of, 316
Juvenile cases, handling of, by county courts, 99, 156
Juvenile offenders, care of, 96

Kansas, type of local government in, 63, 71, 72; townships in, 308; towns in, 329; classification of cities in, 332
Kentucky, pioneer period in, 55; type of local government in, 60; type of county board in, 71
King's highway, maintenance of peace on, 275

Labor, opposition of, to state police, 180
Labor disorders, guards during, 167; difficulties of sheriffs with, 175; state police in charge of, 177, 178
Land, authority of New England town meeting over, 32, 33; use

INDEX

of, in common, 32, 33; transfers of, 41, 53, 107, 108, 111, 112, 118, 158, 159, 160, 161; giving of, for schools, 101; purchase of, for counties, 124, 125; survey of, 134, 161
Law, promulgation and enforcement of, 136, 138
Law enforcement agencies, disorganization of, 199, 200; changes proposed for, 200
Law officers, county, 189–211
Legal adviser, function of public prosecutor as, 190–193
Legal residence, prevention of acquiring of, 243
Legal status of counties and townships, 90, 91
Legislative assembly, districts for election of members of, 5, 7, 8
Legislatures, state, existence of, 4; districts for election of members of, 18; powers of, over local governments, 77–87; limitations on power of, over counties, 78–84, 87; special legislation not to be enacted by, 84, 85, 86
Libraries, counties permitted to establish, 84, 289, 334; maintenance of, 110, 125, 325, 334; control over, 304
Licenses, granting of, by county courts, 51; right of county boards to grant, 134; issuing of, by county clerk, 152, 153
Liens, recording of, 159, 161
Lieutenant, county, appointment of, 54
Lincoln Highway, marking of, 286
Liquor, licenses for sale of, 134; enforcement of laws against sale of, 166, 177, 197, 198
Liquor law, enforcement of, by federal agents, 94, 166; duty of state police to enforce, 177
Litigation, public prosecutor as attorney in, 193–195, 203
Local charities, provision for, 239–257
Local government, definition of, 1; areas of, 1, 3, 42–57; types of, 54, 55, 56, 57, 58–75; development of, in West, 55, 56; effects of state laws on, 56; groups of states by variations in, 58–63; merits of various types of, 63–66; demands on, 65, 66; uniformity in, 72; tendencies affecting, 72–75; powers delegated to units of, 77, 78; functions of, 92–113; probate work of, 98–100; control of poor relief by, 100, 239–257; maintenance of schools by, 101, 102; control of, over highways, 102, 103; administration of taxes by, 103–105; administration of elections by, 105–107; recording of land titles by, 107, 108; provision for, 239–257; reform in, 287–306; definition of, 323 (see also Local self-government)
Local legislation, enforcement of, by local officers, 94, 95
Local officers, enforcement of laws by, 13, 94, 95
Local self-government, substitute for, 9; advantages and disadvantages of, 9, 10, 14; preference of Americans for, 11, 12, 23, 24, 87; results of, 13, 14, 15; areas of, 14, 15, 16, 17, 18, 19, 20; meaning of, 16, 17; combination of, with state government, 18, 19, 20; compromise with, 19, 20; factors in, 21, 23, 24; origin of, 21–41; functions of, 92–113 (see also Local government)
Local self-government areas, election of administrative officers by, 19 (see also Local government)
Louisiana, local government in, 60, 71

Magisterial districts, purpose of, 319, 320
Maine, type of local government in, 58; type of county board in, 71, 72; status of municipalities in, 328, 329
Maintenance of peace, discussion of, as function of local self-government, 92–96
Major areas of government, discussion of, 1–4
Manors, existence of, in New York, 44
Maps, keeping of, by county clerk, 152
Marriage licenses, issuing of, 153, 157

INDEX

Marriages, records of, 41, 47, 99, 157; performance of, by justices of the peace, 316

Marshal, duties of, 331, 336

Marshal, United States, duties of, 166

Maryland, type of local government in, 60; type of county board in, 71, 72

Massachusetts, status of, in federal state, 3; type of local government in, 58; county board in, 71, 72; state police in, 176, 177; status of public prosecutor in, 189; status of towns in, 327, 328

Massachusetts Bay Colony, attitude of, toward local areas, 24, 25

Mayor, status of, as chief executive of cities, 136, 325, 331; consent of, required for work of state police, 178; duties of, 335, 336

Metropolitan district, definition of, 339

Mexican Border, patrolling of, 177

Michigan, pioneer period in, 55; type of local government in, 61; type of county board in, 71; status of townships in, 91, 308, 310, 312

Military districts, service of counties as, 49

Military roads, importance of, 275, 277

Military training, counties as units of, 108

Militia, quota of, from towns, 28; officer in charge of, 50; organization of, by local governments, 108, 109; service of counties in organization of, 111, 112; census of men eligible to, 153; right of sheriff to call for, 168

Milk, inspection of, 260, 261

Minnesota, type of local government, 63; type of county board in, 71, 72; townships in, 308, 310, 312

Minor areas of government, definition of, 4–20

Mississippi, type of local government, 60; type of county board in, 71, 72

Missouri, type of local government in, 63; type of county board in, 71; townships in, 308, 312

Moderator, election of, by town meeting, 29; duties of, 29, 30

Montana, type of local government in, 60; type of county board in, 71, 72; townships in, 308

Mortgages, recording of, 159, 161

Munger, E. E., work of, to establish county hospitals, 258

Municipal corporations, examples of, 88, 89; description of, 89, 90

Municipal function, city to carry on, 4

Municipalities, status of, as minor areas of local government, 6, 16, 17, 59; special legislation concerning, 85, 86; status of, as corporations, 88, 89; relation of, to townships, 310; legal status of, 323, 324; classification of, 328, 329; state laws concerning, 329, 330 (see also Municipalities, small)

Municipalities, small, classification of, 323, 324, 325, 326; emergence of, 326, 327, 328, 329; state laws concerning, 329, 330; incorporation of, 330, 331; internal organization of, 331, 332; reorganization of, as cities, 332, 333; functions of, 333, 334, 335, 336, 337; schools of, 337, 338; status of, as suburbs, 338, 339; absorption of, 339, 340; range of character of, 340 (see also Municipalities)

Murder, verdict of, by coroner's jury, 185; prosecution of, 195

National arteries, 281, 282

National highways, support of, 276, 285, 286

National government (see Federal government)

National Municipal League, purpose of, 290

National Short Ballot Organization, work of, 290

Natural death, verdict of, 184

Nebraska, type of local government in, 61; type of county board in, 71; townships in, 308, 310

Nevada, type of local government in, 60; type of county board in, 71, 72; townships in, 308

New England, importance of towns in, 24, 26, 27, 28, 44, 308, 309,

INDEX

310, 327, 328; right of towns in, to exclude persons, 30, 31, 320; representatives to state assemblies in, 36; significance of town organizations of, 39, 40; modern township evolved from towns of, 41; type of local government in, 43, 54, 58, 59, 60, 63, 64, 70; position of counties in, 47–51, 91; merits of forms of local government in, 63, 64; counties and towns created by states of, 76; position of sheriffs in, 95, 165; poor relief in, 240, 242, 243; provision for schools in, 262, 263, 264

New England type of local government, 54, 63, 64, 70

New Hampshire, type of local government in, 58; type of county board in, 71, 72; status of towns in, 327, 328

New Jersey, type of local government in, 61; type of county board in, 71; townships in, 308, 310

New Mexico, type of local government in, 60; type of county board in, 71, 72; state police organized by, 177

New York, state police in, 11, 180; units of local government in, 44, 45, 54, 55, 61; importance of county in, 47, 51, 52, 53; townships in, 308, 310, 311, 312; villages in, 329

New York City, counties absorbed by, 302

New York State Troopers, account of, 177, 178, 179

Norman Conquest, effect of, on county government in England, 162

North Carolina, type of local government in, 60; type of county board in, 71, 72; townships in, 308

North central states, local governments in, 61, 62; type of county boards in, 70, 71

North central type of local government, 54

North Dakota, type of local government in, 63; type of county board in, 71, 72; townships in, 308, 310, 312

Northwest Ordinance of 1787, provisions of, concerning local government, 56, 57; reference to schools in, 101

Northwest Territory, government of, 56, 57

Nuisances, abatement of, 134, 261, 333

Oaths, administering of, 316

Ohio, pioneer period in, 55; type of local government in, 63; type of county board in, 71, 72; townships in, 308, 312

Oklahoma, type of local government in, 63; type of county board in, 71, 72; townships in, 308, 312

Ordinance of 1787, provisions of, concerning local government, 56, 57

Ordinances, adoption of, by town meetings, 37, 38; adoption of, by county courts, 51; authority of county boards to pass, 134, 300; enforcement of, 325, 333

Oregon, type of local government in, 60; type of county board in, 71; status of public prosecutor in, 189

Origin of local self-government in America, 21–41

Orphanages, reports of, 153; care of dependents in, 248, 249; control over, 304

Orphans, commitment of, 99; census of, 153; classification of, with dependents, 245; care of, 256

Outdoor relief, giving of, by townships, 111; county boards in charge of, 126; plan of, 245, 246; abuses in, 247

Overseer of the poor, office of, 59, 245, 246; proposal to abolish office of, 289; mention of, 293; appointment of, 297, 299; duties of, 297, 298, 313

Parishes, status of, as local government units, 46, 47, 53; delegates from, 54; police jury in, 71; poor relief in, 239, 240

Park districts, creation of, 5, 15, 110; reasons for, 15, 320, 321; status of, as corporations, 89

INDEX

Parks, districts for, 5, 15, 110, 320, 321; control of, 9, 74, 86, 289, 301; maintenance of, 110, 325, 334, 335; records of, 119; tax for, 335
Parliament, election of representatives to, 35
Patents, land, 158, 159
Paving, contracts concerning, 123; control over, 325; provision for, 333
Peace, maintenance of, as a function of local self-government, 92–96, 110, 111, 112; duty of sheriff to maintain, 162, 163, 164, 165, 166, 167, 168; changes in methods of maintaining, 287, 289
Peace officers, possibility of abolition of local offices of, 11; position of, 111; sheriffs as, 166, 167, 168, 173, 174; powers of, in small cities, 333
Penal farms, need of, 96
Pennsylvania, state police in, 11, 177; units of local government in, 44, 45, 55, 63; status of townships in, 45; importance of counties in, 47, 52, 53; type of county board in, 71, 72; status of townships in, 91, 308, 312; poor relief in, 247; boroughs in, 329
Pennsylvania State Constabulary, account of, 177, 179
Personal property, objections to tax on, 235, 236
Philadelphia, county absorbed by, 302
Philippine Islands, police in, 176
Physician, county, investigation of murder cases by, 186, 187; duties of, 257; relation of, to coroner, 257, 258; mention of, 293; appointment of, 298
Plantations, effect of, on local government, 46
Playgrounds, maintenance of, 110, 325, 334
Police, control of, by local authorities, 11, 12; use of, in maintaining peace, 93; duty of, in murder cases, 185, 186; duplication of, 303 (see also City police and State police)
Police chief, duties of, 336
Police courts, jurisdiction of, 335, 336; appeals from 336

Police jury, election of, 71
Police magistrate, duties of, 335, 336
Police power, control of state over, 9, 11; administration of, 10, 11; control of, by counties, 162–188; importance of, in government, 167; extent of, in municipalities, 325, 333
Political parties, local organization of, 107; definition of, 107
Political units, definition of, 1–4
Poll books, provision for, 133
Polling places, location of, 106, 151; provision for, 133, 134; supplies for, 151, 152
Pool rooms, licenses for, 134, 152, 153
Poor, control of state over, 9; care of, by local authorities, 12, 239–241; disadvantage of, in trials, 205, 206, 207, 208
Poor districts, purpose of, 320, 321
Poor farms, control of county board over, 118; establishment of, 253; stewards of, 253, 254
Poor relief, administration of, by towns, 37, 39, 59, 263; supervision of, by vestry, 47; control of townships over, 73; 311, 314, 317, 318, 319; local governments in charge of, 100, 101, 111, 112, 239–257, 288, 289; duties of county board in, 126, 288, 289; common law rule concerning, 239–241; legislation concerning, 240, 241; improvement in, 241; reasons for centralization of, 241; who entitled to, 241–244; methods of, 245–249, 287; farming out of, 247, 248; specialized institutions for, 254–257; state supervision over, 257, 303, 307; department in charge of, 301; districts for, 320, 321
Poorhouses, location of, 81; provisions for, 100; character of, 100; land for, 125; rules concerning, 125, 251, 252; persons committed to, 126, 249, 250; supplies for, 127; care of dependents in, 248–257; maintenance of, 249; control of, 249; evil conditions in, 252, 253; medical attention for inmates of, 252–257; substitutes

INDEX

for, 254; ideal function of, 257; control over, 304
Poor-master, duties of, 165, 307; position of, 245, 246; poorhouse in charge of, 249
Porto Rico, police in, 176
Posse comitatus, power of sheriff to call, 167, 168
Precincts, polling places in, 151; election types of, 320
President, village, position of, 331; duties of, 335, 336
President of the United States, position of, 136, 137; authority of, over law enforcement agents, 196
Printing, contracts for, 120, 121, 124
Prisoners, sheriff's responsibility for, 165, 169, 170-173; maintenance of, 170, 171, 317; segregation of, 171, 172, 173
Prisons, county court in charge of, 50; need of, 96 (see also Jails)
Private corporations, definition of, 88; powers of, 88, 89, 90
Probate, duties of local government in, 98-100; counties in charge of, 110, 111, 112, 156
Probate clerk, appointment of, 161
Probate courts, county, 161
Prohibition laws, enforcement of, by federal agents, 94, 166; duty of state police to enforce, 177
Property, authority of towns over, 32, 33; tax rate on, 131, 132, 230-233; condemnation of, 156, 157, 278; liens against, 159, 161; protection of, by state police, 180; classification of, 232-237; difficulties of assessing, 232, 233, 234, 236, 238; valuation of, 233, 234, 236
Property, personal, assessment of, 235, 236
Property tax, general, reliance on, 131, 237; assessment of, 230-233; difficulties of levying, 232, 233, 234, 235, 236; abolition of, 237; better machinery for collection of, 237
Prosecuting attorney, county, duties of, 14; title of, 189 (see also Prosecutors, public)
Prosecution of criminals, 195-199; steps in, 200-203; emphasis on, 204, 205
Prosecutors, county enforcement of laws by, 13; election of, 19, 83 (see also Prosecutors, public)
Prosecutors, public, election of, 98, 189, 296, 299; position of, 98, 181, 189, 190; relation of, to county board, 117; relations of, with sheriffs, 173, 174, 199; inquests requested by, 183, 184; duty of, in murder cases, 185, 186, 187; relation of, to state government, 189, 190, 196, 197, 198, 289, 298; various titles of, 189; function of, as legal adviser to county officers, 190-193; duty of, to represent county in litigation, 193-195; functions of, in law enforcement, 195-199; criticisms of, 197, 198; responsibilities of, 198, 199; salary of, 198, 199; assistants for, 199; relation of, with other law enforcing agencies, 199, 200, 291, 299; cases presented to grand jury by, 201, 202; need of reform in office of, 203, 204; politics involved in, 204; relation of, to public defender, 208, 209, 210; functions of, 211, 296; mention of, 293
Public corporations, functions of, 88, 89; creation of, 330, 331; status of, 332
Public defender (see Defender, public)
Public health, control of state over, 9, 73; protection of, 134, 325; governmental agencies for, 259, 260, 261; department in charge of, 301; regulations concerning, 333
Public lands, survey of, 56
Public service corporations, definition of, 88
Public utilities, control of, by state, 9; demand of cities for control over, 12; taxation of, 233; status of, in suburbs, 339
Public works, contracts for, 9, 120, 121, 122, 123, 124; department for, 301
Purchasing agent, need of, in counties, 127, 145

Pure food laws, administration of, 10, 109

Quasi-corporations, definition of, 88, 90; powers of, 90
Quorum, of county board, 116

Real estate, taxation of, 236
Recorder, county, election of, 83, 161; duties of, 118, 119, 158-161; claims approved by, 144; land surveys ordered by, 161; substitute for, 161; fees of, 227; records of, 288; relation of, to other officers, 291, 299; mention of, 293; appointment of, 297
Records, keeping of, by county officers, 118, 146, 147
Referendum, requirement of, for changing county seats and boundary lines, 78-81
Reform, public interest in, 289, 290
Reform schools, need of, 96
Register of deeds, supplies for, 126; title of, 158; relation of, to other officers, 291
Registration books, provision for, 151
Representative districts, creation of, 5; status of, as areas of government, 7, 8, 16; counties serving as, 18, 52, 79, 80
Representatives, districts for election of, 5, 7, 8; election of, by town meetings, 35, 36
Republic, significance of term, 3
Resident, definition of, for purposes of poor relief, 242
Resorts, licenses for, 152
Rhode Island, type of local government, 58; no county board in, 71; appointment of sheriffs in, 164; status of towns in, 327, 328
Road commissioners, supervision of, by county board, 118; mention of, 292; duties of, 294, 295, 313; no need of, 295
Road districts, status of, as corporations, 89; function of, 319-320
Road supervisors, township roads in charge of, 278, 279, 307
Roads, control of states over, 9, 11, 73, 74, 276, 277, 278, 285, 307; local control of, 12, 102, 103, 277, 278, 279, 288, 289, 307, 311; maintenance of, 13, 275, 276, 277, 278, 279, 283, 284, 287; control of towns over, 37, 39, 263; tax for, 103, 230, 278, 279, 282, 283; work on, 103, 120, 121, 123, 278, 279, 282, 284, 285, 286; duties of county board in regard to, 119, 120, 123; land for, 125; maps showing, 152; effect of, on extent of crime, 174; attitude of federal government to, 276, 285, 286; neglect of, 276, 277, 278; distances covered by, 277; contracts for, 278; routes of, 278; officials in charge of, 278, 279; importance of, 279, 280; definition of, 280; classification of, 280, 281, 282; cost of, 282, 283, 285, 286; county in charge of, 288, 289; township control over, 311, 314
"Rotten boroughs," meaning of, 35
Rural districts, crime in, 95, 174, 175; state police desired by, 180; hospitals for, 258, 259; need of public health agencies in, 259-261; definition of, 323, 328
Rural schools, organization of, 101, 102

St. Louis, county absorbed by, 302
Salaries, prohibition of reduction of, by legislatures, 83, 84
Sanitary districts, creation of, 110, purpose of, 320, 321
Sanitation, control of state over, 9, 73; governmental agencies for, 259, 260, 261
School board, office of, 60; need of, 272; selection of, 272; size of, 272; mention of, 292; duties of, 272, 273, 295; 337, 338; membership on, 295; pay of, 295; selection of, 295, 299, 337; township board as, 312
School buildings, erection of, 101; maps showing, 152; regulation of, 267, 268, 269, 272, 273
School district, status of, as area of local government, 1, 319; creation of, 101, 102, 265; democracy of, 265; meetings held in, 265; referendum in, 265, 266; trustees of, 266; restrictions

INDEX 357

on, 266, 267; consolidation of, 270; abolition of, 272; meetings in, 337; municipalities as, 337, 338
School officers, supplies for, 126, 127
School superintendent, (see Superintendent of schools, county)
Schools, control of state over, 9, 11, 73, 266, 267, 268, 269, 270, 304; local control of, as a factor in democracy, 12; inefficiency in maintenance of, 13; establishment of, by towns, 37, 39, 59, 262, 263; children required to attend, 37, 267, 269, 272; selectmen in charge of, 40; land set aside for, 57, 125; control of townships over, 73, 311, 314, 317, 318; maintenance of, by local authorities, 101, 102, 111, 112, 337, 338; tax rates for, 230, 263, 266, 267, 272; establishment of, by pioneers, 262; relation of government to, 262-274; social unity promoted by, 264; provision for, outside of New England, 264; variations in, 267, 269; standardization of, 267, 268; provision for, in counties, 262-273; budgets for, 273; statistics of, 273; centralized control over, 269, 270, 271, 272, 273, 274, 304; maintenance of, by municipalities, 337, 338
Schools for the blind, care of dependents in, 249
Selectmen, authority of, 31, 32; duties of, 37, 40, 41, 48; election of, 38; judicial powers of, 48; survival of office of, 59; supervision of, over schools, 263; roads in charge of, 278
Selectmen, board of, election of, 38; development of, 40, 41; duties of, 40, 41
Self-governing dependencies, character of, 3
Self-government (see Local self-government)
Senate, United States, state representation in, 7, 36
Senators (U. S.), districts for election of, 8, 36
Sergeant major, duties of, 50
Sheriff, county, abolition of office of, suggested, 11; selection of, 19, 54, 71, 83, 164, 166, 181, 182, 296, 299; duties of, 52, 93, 94, 95, 96, 163, 164, 165, 166-173, 176, 181, 200, 296; arrest of Governor by, 94; position of, 98, 162, 163, 164; independence of, from county board, 117; claims approved by, 144; report by, 153; jury summoned by, 157; origin of office of, 162, 163; military power of, 163, 168; term of office of, 164, 296; accountability of, 164; relation of, to state government, 165, 166, 176, 178, 179, 189, 190, 298; importance of, on frontier, 167; authority of, to call *posse comitatus*, 167, 168; conflicts of, with city police, 168; duty of, as executive officer of the court, 168-170; pay of, 169, 170, 227, 296; deputy for, 169, 175, 176; responsibility of, for prisoners, 170-173; changes in office of, 173-175, 181, 182; failure of, as peace officer, 173, 174; difficulties of, 174, 175; inquests requested by, 183; relations of, with public prosecutor, 199; relations of, with other officers, 199, 200, 291, 299, 317; duplication of work of, 303
Shire-reeve, sheriff's office derived from, 163
Shires, counties known as, 50; chief officers in, 163; status of, in England, 162, 163
Short ballot, effect of agitation for, 125
Special districts, 15
Special legislation, prohibition of, concerning counties, 84, 85, 86
Speeding, enforcement of laws against, 95, 96, 175, 176, 193
Socialists, opposition of, to state police, 180
Solicitor, city, position of, 331; duties of, 336, 337
South, type of local governments in, 43, 44, 47, 60, 61, 65, 70; status of counties in, 47, 53, 54; office of sheriff in, 165; county districts in, 318
South Carolina, type of local government in, 60; type of county board in, 71, 72; townships in, 308

INDEX

South-central states, local government, status in, 55, 62, 63
South Dakota, type of local government in, 63; type of county board in, 71, 72; townships in, 308, 310, 312
Southern type of local government, 54
Sovereign states, meaning of, 2, 3
Sovereignty, attributes of, 3, 4
State, definition of, 1, 2, 3; qualifications of, 2
State administration, powers of, 9; causes of inefficiency of, 13; service of local governments in, 109, 110; reforms needed in, 203, 204
State agents, use of, in execution of laws, 94
State aid for road building, 285, 286
State aid for schools, 268, 269
State assembly, counties as units of representation in, 52
State boards of education, functions of, 274
State department of justice, need of, 203, 204
State government, attitude of, toward local governments, 56, 111, 112; relation of sheriff to, 165, 166, 189, 190
State highways, creation of, 285
State institutions, care of dependents in, 248
State laws, enforcement of, 13, 19, 94, 95
State penitentiaries, prisoners turned over to, 169
State police, creation of bodies of, 11, 173, 200; use of, in enforcing laws, 94; need of, 96, 204; work of, in foreign countries, 176; legislation concerning, 176; status of, in United States, 176-180; relation of, to sheriffs, 176, 178, 179; opposition to, 179, 180; desire for, 180
State representative districts, status of, as areas of government, 8
State senatorial districts, status of, as areas of government, 8
States (U. S.), status of, as federal units, 3, 4; division of, into minor areas, 4, 5, 14, 15, 16, 58-63, 76; cities created by authority of, 5, 324; judicial districts of, 6, 7; representation of, in Senate, 7, 8, 36; situation in, if organized into administrative districts, 8, 9; authority of, over local affairs, 10, 11, 73, 74, 76, 77-87, 89, 90, 134, 217, 224, 225; centralization of authority in, 10, 11, 73, 74, 76-87, 289, 290; law enforcing agencies in, 13, 14, 166, 167, 173, 174; administrative decentralization in, 14; division of, into congressional districts, 18; relation of counties to, 18, 19, 20, 76-87, 89, 90; collection of taxes by, 19, 104, 105, 237; representatives to legislatures of, 36; counties and townships created by, 76; political power of, 77; maintenance of peace by, 93; care of dependents by, 100, 240; control of, over schools, 102, 103, 266, 267, 268, 269, 270, 271, 272, 274; authority of, over roads, 103, 276, 277, 278; control of, over elections, 106, 107; authority of, over militia, 109; contracts made by, 121; budget systems for, 128; accountability of sheriff to, 164, 181; offenses against, 195, 196; auditing to be done by, 228, 229; public health agencies of, 259, 261; importance of education to, 271; boards of education maintained by, 274
State's attorney, title of, 189
Stewards of the poor farms, 125, 249, 253, 254
Stocks and bonds, taxation of, 236
Streets, care of, 325
Strikes, work of state police in, 180
Subpoenas, serving of, 157
Suburbs, small municipalities as, 338-340
Suicide, verdict of, 184, 185
Superintendent of county institutions, appointment of, 125
Superintendent of education, duties of, 274
Superintendent of poorhouse, 249, 251, 252, 253
Superintendent of schools, county, claims approved by, 144; authority of, 271, 272; selection of,

INDEX

273, 297, 299; duties of, 273, 338; accountability of, to state authorities, 289; relation of, to other officers, 291, 299, 301; mention of 293

Superintendent of schools, state, authority of, 271

Supervisors, board of, origin of, in New York, 52; duties of, 52; types of, 70, 71, 72; number on, 114

Supervisors, county, number of, 66, 67, 68, 69, 70; types of boards of, 70, 71, 72; fees of, 227; poor relief in charge of, 246; persons committed to poorhouse by, 250

Supervisors, township, organization of board of, 312; duties of, 312, 313, 319; service of, on township board, 312

Supplies, contracts for, 120; purchase of, by county boards, 126, 129

Supreme Court of the United States, decision of, concerning grand jury, 202, 203

Surveyor, county, appointment of, 54, 125, 298, 299; duties of, 161; relation of, to other officers, 291, 299; mention of, 293

Surveyor, town, duties of, 41

Surveyors, employment of, on roads, 284

Tax books, preparation of, 148
Tax gatherers, hatred of, 104
Tax rate, fixing of, 33, 34, 86, 128, 300, 311, 312, 318, 321, 335, 340; authorization of, 131, 132

Taxation, control of, by town meetings, 33, 34; need of better machinery for, 105; function of county in administration of, 130–132

Taxes, control of state over, 9; control of, by local authorities, 12, 19, 33, 34, 39, 46, 103–105, 111, 112, 137, 226, 227; towns in charge of, 28, 33, 34, 39, 59; collection of, by parish, 46; collection of, by counties, 49, 50, 59, 137, 226, 227; justice supported by, 98; service of county clerks in collection of, 147, 148, 149, 152; sale of property for, 148, 149; payment of, to treasurer, 214; delayed entries of, 221; collection of, by collector, 225; percentage paid for collection of, 226; assessment of, 229, 230, 231, 232, 233; separation of sources of, 237; control over, 303, 304 (see also Assessment of taxes)

Teachers, employment of, 266, 273; pay of, 267, 268, 269, 272; qualifications of, 272, 273

Tellers, election, appointment of, 106

Tendencies affecting local government, 72–75

Tennessee, pioneer period in, 55; type of local government in, 60; type of county board in, 71

Texas, state police in, 11, 177; type of local government in, 60; type of county board in, 71

Texas Rangers, account of, 177

Titles to land, recording of, 107, 108

Town clerk, town meeting called to order by, 29, 30; election of, 38; duties of, 41; office of, 59; land titles recorded by, 159

Town hall, tax for, voted by town meeting, 33; care of dependents in, 248

Town meeting, description of, 28; powers of, 28, 29, 31, 32, 33, 34; calling of, 28, 29; procedure in, 29; officers of, 29, 30; influence of, 30, 39, 40; functions of, 30–38; selection of representatives by, 35, 36; local affairs administered by, 36, 37; ordinances passed by, 37, 38; officers chosen by, 38, 39; status of, in New England, 59, 60; school established by, 263; township meeting similar to, 311

Town officers, enforcement of state laws by, 13; salaries of, 34; selection of, by town meetings, 38; duties of, 38, 39, 40, 41; authority of county court over, 50, 51

Towns, status of, as areas of local government, 6, 54, 55, 56, 58, 59, 65, 323; importance of, in New England, 24, 26, 27, 28, 58, 59; origin of, 25, 326, 330;

distinction between townships and, 25, 26; definition of, 25, 329; jurisdiction of, 25, 26, 47, 48; attitude of American colonies toward, 27, 28; judicial powers of, 28; right of, to exclude persons, 30, 31, 32; lands owned by, 32, 33; representatives of, in colonial assembly, 35; local affairs of, 36, 37; organization of, 39, 40, 42, 325, 326, 330; functions of, 39, 40, 325, 327, 328, 329; officers of, 40, 41, 331, 339; origin of townships from, 41; characteristics of, outside of New England, 42, 43, 44, 45; lack of, in Pennsylvania, 45, 46; authority of county court over, 50, 51; use of, as administrative districts, 59; status of, as corporations, 88, 89; duty of, to care for dependents, 239, 240, 242, 243, 249; schools in, 262, 263; comparison of, with cities, 324, 325, 326; classification of, as urban centers, 327, 328, 329; incorporation of, 330, 331, 332; government of, 331, 332; powers of, 332; reorganization of, as cities, 332, 333; powers of councils in, 333, 334, 335; status of, as city suburbs, 338, 339, 340; public utilities in, 339; absorption of, into cities, 339, 340; variations in, 340

Township chairmen, duties of, 312, 313

Township meetings, states in which held, 310, 311; function of, 311, 312; degeneration of, 311, 312

Township officials, taxes collected by, 19; indefinite status of, 19; information concerning, 153; election of, 311

Township trustees, services of, as board of review, 132, 133; persons committed to poorhouse by, 250; roads controlled by, 278; types of boards of, 312; functions of, 312, 313

Townships, status of, as area of local government, 1, 15, 16, 17, 54, 55, 60, 61, 62, 63, 64, 65, 66, 309, 310, 324, 325; jurisdiction of, 5, 26; reason for maintenance of, 13, 313, 314; chief characteristics of, 16, 20; functions of, 17, 18, 34, 39, 77, 92–113, 288, 289, 290, 331; use of, as administrative districts, 18, 19, 20; definition of, 21; origin of, 24, 25, 41, 308, 309, 310; distinction between towns and, 25, 26; organization of, 44, 45, 53, 325; powers of, in New York, 45; status of, in Pennsylvania, 45, 53, 91; absence of, in Virginia, 45; place of, taken by counties, 47; loss of authority of, 52, 72, 73, 82, 83, 288, 289, 290, 310; status of, in South, 53, 60, 61; development of, in West, 55, 56, 60, 61; creation of, 56, 324; naming of, 56; granting of, for school purposes, 57; number of, in United States, 57; service of, as justice of the peace districts, 60; status of, in central states, 61, 62, 63, 64, 65, 66; relation of, to counties, 66–72, 307; state control over, 76, 87; legal status of, 76–91, 310; changes in boundaries of, 80, 81, 116, 134; status of, as bodies corporate and politic, 87–91; status of, in Michigan, 91; maintenance of schools by, 101, 102, 264, 270; control of, over highways, 102, 103, 278, 279, 280, 282; part of, in collection of taxes, 104, 105; control of, over elections, 106, 107; service of, as state administrative districts, 109, 110; assessors appointed by, 229, 230; duty of, to provide for dependents, 239, 240, 244, 249; existence of, in United States, 307, 308; relation of municipalities to, 310; meetings in, 310, 311, 312; boards of, 312; officers of, 312, 313, 314, 315, 316, 317; no need for, 317, 318; comparison of county districts with, 318, 319; relations of, with municipalities, 331, 334

Treasurer, county, duties of, 50, 165, 212, 213–218, 227, 297; selection of, 83, 212, 222, 224, 225; deputy of, 126, 216, 297, 299; claims approved by, 144; warrants paid by, 146; taxes collected by, 148, 149, 227; re-

INDEX

port by, 153; public prosecutor as legal adviser to, 191, 192; term of, 212; bond of, 213; pay of, 213, 227; records of, 215, 216, 288; funds in charge of, 217, 218, 219, 223, 224; interest retained by, 219, 220; depositories selected by, 220, 221, 224; opportunity of, for spoils, 221, 222, 223, 224; need of reform in office of, 222, 223, 225; reasons for defalcations of, 223–225; audit of books of, by state authorities, 222, 225, 297; relation of, to other officers, 291, 299; mention of, 293

Treasurer, municipal (see Treasurer, town)

Treasurer, town, election of, 39; office of, 59, 331; duties of, 336

Treasurer, township, duties of, 307, 312, 313

Trial, procedure in, 203

True bills (see Indictments)

Trustees, municipal, board of, 331

Trustees, school, office and duties of, 266, 271, restrictions on, 266, 267, 268; substitutes for, 270, 271, 272

Trustees, town, duties of, 37

Trustees, township, board of, service of, as board of review, 132, 133

Tuberculosis sanitariums, maintenance of, 256, 257

Types of local government, 63–66, 70

United States, status of, as political unit, 2, 3, 4; creation of cities in, 5; representative districts in, 7, 8; administrative districts in, 8, 9, 10, 11; preference of, for local self-government, 11, 12, 13; areas of local self-government in, 15, 16, 17; number of counties and townships in, 57, 134, 135; peace officers in, 166; early poor relief in, 240, 241; justice of the peace in, 315

Unity, need of, for local self-government, 21, 22; factors in, 22, 23, 24

Urban population, definition of, 327, 328

Utah, type of local government in, 60; type of county board in, 71, 72

Verdicts, types of, in coroner's juries, 184, 185

Vermont, type of local government, 58; type of county boards in, 71; status of municipalities in, 328, 329

Vestry, parish, election of, 46; duties of, 46, 47

Villages, status of, as areas of local government, 1, 6, 323; existence of, in New York, 44; towns similar to, 59; status of, as corporations, 88, 89; presidents of, 136; duty of, to provide for poor, 239, 240, 243, 244; relation of, to townships, 310; similarity of, to cities, 324, 325, 326; organization of, 325; functions of, 325, 327, 328, 329; creation of, 326, 330; definition of, 329; incorporation of, 330, 331, 332; government of, 331, 332; officers of, 331, 339; powers of, 332; reorganization of, as cities, 332, 333; powers of councils in, 333, 334, 335; status of, as city suburbs, 338, 339, 340

Virginia, local government in, 44, 45, 46, 60; importance of counties in, 54; type of county board in, 71; magisterial districts in, 319

Vital statistics, records of, 41, 47, 99, 110, 157

Voters, registration of, 151, 152; grand jury selected from, 201

Voting, methods of, 106, 107

Warrant book, keeping of, by county board, 119

Warrants, financial, county clerk in charge of, 146, 152; signing of, by auditor or clerk, 217; payment of, by treasurer, 217, 218, 221; drawing of, 336; warrants for arrests, service of, 168; issue of, for criminals, 200, 316

Washington, type of local government in, 60; type of county board in, 71, 72; absence of townships in, 308

Watchers at elections, appointment of, 106

Water, supply of, 9, 325, 333; need of inspection of, 260

West, local government institutions

in, 55, 56, 60; county districts in, 318

West Virginia, type of local government in, 60; type of county board in, 71, 72

Wills, probation of, 99

Wisconsin, type of local government in, 61; type of county board in, 71; townships in, 308, 310, 311, 312; township board in, 312; township chairman in, 312

Witnesses, subpoenas for, 157; sheriff in charge of, 168, 169

Wyoming, type of local government, 60; type of county board in, 71, 72

Yellowstone Trail, marking of, 286